Behavioural Public Policy

Edited by

ADAM OLIVER
London School of Economics and Political Science

CAMBRIDGE
UNIVERSITY PRESS

CAMBRIDGE
UNIVERSITY PRESS

University Printing House, Cambridge CB2 8BS, United Kingdom

Published in the United States of America by Cambridge University Press, New York

Cambridge University Press is part of the University of Cambridge.

It furthers the University's mission by disseminating knowledge in the pursuit of education, learning and research at the highest international levels of excellence.

www.cambridge.org
Information on this title: www.cambridge.org/9781107617377

© Cambridge University Press 2013

First published 2013
Reprinted 2014

Printed in the United Kingdom by CPI Group Ltd, Croydon CR0 4YY

A catalogue record for this publication is available from the British Library

Library of Congress Cataloguing in Publication data
Behavioural public policy / edited by Adam Oliver, London School of Economics and Political Science.
   pages   cm
ISBN 978-1-107-04263-6 (Hardback) – ISBN 978-1-107-61737-7 (Paperback)
1. Policy sciences–Psychological aspects.   2. Economics–Psychological aspects.
3. Economic policy–Psychological aspects.   4. Social policy–Psychological aspects.
I. Oliver, Adam J.
H97.B435 2013
320.6–dc23   2013021436

ISBN 978-1-107-04263-6 Hardback
ISBN 978-1-107-61737-7 Paperback

Behavioural Public Policy

How can individuals best be encouraged to take more responsibility for their well-being and their environment or to behave more ethically in their business transactions? Across the world, governments are showing a growing interest in using behavioural economic research to inform the design of nudges which, some suggest, might encourage citizens to adopt beneficial patterns of behaviour. In this fascinating collection, leading academic economists, psychologists and philosophers reflect on how behavioural economic findings can be used to help inform the design of policy initiatives in the areas of health, education, the environment, personal finances and worke   shorter
'response' t   **DATE DUE**   perspec-
tive. This   graduate
students and policy-makers across a range of disciplinary perspectives.

ADAM OLIVER is a reader in the Department of Social Policy at the London School of Economics and Political Science. Dr Oliver's principal research interests focus upon behavioural economics and its applications to public and private decision-making, on which he has published extensively. He is founding editor of the journal *Health Economics, Policy and Law*.

Contents

Figures

Tables

Contributors

GILES ATKINSON is Reader in Environmental Policy in the Department of Geography and Environment and Associate of the Grantham Research Institute on Climate Change and Environment at the London School of Economics and Political Science. His main research interests are within the fields of the economics of sustainability, particularly greening the national accounts, environmental valuation and environmental equity. He is currently a member of the (UK) Natural Capital Committee, an independent body providing advice to HM Government on the sustainable use of natural capital.

GWYN BEVAN is Professor of Policy Analysis and head of the Department of Management at the London School of Economics and Political Science. He has worked as an academic at Warwick Business School, St Thomas's Hospital and Bristol Medical School, and in industry, consulting, the Treasury and for the Commission for Health Improvement (2001–3), where he was director of the Office for Information on Healthcare Performance. His current research includes studies of outcomes of the natural experiment of different policies in UK countries for the NHS and schools following devolution.

LUC BOVENS taught in the University of Colorado at Boulder from 1990 to 2003. Since 2004 he is a Professor at the London School of Economics and Political Science, Department of Philosophy, Logic and Scientific Method. From 2002 to 2005 he was director of the Philosophy, Probability and Modelling Research Group in the University of Konstanz, Germany. He was an editor of *Economics and Philosophy* from 2002 to 2007. He has published widely in the areas of moral and political philosophy, philosophy of public policy, moral psychology, Bayesian epistemology, philosophy of science, voting theory, and rational and social choice theory.

DAYLIAN M. CAIN is Assistant Professor of Organizational Behavior at the Yale School of Management. His research focuses on decision-making and behavioural business ethics. Cain is a leading expert on conflicts of interest and 'reluctant' altruism, exploring the psychological tension between selfish and altruistic preferences.

RICHARD COOKSON is a reader at the Centre for Health Economics, University of York, and his main research interests are in equity in health and health care. He has also served as a technical adviser to the UK Department of Health, the National Institute for Health and Clinical Excellence, and the Prime Minister's Delivery Unit.

KATE DISNEY is interested in self-determination theory and the relationship between economic approaches to behaviour change and motivation. The plastic bag charge at M&S was researched as part of her PhD studies at the London School of Economics and Political Science.

PAUL DOLAN is a professor in the Department of Social Policy at the London School of Economics and Political Science. There are two main themes to his work. The first focuses on developing measures of subjective well-being that can be used in policy. The second considers ways in which the lessons from behavioural economics can be used to understand and change individual behaviour. Paul Dolan has advised various government departments, including Defra, Department of Health, Department for Communities and Local Government and the Home Office.

CHRISTOPHER EXETER is a Senior Fellow in the Faculty of Medicine at Imperial College London. Prior to this he was a public servant, holding posts at the Department of Health and most recently at the Design Council where he was Executive Director of Policy. He also held various roles at the global professional services firm Deloitte LLP. His current research interests centre on health and clinical technology.

BARBARA FASOLO is Senior Lecturer in Behavioural Science at the London School of Economics and Political Science and head of the Behavioural Research Lab of the Department of Management. Her expertise is choice and choice architecture. She studies how people react to choice and make decisions in the domains of health, wealth and well-being, with a particular interest in understanding how and when choice architecture can allow people to be good and informed decision-makers in the presence of tradeoffs and complexity.

BRUNO FREY is Professor of Economics at the University of Zurich, Distinguished Professor of Behavioural Science at the University of Warwick, and research director of the Centre for Research in Economics, Management and the Arts, Switzerland. He is also managing editor of *Kyklos*. Professor Frey seeks to extend economics beyond standard neoclassics by including insights from other disciplines, including political science, psychology and sociology. According to the Institute for Scientific Information, Professor Frey is among the 'the most highly cited researchers'.

MATTEO M. GALIZZI is LSE Fellow in the Department of Social Policy and LSE Health and Social Care, London School of Economics and Political Science, and former Post-Doctoral Research Fellow at the Centre for the Study of Incentives in Health, King's College–LSE–Queen Mary London. His main interests are in the design of lab and field experiments in the areas of health and social policy.

JULIAN LE GRAND is Richard Titmuss Professor of Social Policy at the London School of Economics and Political Science. He has served in a number of government advisory positions, most notably as a chief adviser on health policy to UK Prime Minister Tony Blair. Professor Le Grand's research interests include health and community care policy, welfare reform and social justice in theory and practice. His current research is concerned with motivation, agency and the reform of public services.

GEORGE LOEWENSTEIN is the Herbert A. Simon University Professor of Economics and Psychology at Carnegie Mellon University. He received his PhD from Yale University in 1985 and since then has held academic positions at the University of Chicago and Carnegie Mellon University, and fellowships at the Center for Advanced Study in the Behavioral Sciences, the Institute for Advanced Study in Princeton, the Russell Sage Foundation and the Institute for Advanced Study in Berlin. He is one of the founders of the field of behavioural economics and more recently of the field of neuroeconomics. He is past president of the Society for Judgment and Decision Making, and a Fellow of the American Academy of Arts and Sciences. Loewenstein's research focuses on applications of psychology to economics, and his specific interests include decision making over time, bargaining and negotiations, psychology and health, law and economics, the psychology of adaptation, the role of emotion in decision-making, the psychology of curiosity, conflict of interest, and 'out of control' behaviours such as impulsive violent crime and drug addiction. He has published over 200 journal articles and book chapters, and has written or edited six books on topics ranging from inter-temporal choice to behavioural economics to emotions.

ADAM OLIVER is a reader in the Department of Social Policy at the London School of Economics and Political Science. He teaches to postgraduates a range of health policy and health economic-related topics. His principal research interests focus upon behavioural economics and its applications to public and private policy-making.

DRAZEN PRELEC is the Digital Equipment Corporation LFM Professor of Management in the Sloan School of Management at MIT. His research deals with the psychology and neuroscience of decision-making: specifically, behavioural economics and neuroeconomics, risky choice, time discounting, and self-control and consumer behaviour. He works both on the development of normative decision theory and the exploration of the empirical failures of that theory.

MATTHEW RABIN is the Edward G. and Nancy S. Jordan Professor of Economics in the Department of Economics at the University of California, Berkeley. He has contributed extensively to the field of behavioural economics, and was the recipient of the 2001 John Bates Clark Medal, awarded to that American economist under the age of forty who is judged to have made the most significant contribution to economic thought and knowledge.

SUNITA SAH is an assistant professor of Business Ethics at Georgetown University and a Research Fellow at the Ethics Center, Harvard University. Her research focus is on organizational corruption, business ethics and advice – in particular, how professionals who give advice alter their behaviour as a result of conflicts of interest and the policies designed to manage them. Dr Sah has won numerous awards for her research from the Academy of Management, Society of Business Ethics, Society of Judgment and Decision Making and the Society of Personality and Social Psychology. More information on Dr Sah can be found at www.sunitasah.com.

PAUL SLOVIC is one of the leading behavioural decision theorists in the world. He is a pioneer in the field of constructed preference, and, among decades of other important contributions, he edited classic texts on heuristics and biases with Daniel Kahneman and Amos Tversky in the 1980s. His own empirical work has examined judgement and decision processes with an emphasis on decision-making under conditions of risk, the influence of affect on judgements and decisions, and the factors that underlie the management of risk in society. More information on Professor Slovic can be found at www.decisionresearch.org.

CHARITINI STAVROPOULOU is a Lecturer in Health Care Management at the University of Surrey. Her main research interests focus on understanding individual behaviours, such as adherence to medication, lifestyle choices and involvement with health safety. In particular, she is interested in the role that the doctor–patient relationship plays in explaining these behaviours.

ROBERT SUGDEN is Professor of Economics at the University of East Anglia, Norwich. His research uses a combination of theoretical, experimental and philosophical methods to investigate issues in welfare economics, social choice, choice under uncertainty, the foundations of decision and game theories, the methodology of economics and the evolution of social conventions.

SANDER VAN DER LINDEN is a PhD candidate at the Grantham Research Institute within the London School of Economics and Political Science (Department of Geography and the Environment) and currently a Visiting Research Fellow at Yale University (2012–13). His PhD is in environmental psychology; he specializes in the process of behavioural change and is particularly interested in modelling and predicting pro-social and pro-environmental behaviours.

DANIEL VÄSTFJÄLL is a research scientist at Decision Research and Professor of Cognitive Psychology at Linköping University in Sweden. His research focuses on the role of affect, and especially mood, in judgement and decision-making, perception and psychophysics. A common theme for his research is how affective feelings serve as information for various judgements, including judgements about consumer products, health, the self and auditory characteristics of objects.

ALEX VOORHOEVE is Senior Lecturer in Philosophy at the London School of Economics and Political Science and teaches in its philosophy and public policy programme. He writes on liberal egalitarian ideals of equality, responsibility and state neutrality and on the theory of rational choice. He has applied his conclusions to health care resource allocation in developed and developing countries. His articles have appeared in *Philosophy and Public Affairs*, the *Journal of Political Philosophy*, the *American Journal of Bioethics* and *Economics and Philosophy*, among others.

JONATHAN WOLFF is Professor of Philosophy at University College London. His books include *Philosophy and Public Policy: A Philosophical Inquiry* (2011) and *The Human Right to Health* (2012). He is a member of the Nuffield Council on Bioethics, and he writes a monthly column for Education Guardian.

Introduction

ADAM OLIVER

For much of the nineteenth century, a discursive, almost exclusively theory-driven style of political economy dominated the economics discourse. Among much else, for instance, David Ricardo had stated that the value of a good is proportional to the cost of the labour taken to produce it, Thomas Malthus believed that population growth would inevitably lead to famine, and J. S. Mill and Karl Marx warned that wages would never rise much above subsistence levels. However, in many cases, of course, brilliantly prosecuted, empirical analysis to test the often competing claims was somewhat lacking. Due to the absence of tools to provide seemingly objective answers, the perceived usefulness of political economy for informing and assessing policy was ultimately undermined.

Alfred Marshall aimed to address this state of affairs by making economics more scientific, that is, more testable and tested. Recognizing that the world is complex and changing, and that preconceptions may be less than valid, he undertook ground-breaking empirical work to demonstrate that, in contrast to the forewarnings of Mill and Marx, wages were in fact increasing over time, as a consequence of greater productivity necessitated by competition. Marshall may have paid insufficient attention to the possibility that not all workers receive an equitable share of the fruits of competition, but, by empirically addressing testable theoretical propositions, he revolutionized economics. From that point onwards, mathematical and applied empirical economics superseded political economy as the dominant force within the mainstream economics community.

The measurement of expected utility is an important branch of economics that benefited substantively from the introduction of mathematics. By the end of the nineteenth century, many economists had turned away from the attempt to derive cardinal measures of utility, and, in subsequent decades, built welfare economics instead upon Vilfredo Pareto's famous ordinal criterion, a development that Luigino

1

Bruni and Robert Sugden (2007) have coined the Paretian turn. However, between the 1920s and the early 1950s, a number of remarkable mathematicians and mathematically minded economists, including Frank Ramsey, Leonard Savage, John von Neumann, Oskar Morgenstern, Jacob Marschak and Paul Samuelson, contributed towards developing axiomatic systems of formal logic that prescribed how people ought to choose under risk and uncertainty if they are expected utility maximizers. This movement culminated in the specification of expected utility theory.

The standard gamble, a tool that theoretically enables the elicitation of an individual's cardinal utilities for goods, was developed from the axioms of expected utility theory, and thus appeared to provide a solution for the derivation of strength of preference indices. However, eliciting individuals' preferences relies principally upon how they do choose (i.e. on descriptive behaviour), rather than on the normative proposition of how they ought to choose if they are expected utility maximizers, and thus the validity of the theory for utility elicitation is informed by observed choice. The axioms of expected utility theory offered themselves to formal testing, and, as early as the 1950s, findings that undermined the descriptive validity of expected utility theory – perhaps the first empirical behavioural economics results – were published. The most frequently tested and contested assumption of the theory has proven to be the independence axiom, which essentially states that the subjective value that people attach to any particular outcome ought not to be affected by the probability with which that outcome occurs, and that their perception of any particular probability ought not to be influenced by the outcome that is attached to that probability. The implication of independence is that when an individual is presented with a choice of two or more options, he or she should deem any outcome common to the options as irrelevant to his or her decision.

The earliest and most famous violation of the independence axiom was postulated in print by Maurice Allais in 1953. To illustrate, consider the following four options, A, B, A^* and B^*:

A: $1m for certain

B: 10% chance of $5m; 89% chance of $1m; 1% chance of $0

A^*:   11% chance of $1m; 89% chance of $0

B^*:   10% chance of $5m; 90% chance of $0

Allais contended that if individuals were faced with two choice contexts – i.e. A or B and A* or B* – they would show a tendency to choose A and B*. However, close examination reveals that A and B share the common outcome of an 89 per cent chance of $1m, and therefore, according to the independence axiom, the chooser should consider this common consequence as irrelevant to his decision. Similarly, A* and B* share a common outcome of an 89 per cent chance of $0. If common consequences are ignored in both choice tasks, A is identical to A* and B is identical to B*; therefore expected utility theory requires the individual to choose A and A* or B and B*, or neither in both contexts. Allais's conjecture of frequent observance of people choosing A and B* has been confirmed in much subsequent empirical testing, and has been labelled the common consequence effect.

The Allais paradox is attributed to the certainty effect – the high weight that individuals tend to attach to certainty, higher than that allowed by expected utility theory. Ambiguity, where the exact probability of an uncertain event is unknown, is even less certain than risk (where the probability is clearly specified), and ambiguity aversion can cause further violations of independence. Daniel Ellsberg's classic thought experiment, published in 1961, is an example of this. Ellsberg posed a scenario where an individual is presented with an urn containing 30 black balls and 60 red and blue balls of an unspecified mix and is requested to pick one ball from the urn. Before picking a ball, the individual is asked to consider the following two choices, A or B and A* or B*, where:

A: $100 if the ball is black, $0 if red or blue

B: $100 if red, $0 if black or blue

A*: $100 if black or blue, $0 if red

B*: $100 if red or blue, $0 if black

In the choice between A and B, A therefore offers a definite one-third chance of winning $100 (30 of the 90 balls will be black); B an ambiguous zero to two-thirds chance of winning $100 (anything between 0 and 60 of the 90 balls will be red). As to A* versus B*, A* offers an ambiguous one-third to certain chance of winning $100; B* a definite two-thirds chance of winning £100. If a blue ball is picked in A or B, $0 is won, and thus, according to the independence axiom, the chooser should perceive the possibility of picking a blue ball as irrelevant to their decision in the first choice context. The same applies in the second choice context, where a blue ball in both A^* and B^* offers a common consequence of \$100. If consideration of the blue ball is eliminated from both choice contexts, then A is identical to A^*, and B is identical to B^*; thus, according to expected utility theory, the individual should choose A and A^* or B and B^*, or consistently neither. However, Ellsberg hypothesized that many people will be ambiguity averse, and will therefore demonstrate a systematic preference for the risky but unambiguous options, A and B^*, a conjecture that has since been amply confirmed. In this volume, I offer a chapter that discusses ambiguity aversion in a little more detail, and which uses the concept as an explanation for the UK government's arguably excessive response to the 2009 swine flu outbreak.

During a period concurrent with publication of the early literature that demonstrated specific violations of the axioms of expected utility theory, Herbert Simon (1956) offered a challenge to the broader under-lying assumption, common to welfare economics and much of rational choice theory, that people are optimizers who always seek to maximize utility. Simon argued that, due to bounds on their rationality and time, people do not expend the effort required to optimize, and instead use relatively simple rules of thumb, or heuristics, to help them reach deci-sions. In short, they 'satisfice', or make do with something that is good enough. Psychologists have since reported a great many heuristics that drive decision-making in particular contexts. Some of the most promin-ent of these rules of thumb include the representativeness, availability and anchoring heuristics. Representativeness, for instance, is the finding that people may overlook the objective probability of something happening, and resort more to preconceptions or stereotyping; availabil-ity is the tendency for people to assess the probability of an event by the ease with which similar instances can be brought to mind; and anchoring is the finding that people often place a heavy emphasis on particular salient features of a decision context – or even on entirely irrelevant prompts – and insufficiently account for less prominent characteristics.

The early concerns with expected utility theory were not initially treated with a great deal of respect by the mainstream economics community. Leonard Savage, on violating his own sure thing principle (essentially the independence axiom under conditions of uncertainty), attributed his choices to mere error, rather than a deliberate, systematic preference pattern. Nonetheless, during the 1960s and 1970s, psychologists continued to compile a growing body of evidence that placed serious question marks against, at the very least, the descriptive validity of the theory. Prominent among this evidence was the reporting of preference reversals, which, in their classic form, involve the offering of two bets, referred to as the *P-bet* and the *$-bet*. The *P-bet* offers a high probability of winning a modest amount, the *$-bet* offers a modest probability of winning a relatively large amount, and the two bets have similar expected values. People are asked to choose directly between the *P-bet* and the *$-bet*, and are also asked for the value, in the form of approximate certainty equivalents, that they place on each of the two bets. It has been frequently reported that a substantial percentage – often a majority – of respondents choose the *P-bet* over the *$-bet*, but value the *$-bet* higher than the *P-bet*. For illustrative purposes, consider the following two bets, taken from the classic 1971 study by Sarah Lichtenstein and Paul Slovic:

P-bet: ($4, 35/36; –$1, 1/36)

$-bet: ($16, 11/36; –$1.50, 25/36)

Thus, the *P-bet* offers a 35/36 chance of winning $4 and a 1/36 chance of losing $1. The *$-bet* can be similarly read. In three tests, Lichtenstein and Slovic observed systematic preference reversals, in the direction of people choosing the *P-bet* but valuing the *$-bet* higher, in something between 50 and 80 per cent of their respondents. It is unlikely that such a substantial, systematic pattern can be attributed to random error.

Several explanations for preference reversals have been suggested, but the most likely cause is that people use different heuristics across elicitation procedures. Choice tasks might encourage greater focus on the probability of winning, which favours the *P-bet*, while valuation tasks may tend to focus attention on the payoffs, which of course favours the *$-bet*. Specifically, when valuing the *$-bet*, people often anchor on its best outcome, but then fail to adjust the overall value of the bet downwards sufficiently to take account of its other less favourable attributes. This notion of anchoring and insufficient adjustment to account for the less desirable features of a choice option is, as earlier noted, a key finding in the behavioural economics literature, and resonates to some extent in the chapter in this volume by Sunita Sah, Daylian M. Cain and George Loewenstein, where they argue that if financial advisers exaggerate, or further exaggerate, the usefulness of their advice due to having to disclose any conflicts of interest, their clients might anchor on the biased advice and insufficiently adjust their decisions to account for the bias. More generally, psychologists, in contrast to standard economic theory, became increasingly convinced that preferences are not always fixed and stable, but are often constructed in response to how they are elicited and how choice contexts are framed. Paul Slovic today still continues to study the psychological processes that can cause people to violate the assumptions of rational economic man, and in this volume, together with Daniel Västfjäll, he provides a chapter that partially attributes the insufficient sensitivity that most people feel towards large numbers of statistical deaths to psychic numbing, i.e. the observation that it is impossible to multiply the intensity of our feelings towards good or bad events by very large magnitudes.

Scepticism towards the preference reversal findings by members of the economics community somewhat ironically led to a degree of acceptance that phenomena that cannot be explained by mainstream theory are, indeed, genuine. In 1979, the economists David Grether and Charles Plott reported a study that controlled or corrected for many of the problems that they, possibly somewhat unfairly, perceived as inherent to the psychologists' work on preference reversals. For example, responding to what they saw as flaws in the methods of prior studies, Grether and Plott included real financial incentives (although Sarah Lichtenstein and Paul Slovic had actually already included financial incentives in field experiments on gamblers in Las Vegas), refrained from forcing people to make a choice between bets by allowing them to express indifference and attempted to remove the motivation for respondents to hedge their bets, by informing them that at the end of the experiment only one of the questions, chosen randomly, would be played out for real. Preference reversals were as significant and systematic as they were in the earlier psychologists' work, which convinced at least some mainstream economists that the phenomena could not be casually brushed aside.

Also in 1979 came the publication of a monumental work in the history of behavioural economics, namely Daniel Kahneman and Amos Tversky's prospect theory. In prospect theory, Kahneman and Tversky proposed two major modifications to expected utility theory. The first is that in prospect theory, the carriers of value are gains and losses around a reference point, rather than final assets, and losses are weighted substantially more – at least twice as much – as gains of the same magnitude. Second, people transform probabilities in an inverse S-shaped pattern, such that they overweight small probabilities, underweight large probabilities and perceive subjective probability to equal objective probability at approximately 0.4. Perhaps rather ambitiously, Kahneman and Tversky claimed that prospect theory could account for most of the major violations of expected utility theory. The latter nonetheless remains the dominant theory of rational choice, a state of affairs that in 1990 caused Maurice Allais to complain that for 'nearly forty years the supporters of [expected utility theory] have exerted a dogmatic and intolerant, powerful and tyrannical domination over the academic world; only in very recent years has a growing reaction begun to appear. This is not the first example of the opposition of the "establishments" of any kind to scientific progress, nor will it be the last' (Allais, 1990, p. 8). For a discipline that had for a century been developed with scientific credentials in mind, the cursory dismissal by the majority of mainstream economists of empirical evidence that falsified the axioms on which much of standard theory is based was not particularly edifying. Subsequent to Allais's statement, however, behavioural economics has gained more acceptance as a sub-branch of economics, culminating in Kahneman being awarded the 2002 Nobel Memorial Prize in Economic Sciences.

The growing 'reaction', which gathered momentum during the 1980s, produced a cottage industry of behavioural economics, encompassing theory-driven work, such as the development of several alternatives to expected utility theory, and research that further tested and questioned the axioms of standard theory. Some of the alternatives to expected utility theory were mathematically motivated in that they directly weakened the axioms underlying the theory so as to allow a wider array of preference patterns; others, such as prospect theory, were modifications based on observed psychological processes, arising from the view that the logic-based axioms of standard theory overlooked the fact that people are human. Of all the alternatives, prospect theory, although still deep in the shadow of expected utility theory, is the most influential, at least partly because Kahneman and Tversky offered numerical parameters for loss aversion and probability weighting, which gives the theory predictive power, and partly because the theory does indeed resonate with how people often appear to reach their decisions. A substantial literature on the anomalies to standard economic theory was published during this time, many of which were reviewed by Richard Thaler in a series of articles in the *Journal of Economic Perspectives*, later collectively printed in his book, *The Winner's Curse* (Thaler, 1994). Thaler was an early pioneer in empirical behavioural economics, and worked with Kahneman and Tversky on experiments on loss aversion, for example. He paved the way for other luminaries in the field, including George Loewenstein, Drazen Prelec and, later, Matthew Rabin, all of whom contribute, or contribute to, chapters in this volume.

During the 1990s, George Loewenstein wrote extensively on people's attitudes towards discounting time. One particular aspect of this general area of interest that has attracted much attention in the behavioural economics discourse is present bias, otherwise known as hyperbolic discounting. Present bias is the observation that people attach an enormous weight to the immediate moment, irrespective of whether that moment is pleasurable or painful, and consequently underplay the importance of all subsequent moments. Present bias may well explain why many people consume too much tasty but unhealthy food, drink excessive quantities of alcohol, refrain from exercise and accumulate substantial debts, overlooking the long-term consequences of their actions. In his chapter, Matthew Rabin argues that a combination of present bias and projection bias, where people do not rationally predict future tastes and overlook the extent to which current behaviours are likely to become habits, can cause people to embark upon and maintain unhealthy lifestyles.

A further issue that has attracted much attention in the behavioural economics community is the notion of motivational crowding out, an area over which Bruno Frey has been a leading researcher since at least the 1990s. Motivational crowding out is the observation that paying people to do something may crowd out their intrinsic or altruistic motivation to do that very thing. For example, to allude to Richard Titmuss's classic 1970 study, *The Gift Relationship*, if a person is altruistically motivated to donate blood voluntarily, that motivation may be eroded if he or she is offered monetary recompense for the donation, because the act would no longer be altruistic, and would more closely resemble a market exchange. For such acts, therefore, the offer of money could lead to less action. This is potentially at odds with the relative price mechanism of standard economic theory, which implies that offering people money, or more money, to do something will increase the likelihood that they will do it. In this volume, Kate Disney, Julian Le Grand and Giles Atkinson argue that an external reward may crowd in altruistic behaviour if it is perceived as supporting or reinforcing an autonomous action, but crowd out altruism if the reward is perceived as controlling. By analysing data in relation to a small charge – i.e. a negative payment – for plastic bags imposed on shoppers in a supermarket, they claim that the charge reinforced a moral norm that people should be reusing their shopping bags, which, they argue, may rebut the idea that charging for environmental goods crowds out intrinsic concern and creates a society of selfish individuals who have no social awareness. Bruno Frey also offers a chapter in this volume, and argues that non-monetary incentives, such as awards and honours, may often be a more powerful tool for motivating people than money, because such incentives might strengthen people's identity with the organization for which they work. Awards may therefore crowd in intrinsic motivation.

From the 1990s to the present, a number of behavioural economists have come onto the scene, many inspired no doubt by those who are these days thought of as the old masters, Kahneman, Tversky and Thaler. Among these are Dan Ariely, David Laibson and Sendhil Mullainathan, but there are also of course a host of others doing interesting and potentially important work in the area. Not all of these are based at US institutions, and some have been undertaking work in behavioural economics for almost as long as the pioneering figures. For example, Ernst Fehr in Switzerland and Robert Sugden in the UK, to name but two, have made significant contributions to behavioural economics over the last three decades. A thorough review of behavioural economics over even the last ten years is beyond my scope here, but three developments will be highlighted. The first relates to some extent to Bruno Frey's chapter mentioned above, namely George Akerlof and Rachel Kranton's work on identity economics in the 2010 book of the same name. Akerlof and Kranton propose that people will experience positive utility from working for an organization with which they identify, and negative utility if they perceive themselves to be outsiders, and yet this utility, experienced from feeling that one belongs or otherwise, is not incorporated into standard economic theory. According to Akerlof and Kranton, our identity defines who we are – our social category – and will influence our behaviours, because different behavioural norms are associated with different social categories. If we take firms, for example, good managers, according to the theory of identity utility, will want their workers to be motivated insiders who identify with the goals of the firm, rather than alienated outsiders. If this is achieved, then employees will want to work enthusiastically towards the objectives of the firm, irrespective of additional personal financial rewards, because they will intrinsically support the firm's mission. This theory can be applied across all conceivable public and private organizations, and may, in monetary terms, offer an inexpensive way to motivate individuals.

A second notable development, or, rather, event, of the past decade was the publication of Daniel Kahneman's intellectual autobiography in 2011. There will of course be many who dispute the general importance of Kahneman's many contributions, but there can be little argument that he is the greatest living behavioural economist, all the more remarkable since he openly admits to having a limited knowledge of economic theory. His substantial impact is and will remain beyond doubt, from his development of prospect theory with Amos Tversky, to his work with a number of colleagues on the gestalt characteristics, or in other words his observations that people's remembered and decision utility often fail to correspond in systematic ways to the utility that they experience. This latter observation cuts a chink in the armour of welfare economics, and has informed, for good or ill, the development of the new economics of happiness. At my own institution, the London School of Economics and Political Science, Kahneman's book is required reading on a number of courses, and everyone who wants to engage with behavioural economics ought to read it.

However, perhaps the most significant development in behavioural economics since 2000 has been the increasing efforts to apply approximately three decades of behavioural economics observations to practical policy concerns. These policy efforts have been principally underpinned by philosophical frameworks – essentially, soft forms of paternalism – developed by some of the world's leading behavioural economists, and include asymmetric paternalism, formulated by Colin Camerer, Samuel Issacharoff, George Loewenstein, Ted O'Donoghue and Matthew Rabin in 2003. The most famous and influential of these frameworks is libertarian paternalism, developed by Richard Thaler and Cass Sunstein and outlined in their 2008 applied behavioural economics book, *Nudge*. Libertarian paternalism may sound like an oxymoron, but Thaler and Sunstein state that they use the term libertarian to modify the word paternalism in order to signify that their approach is liberty-preserving. That is, there should be no burden on those who want to continue their prevailing actions, and the approach does not allow regulation or bans. It is only paternalistic in the sense of wanting to make choosers alter their behaviours such that they would be better off, as judged by their reflective selves. The core essence of the approach is that behavioural economic insights – such as loss aversion, probability weighting, present bias and a host of other findings – can and should inform the design of what Thaler and Sunstein call the choice architecture, or in other words, the context or the environment, so that people are more likely to make voluntary decisions that, on reflection, they would like to make and yet, due to bounds on their economically defined rationality and human error, ordinarily fail to do so. Essentially, libertarian paternalism is based on the observation that people often construct their non-reflective preferences according to how choice tasks are presented to them, a concept discussed earlier in relation to preference reversals. By appealing to the cognitive affects and processes that people employ when making automatic decisions, we might expect that behavioural economic-informed interventions will have more effect than interventions that are otherwise informed. A much discussed example of such an intervention is to place fruit and vegetables at the front and at eye level on canteen counters if one wants to motivate healthier eating habits – assuming, of course, that at least some of those targeted would, on reflection, prefer to eat more fruit and vegetables – because it has been observed that greater salience increases the likelihood of these foodstuffs, or indeed anything, being chosen. Such behavioural economic-informed interventions are now known as nudges.

There is a growing international interest in and awareness of these ideas. For instance, a number of governments, mostly although not exclusively right of centre, are considering or experimenting with nudge-type interventions, including Sweden, the Netherlands, France and Denmark, attracted to the anti-regulatory ethos of the approach. Moreover, Cass Sunstein served as Administrator of the Office of Information and Regulatory Affairs in the Obama Administration up until the summer of 2012, and Richard Thaler is an adviser to the UK government's Behavioural Insights Team, colloquially known as the Nudge Unit. The Nudge Unit was established by David Cameron soon after he came to power in 2010, and, although modest in size with only a handful of staff, it is, from a central government policy perspective, the global leader in developing and applying nudge interventions. The unit has released a number of reports on nudge applications, focusing on areas such as health, personal energy use and tax payment behaviours, all downloadable from its website (www.cabinetoffice.gov.uk/behavioural-insights-team). Paul Dolan helped to develop the intellectual foundation of the Nudge Unit's proposals, and in this volume he discusses the relevance of this work for motivating people to take more responsibility over their personal finances.

The nudge approach, with, for example, its emphasis on feeding into unconscious automatic thought processes and concerns about whether this equates to manipulation, provides fertile ground for moral argument. Despite being one of the world's leading behavioural economists, Robert Sugden is, for instance, wary of using its findings to help inform policy in the manner that Richard Thaler, Cass Sunstein and Paul Dolan advocate. Sugden argues that we ought to be cautious about that which the libertarian paternalist judges to be best for the individual, because there is no guarantee that the limitations on attention, cognitive ability and self-control that affect the individual's automatic responses are absent from their deliberative decision-making. This view is shared by Drazen Prelec, who, writing in this volume, expresses scepticism about people's ability to introspect desires and beliefs. Prelec argues that the values that define a society are not fully accessible by collective reflection, and that even if we could elicit information about deep characteristics, there is a question of credibility that affects both members of the general public – e.g. smokers' expressed intentions to quit smoking cannot be trusted – and public officials, who have incentives to disguise the real picture. Sugden maintains that behavioural welfare economics, of which nudge theory is a part, tends to keep well-being as the normative criterion, but detaches the definition of well-being from individual choice. He advocates the opposite approach by proposing that opportunity should be the normative criterion, without necessarily claiming that increases in opportunity improve well-being.

Although the nudge approach has to a considerable degree comman-deered the policy relevance of behavioural economics over recent years, behavioural economics can be of use, and arguably of more profound use, for informing policies that fall outside the scope of nudging. For example, behavioural economics can potentially provide insights into how private sector corporations implicitly use human cognitive processes, such as present bias, to encourage people to buy more of a particular product than they really want, and thus can help governments to decide on when and how the private sector ought to be regulated. Therefore, consideration of behavioural economics is not merely of use to those who wish to introduce anti-regulatory approaches aimed at influencing the behaviour of citizens, but can and arguably should be used also – or perhaps instead – to inform regulations that essentially define the acceptable limits of corporate actions. Moreover, the findings of behavioural economics can be used to explain the success or otherwise of previous policies. An example of this in the current volume is my own chapter that attributes ambiguity aversion as a cause of the UK government's arguably excessive response to the swine flu outbreak. Another example is given by Gwyn Bevan and Barbara Fasolo, who argue in their chapter that the public reporting of performance in the health and education sectors, by creating widely observable reference points and instilling a fear of reputational losses, has motivated performance improvements.

Behavioural economics has travelled a long way, particularly in the last thirty years, and is now being considered seriously in policy dialogues. This volume, it is hoped, contributes importantly to thought on the policy implications of the subdiscipline. All of the main chapters that follow were presented at a seminar series funded by the UK Higher Education Innovation Fund, and hosted at the London School of Economics and Political Science during the 2010–11 academic year. Responses to each of the chapters were solicited from relevant scholars, and they are included within the volume so as to enrich the issues presented.

The authors of the chapters were asked to relate an aspect of behavioural economics to a policy concern of their choosing, and therefore a disparate range of policy areas are included here, from health and education to environmental concerns, to name but three. It would be somewhat artificial to group chapters together according to particular issues, but, loosely, the chapters by myself and Bevan and Fasolo attempt to use established behavioural economics findings to explain the success or otherwise of previously implemented policies; Disney, Le Grand and Atkinson report a pilot study that specifically tests various aspects of motivational theory; Slovic and Västfjäll, Rabin, Sah, Cain and Loewenstein, and Frey hypothesize how behavioural economics might inform future policy design; and Dolan and Prelec present arguments more closely focused on nudge theory, the former as an advocate and the latter, implicitly, as a critic. It is in this order that the chapters are presented, and if read together they will, it is hoped, strengthen the reader's knowledge of the findings of behavioural economics, and his or her understanding of how these findings might inform policy.

References

Akerlof, G. A. and Kranton, R. E. (2010). *Identity Economics: How Our Identities Shape Our Work, Wages, and Well-Being.* Princeton University Press.

Allais, M. (1953). Le Comportement de l'Homme Rationnel Devant le Risque: Critique des Postulats et Axiomes de l'Ecole Américaine. *Econometrica* 21: 503–46.

(1990). Allais Paradox. In J. Eatwell, M. Milgate and P. Newman (eds.), *The New Palgrave: Utility and Probability.* New York: Macmillan, pp. 3–9.

Bruni, L. and Sugden, R. (2007). The Road Not Taken: How Psychology was Removed from Economics, and How it Might be Brought Back. *Economic Journal* 117: 146–73.

Camerer, C., Issacharoff, S., Loewenstein, G., O'Donoghue, T. and Rabin, M. (2003). Regulation for Conservatives: Behavioral Economics and the Case for 'Asymmetric Paternalism'. *University of Pennsylvania Law Review* 1151: 1211–54.

Ellsberg, D. (1961). Risk, Ambiguity and the Savage Axioms. *Quarterly Journal of Economics* 75: 643–69.

Grether, D. M. and Plott, C. R. (1979). Economic Theory of Choice and the Preference Reversal Phenomenon. *American Economic Review* 69: 623–38.

Kahneman, D. (2011). *Thinking, Fast and Slow.* London: Allen Lane.

Kahneman, D. and Tversky, A. (1979). Prospect Theory: An Analysis of Decision Under Risk. *Econometrica* 47: 263–91.

Lichtenstein, S and Slovic, P. (1971). Reversals of Preferences Between Bids and Choices in Gambling Decisions. *Journal of Experimental Psychology* 89: 46–55.

Simon, H. A. (1956). Rational Choice and the Structure of the Environment. *Psychological Review* 63: 129–38.

Thaler, R. H. (1994). *The Winner's Curse: Paradoxes and Anomalies of Economic Life.* Princeton University Press.

Thaler, R. H. and Sunstein, C. R. (2008). *Nudge: Improving Decisions about Health, Wealth and Happiness.* New Haven: Yale University Press.

Titmuss, R. (1970). *The Gift Relationship: From Human Blood to Social Policy.* London: New Press.

1 | *Ambiguity aversion and the UK government's response to swine flu*

ADAM OLIVER

Introduction

In April 2009, an outbreak of the H1N1 swine flu virus captured the attention of the world. The UK government quickly claimed that the country was well prepared to respond to this potential global pandemic. Indeed, ever since (and even before) the 2002 H5N1 avian flu outbreak, the government had been laying the foundations for action. The Chief Medical Officer (CMO) for England, Sir Liam Donaldson, was deeply involved in the response, having himself published a 2002 policy document entitled *Getting Ahead of the Curve: A Strategy for Combating Infectious Diseases* (Department of Health, 2002), and in 2007 the government published *A National Framework for Responding to an Influenza Pandemic* (Cabinet Office/Department of Health, 2007). The *Framework* was geared towards a worst case scenario, and planned for between 55,500 and 750,000 fatalities. It said that there should be a stockpile of antiviral medications sufficient to treat 50 per cent of the population, and in the event of a pandemic, stated that the government should purchase sufficient vaccine to immunize everyone in the country and should establish a national pandemic flu service so that people can have antivirals authorized over the phone. The government's response to the 2009 outbreak was directly informed by the *Framework*.

The initial response focused on containing the virus, principally so as to try to buy some time to better understand the virus before a treatment stage was initiated. Among the first people infected were schoolchildren, and the schools affected issued antiviral medications in many cases to all those in the same year as the infected pupil, and in some cases to the whole school. In several instances, schools closed for a week. On 29 April, two days after the first cases of swine flu were detected in the UK, the government announced plans to increase its stockpile of antivirals from levels sufficient to treat 50 per cent of the population to levels sufficient to treat 80 per cent, and people were advised to take these medications if they had come into contact with an infected person. Moreover, a mass public health media campaign was launched, and leaflets were sent to every household in the country advising on what swine flu is, and how to respond to it (e.g. to cover noses and mouths when sneezing and to undertake regular hand-washing, captured under the slogan, 'Catch it. Bin it. Kill it').

In May 2009, the government announced that it had in place advanced purchase agreements with pharmaceutical manufacturers to provide a flu vaccine for the entire UK population, which would be activated automatically in the event of the World Health Organization (WHO) classifying the outbreak as a pandemic (which it did in June 2009). In July, the government, recognizing that the spread of the virus could no longer be efficiently controlled, moved from a policy of containment to a treatment stage, of which it was hoped that the vaccine would form the central component. Also in July, the National Flu Pandemic Service (NFPS) became live in England, and provided a website and call centres for those concerned that they had contracted the illness. Anyone who indicated relevant symptoms was given a unique reference number allowing them or someone acting on their behalf to collect antiviral medications without first visiting their general practitioner (GP), which relieved some of the pressure on primary care services.

As noted, the response was informed by the *Framework*, and the *Framework* was based upon a feared outbreak of avian flu. Swine flu ultimately proved much milder and less deadly than a worst case avian flu outbreak, which has led some to conclude that the government overreacted to the 2009 threat (*The Independent*, 22 April 2010), insufficiently moderating its response as the nature of swine flu became clearer. One possible explanation for any 'excessive' response from the government is given by ambiguity aversion. That is to say that when it arrived, the behaviour of swine flu (its infectivity, severity, etc.) was highly uncertain (or, synonymously, ambiguous), and as a consequence, the government attached disproportionate weight to the worst possible outcome of the threat. A dislike of uncertainty implies that people will pay a high price to avoid it, or, when uncertainty cannot be avoided, they adopt a pessimistic approach and overweight the slight possibility of the worst outcome happening. The latter is an explanation for why people are often attracted to the precautionary principle, particularly when the worst possible outcome is catastrophic.

This chapter is organized as follows. First, ambiguity aversion is described by means of a hypothetical thought experiment, and then the precautionary principle is defined. Following this definition, further details of, and suggested reasons for, the UK government's containment and treatment response to the 2009 swine flu pandemic are offered. The chapter finishes with a short conclusion.

Ambiguity aversion

In economics, a distinction is made between risk and uncertainty. An event that is risky has a known probability of occurrence. For instance, if a die is rolled, the probability of a six is 0.116. When an event is uncertain (or, equivalently, ambiguous), however, the probability of an event occurring is not known, and will fall within a probability range. For instance, the probability of rain in London tomorrow might be somewhere between 0.05 and 0.15. Economic theory assumes that when people are faced with uncertain events they will behave as if well-specified probability distributions exist. If so, uncertain events reduce to risky events, and the same behavioural axioms underlie both types of scenario.

Economic theory of course allows for risk attitude. If someone is risk averse (say, in the case of insurance), they will pay a premium to avoid the risk, or if they are risk seeking (if they like gambling), they will pay to accept the risk. However, behavioural economists have observed that people are willing to pay an additional premium, over and above that implied by risk aversion and outside the framework of standard economic theory, in order to avoid ambiguity. This can be best illustrated by Ellsberg's original demonstration of this phenomenon, which he presented as a thought experiment at a dinner party fifty years ago (Ellsberg, 1961).

Ellsberg used money outcomes; in Table 1.1 his paradox has been adapted to a hypothetical influenza scenario. The example is not intended to be a representation of a realistic flu-related decision context. It is merely meant to illustrate the phenomenon of ambiguity aversion. Assume that there are three strains of flu: A, B and C. The government knows that there is a 1/3 chance that strain A prevails. It also therefore knows that there is a 2/3 chance that either

Table 1.1 *The Ellsberg paradox*

	Strain A	Strain B	Strain C
	1/3	2/3	
Strategy X	10,000	0	0
Strategy Y	0	10,000	0
Strategy X′	10,000	0	10,000
Strategy Y′	0	10,000	10,000

strain B or strain C prevails, but is uncertain of the exact chance of either of these strains. That is, there is a zero to 2/3 chance of B; likewise for C.

Assume that the government is considering implementing either Strategy X or Strategy Y in response to a flu outbreak. If X is followed, there is a 1/3 chance that 10,000 lives will be saved and a 2/3 chance that no lives will be saved. If Y is followed, there is an uncertain zero to 2/3 chance that 10,000 lives will be saved, and a 1/3 to certain chance that no lives will be saved.

Next assume that the government is considering X′ or Y′. For X′, there is a 1/3 to certain chance that 10,000 lives will be saved, and a zero to 2/3 chance that no lives will be saved. For Y′, there is a 2/3 chance that 10,000 lives will be saved, and a 1/3 chance that no lives will be saved.

Now, in the event of strain C, X and Y share a common outcome of no lives being saved. Therefore, according to the independence axiom of standard economic theory, strain C should be irrelevant when considering X or Y; likewise when considering X′ or Y′, where strain C gives a common outcome of saving 10,000 lives. If C is considered irrelevant in both choice contexts, then X is identical to X′ and Y is identical to Y′, and thus, in the choice between X and Y and X′ and Y′, the decision-maker should choose X and X′ or Y and Y′ (or be indifferent in both choices). However, Ellsberg's hypothesis implies that decision-makers will lean towards X and Y′, an expectation that, in the context of money outcomes, has been confirmed empirically (e.g. Bernasconi and Loomes, 1992; Curley and Yates, 1989; Einhorn and Hogarth, 1986).

The reason for the Ellsberg paradox is that decision-makers may not like the uncertainty embedded in Y and X′; that is to say, they are ambiguity averse, which can lead to systematic violations of standard economic theory. As noted in the previous section, when events are uncertain, people may often adopt a form of pessimism, particularly when the magnitude of the associated threat is large, which leads them to lean towards the worst case scenario. This will in turn cause them to take action – arguably, sometimes too much action – to mitigate the uncertainty, and could lead them to adopt a strong version of the precautionary principle.

The precautionary principle

Henry and Henry (2002) maintain that the crucial concept underlying the precautionary principle is not the resolution of uncertainty, but uncertainty itself. That is to say that reaction to uncertainty drives the precautionary principle, with O'Riordan and Jordan (1995) stating that 'the principle of precaution ... implies committing human activity to investments where the benefits of action cannot, at the time of expenditure, be justified by conclusive scientific evidence'. Sunstein (2005) argues that a strong version of the precautionary principle is voiced when regulators are called to take steps to protect fully against all potential harms, a concept that he views as literally incoherent, because regulation itself introduces its own risks and thus the strong version is paralysing, because it forbids the very steps that it requires.

A weaker version of the precautionary principle contends that a lack of decisive evidence of harm should not offer grounds for refusing to act. This is, for Sunstein (2005), something to which no reasonable person could object. Given the uncertainty and the potentially catastrophic effects of the 2009 swine flu outbreak, a policy response that reflected some notion of the precautionary principle was necessary. That is, the government had to act to protect in the face of uncertainty, but was its action too strong? In addressing this question, one has to consider the opportunity costs and unintended consequences of the response, such as the possibility of provoking unnecessary fear within the population in the short term and, conversely, causing widespread insensitivity to legitimate potential harms in the longer term (the 'cry wolf' effect). Further, if the response was too strong, was it because of an aversion to ambiguity? A consideration of these issues, among others, will occupy the rest of this chapter.

The response

The strength of the government's initial and, until early 2010, continuing response to the swine flu pandemic has multiple causal factors. As mentioned in the introduction, Sir Liam Donaldson had for many years invested much effort in highlighting the threat of pandemics, and postponed his retirement to tackle the outbreak in the spring of 2009. In England, unlike Wales and Scotland, the CMO was used as the chief spokesperson during the outbreak, and his voice attracted much attention. Moreover, something akin to 'institutional memory' may have also played a role, in that Sir Liam's predecessors, Sir Donald Acheson and Sir Kenneth Calman, were publicly criticized in the *Phillips Report* (2000) for responding inadequately to the bovine spongiform encephalopathy (BSE)/variant Creutzfeldt-Jakob disease (vCJD) (i.e. mad cow's disease) scare in the 1980s and 1990s (see also Klein, 2000), and across broader government policy, more recent responses to, for example, foot and mouth disease in 2001, had been criticized severely (*The Guardian*, 16 May 2001).

More tellingly, perhaps, the initial information from Mexico (the first cases were confirmed in Mexico and the United States on 23 April 2009) appeared to suggest that the virus was associated with rapid spread and high fatality. The quality of that data was later considered dubious (Hine, 2010), but nobody knew that at the time and it triggered an all-out response from the UK government. Once the response had been set in motion, the government seemingly found it difficult to scale down its actions, perhaps indicating that once it had 'bought into' the threat and had started to apply the *Framework*, the actions became the 'default', and deviating from those proved sticky.

As noted, the *Framework* was a response to avian flu. In parallel, the modellers that the government relied on to predict the outcome of the 2009 outbreak used parameters that reflected more accurately the greater severity of the avian flu outbreak. More specifically, three groups of modellers heavily influenced the Scientific Advisory Group for Emergencies (SAGE), which was tasked with advising the government on the basis of the scientific evidence. SAGE, and thus the government, therefore adopted a worst case scenario. It has been suggested that policy-makers may over-rely on modellers because they are 'credible' (i.e. mathematical and academic), and give concrete, easily understood, seemingly robust answers (Hine, 2010).

Unfortunately, the emphasis on modelling may have somewhat blinded the decision-makers to the contribution that those with other expertise could have made, including those experienced in dealing with previous pandemics and those who were dealing directly and practically with clinical cases who quickly saw that the virus was mild and associated with low mortality (Hine, 2010).

In addition to avian flu, fears provoked by previous pandemics had a significant influence on the government's response to swine flu. The 2002 avian flu outbreak, although infecting only 495 humans globally, had a mortality rate of 59 per cent (*The Independent*, 3 May 2010), and pandemics on a catastrophic scale in the more distant past still loomed large. For instance, the Asian flu and Hong Kong flu outbreaks in 1957 and 1968–9, respectively, had each killed 1 million to 4 million people, and the mother (in terms of magnitude, not composition) of all pandemics, the Spanish flu outbreak in 1918–19, is estimated to have killed up to 40 million people (Hine, 2010), 3 per cent of the world's population at that time.[1]

In addition to not wanting to be seen to repeat the mistakes of the past and relying on evidence that predicted the worst case scenario, the shadow of previous pandemics, the uncertainty and the potentially catastrophic outcome may therefore give reason for an element of ambiguity aversion and possible over-response from the government to the 2009 outbreak. However, to judge more confidently whether the response was indeed excessive requires us to delve a little further into its details.

The containment phase

Between 27 April and 2 July 2009, the government focused upon a containment strategy, the focal point of which centred on the use of antiviral medications. In order to increase the stockpile, two types of antivirals were purchased: the primary stock, Tamiflu, and a

---

[1] As an aside, the origins of the Spanish flu outbreak are debated, but it has been hypothesized that the virus gained a foothold among immuno-compromised soldiers in the hospital and army training complex near Etaples in northern France during the First World War (Oxford et al., 2007). Many of the soldiers had been weakened by gas used in the Somme battlefields, and the camp was overcrowded and under the flight path of flu-carrying geese and ducks. Moreover, there is photographic evidence of soldiers plucking geese and turkeys.

secondary stock, Relenza, which was bought in case the virus became resistant to Tamiflu. Antivirals relieve the symptoms of flu by an average of one day if they are taken within the first 48 hours of the onset of symptoms. It is thus possible that they can prevent some people from developing more serious illness than they would develop in the absence of the drugs (Oxford et al., 2007).[2] Moreover, if people act quickly and take antivirals within a day of the symptoms developing, there is a chance of reduced transmission (Ferguson et al., 2006). The government therefore implemented a policy of recommending antiviral use by those who had come into contact with anyone infected with the virus, in the hope that this would slow the spread and thus give more time to learn about the virus's characteristics (and thus develop further measures to combat the virus effectively) before it had spread extensively throughout the population.

The English government adopted a 'treat all' approach with respect to antivirals, meaning that all those with swine flu symptoms were advised to take the medications. In the three devolved countries of the UK, only those considered most at risk from developing serious illness as a result of contracting the virus were recommended to take the drugs. As early as 30 April, it was noted that the virus appeared to be mild and self-limiting outside of Mexico (Hine, 2010), and by mid-May the Health Protection Agency recommended that the use of antivirals be cut back, due to the observed side-effects of the medications (particularly in children), the large number of people who were not completing the courses of the drugs and the risk of causing drug resistance (Hine, 2010). The English government did not change its policy until the beginning of July, and thus its actions regarding the use of antivirals, from a purely 'health' perspective, can quite reasonably be viewed as excessive (indeed, there is no evidence that the antiviral policy slowed the spread of the illness). However, in this case, any excessive reaction is perhaps less likely to have been motivated by ambiguity aversion (i.e. a focus upon the worst case scenario) *per se*; rather, the action was probably undertaken to show the general public that *something* was being done in response to the threat, and to show that everything possible had been done should

---

[2] Although see Epstein (2011) for a critique of the purported effectiveness of antiviral medications.

the worst case scenario be realized.[3] Thus, the principal motivation behind the treat-all approach may well have been to maintain public confidence, to placate the 'worried well'.

Losing public confidence is a possible opportunity cost of *not* acting aggressively, but there are also opportunity costs of acting too aggressively that the government may have insufficiently considered.[4] As noted in the introduction, a mass media campaign was another part of the government's strategy, a campaign that included regular media briefings from the CMO that continued throughout the response. By July, the briefings included a 'reasonable worst case' scenario, an unfortunate turn of phrase as it was used by some to mean 'relatively likely to occur'. In fact, the reasonable worst case was a highly pessimistic scenario, possibly motivated by ambiguity aversion. Initially, the reasonable worst case specified 65,000 deaths, intended for planning purposes,[5] but used by some of the media as a prediction. Sir Liam Donaldson later lamented this misuse, but the behaviour of the media should have been easy to predict. The sensationalist worst case scenario would be expected to sell most copy and maximize viewing numbers; as Ariely (2008) has pointed out, in press circles 'if it bleeds, it leads'.

It is not a good thing to incite fear unnecessarily. Anxiety has never been a foundation for rational action (Beck, 1992). Fear can spread much quicker than the virus itself, with people becoming fearful of the virus just because they observe a degree of fear in others. The fear was

---

[3] An aggressive response to the outbreak caused by anxiety of a public backlash should the worst happen is, in theory, fuelled by 'anticipated regret', a phenomenon that has a long history in the behavioural economics literature (Loomes and Sugden, 1982). That is, although the worst case was unlikely to happen, the repercussions for the government if it had happened and they had not done everything possible would plausibly have been very large, which led it to focus very heavily on this possible outcome. Like ambiguity aversion, anticipated regret can cause violations of standard economic theory.

[4] The consideration of opportunity costs is a key feature of economics. As far as I can gather, the official committees convened for the swine flu response included only one economist – the Chief Economist at the Department of Health, Barry McCormick.

[5] The reasonable worst case was revised down to 19,000 deaths in September 2009, and to 1,000 deaths in October. In total, 457 people died of swine flu in the UK. Most of these had underlying health problems, but there were some deaths among pregnant women.

possibly compounded by stories that people construct from the visual images that the media present (e.g. the stressed yet determined mothers clinging to their antiviral medications as they steer their children away from school). All of this feeds the 'availability heuristic', where threats that people deem as relevant are those that are foremost in their consciousness, with other potential harms becoming barely visible to them. Policy-makers as well as the general public are likely to suffer from the availability heuristic. People may then disproportionately focus on information that reinforces the conscious threat, and the escalating concern within the populace further compels governments to act in the strongest possible way, or face accusations of not doing enough.

Aside from the disutility felt from personal anxiety, fear can lead to attention and resources being directed away from interventions that are more health-enhancing and life-saving. It is perhaps instructive to note that normal seasonal flu kills 2,000–4,000 people in the UK; swine flu killed 457 people. Since swine flu very likely drove out the normal seasonal flu virus, the 2009 outbreak probably saved lives, although that is, of course, to speak with hindsight. Nonetheless, Hine (2010), in her independent review of the response to the swine flu outbreak, estimated that £1.2 billion was spent on the containment and treatment (discussed below) phases, equivalent to a little over 1 per cent of the annual National Health Service (NHS) budget, a not insubstantial amount of additional money to be found at the margin, particularly at a time of public sector spending constraint. This figure mainly appertains to the costs of pharmaceuticals and vaccines and did not factor in opportunity costs, but even taken at face value, if a part of this spending had been avoided with a more measured response, it could have probably been used to significant effect elsewhere.

On the flipside of provoking short-term fear is the danger of desensitizing people to risk in the longer term, which may be more likely to occur if the policy is to emphasize initially the worst case scenario, but then to revise down the threat. That is, in the longer term, the government could face accusations of 'crying wolf', which may even occur in the short term as the number of threats that are not as catastrophic as originally feared multiplies over time (e.g. vCJD, SARS, avian flu, swine flu). There is some limited evidence that this occurred with respect to the swine flu outbreak, in that a telephone survey of a sample of the general public just a few weeks after the initial outbreak of the virus revealed that only 24 per cent of respondents reported any anxiety with respect to swine flu, 68 per cent believed the media had exaggerated the threat and 72 per cent reported no change in simple preventive measures, such as increased hand-washing (Rubin et al., 2009). A survey conducted in the United States reported similar findings (Holland Jones and Salathe, 2009).

The government's focus on the worst case scenario, and the potential unintended (but predictable) negative consequences of that strategy, can plausibly be explained by ambiguity aversion (among the other factors discussed earlier), but the excessive promoted use of antivirals was, it is contended here, consequent on a desire to maintain public trust. By July 2009, the government decided that it was no longer possible to efficiently contain the spread of the swine flu virus, and therefore moved on to a treatment phase.

The treatment phase

By 2 July, after much delay, the government adopted a more targeted antiviral strategy, and then on 23 July, the NFPS was launched in England, relieving some of the pressure on primary care services (the NFPS was closed on 11 February 2010, by which time it had undertaken 2.73 million assessments and prescribed 1.16 million courses of antivirals (Hine, 2010)). However, the stand-out feature of the treatment phase was the development and later use of a swine flu vaccine.

When WHO upgraded swine flu to phase 6 pandemic status on 11 June 2009,[6] the government had to make a decision on activating the advance vaccine purchase agreements that it had in place with two pharmaceutical companies, Glaxo SmithKline (GSK) and Baxter. Ministers had to choose between buying 30 million doses and 132 million doses of the vaccine, with the latter being sufficient to vaccinate the whole population effectively. The decision to purchase

[6] WHO has been criticized for its response by parliamentarians in a Council of Europe probe, who questioned whether the pharmaceutical industry unduly influenced its decisions in relation to swine flu. WHO officials have denied these claims (*The Independent*, 15 April 2010), and the organization convened an independent committee to review the international response to swine flu, which reported in 2011: www.who.int/csr/disease/swineflu/notes/briefing_20100610/en/.

132 million doses was confirmed on 17 June. This quantity of vaccine was ultimately not required. Due to the uncertainty at the time, the government ought to have been more forceful in negotiating break clauses in their contracts with the pharmaceutical manufacturers, a highly visible recommendation in the *Hine Review* (Hine, 2010). To their credit, Baxter agreed to a break clause; GSK did not. In July 2010, GSK issued the following statement: 'A break clause that allows one country to exceed their allocation when supplies are limited and then pulls out later would not be ethical' (*The Guardian*, 1 July 2010). However, since the worst case scenario did not materialize, the UK's purchase did not presumably deny the populations of other countries needed vaccines. GSK's response is more likely to have been motivated by concerns for profit than for ethics. In future national emergencies (such as a 'worst case' viral outbreak), is it going too far to recommend that governments be instilled with powers to commandeer privately produced vaccines and medications at production prices? In such an eventuality such action may well be in the health-related interests of everybody, including those who work in the commercial pharmaceutical sector.

Although the swine flu vaccine was available for use while the virus was still causing some disease, it took until 21 October before the vaccine had been developed and cleared to administer, almost six months since the first UK cases of the illness had been recorded on 27 April. The process could not have been significantly quicker. However, it is likely that a worst case pandemic would largely be over within four months of the first cases being recorded (Ferguson et al., 2006), and after that time much of the surviving population would probably have built up some natural immunity. The government anticipated that the virus could have peaked again in the winter of 2009/2010, but even without the benefit of hindsight, one can reasonably contend that a more moderate approach of purchasing sufficient vaccine to cover only those at high risk of susceptibility would have been a more appropriate decision.

Since the full quantity of vaccine purchased only became available gradually from late October onwards, the government announced that the high-risk groups would indeed be targeted for vaccination first. These included those aged between six months and sixty-five years with low immunities or certain chronic illnesses, pregnant women, the non-healthy over sixty-fives and frontline health care workers: in total, 13 million people. The government anticipated that 75 per cent of these would get their vaccinations. In the event, only 5.5 million people in total vaccinated themselves against swine flu; 70 per cent of frontline health care workers did not go for vaccination (*The Independent*, 22 April 2010). Although more people would no doubt have vaccinated themselves had the full threat been realized, the government would have been well advised of the likelihood that a significant percentage of the population would not have done so, quite apart from natural immunity rendering vaccination obsolete in many cases.

The government thus purchased sufficient vaccine for a worst case scenario, which appears to lend itself to ambiguity aversion (i.e. recognizing that anything could happen, but nevertheless acting as if the worst would happen), but even if the worst case is certain to happen, a policy of purchasing vaccine for the whole population is questionable. By the time the vaccine is ready, the pandemic is likely to be over, many will have natural immunity and a great number will not vaccinate themselves in any case. It would seem that, at most, a policy to vaccinate the high-risk groups – 13 million people or 26 million doses if two vaccinations are required – will suffice, and even then contracts with manufacturers that better protect the public purse are advisable.

Conclusion

Many – perhaps most – of us are ambiguity averse, and more of us will be so when the worst case consequences are catastrophic. Pandemics provoke this 'dread factor'; we fear the worst, and will anchor on it. We will think of the opportunity costs of *not* acting, and will be influenced by a 'what if' effect. Erring on the side of caution in such cases feeds into a basic human need for security. However, although Henry (2006, p. 9) has stated that 'uncertainty should not be inflated and invoked as an alibi for inaction', caution should be exercised when faced with acting in the face of uncertainty. That is to say that all of us, and particularly the policy-makers among us, ought to recognize that in addition to the opportunity costs of not acting (e.g. the potential political costs, the possible loss of public confidence, the loss of life *if* the worst happens), there are opportunity costs of acting (e.g. provoking unnecessary fear, the repercussions from 'crying wolf', the lives and health lost by diverting resources away from other services) that should not be overlooked.

Clearly, the government had to act in the face of the swine flu pandemic, but did it act too much? The *Hine Review* concluded that given the initial uncertainties with respect to the behaviour of the virus, the development of resistance to antivirals and the possibility of a more virulent second wave, there would inevitably be calls from some to assume the worst case scenario and resource the response accordingly (Hine, 2010). That is what happened. The response was tailored to fit the *Framework* rather than to the nature of the swine flu virus, and was thus arguably directed in part by some kind of 'sunk cost bias' or 'status quo bias', both of which compounded the ambiguity aversion. There was also an over-reliance on modellers who populated their trees with 'worst case' data, and insufficient consideration of other branches of expertise and of the experiences of those directly involved with clinical cases. Hine (2010) goes on to say that there was an alternative viable approach, which would have been for the government to take a view on the most likely outcome of the pandemic, while monitoring events closely and changing tack as necessary. Had this been done, it is the contention of this chapter that the government in the UK was sufficiently informed at the time to promote a more targeted use of antivirals much earlier than they did, and to buy far less vaccine when a decision on purchasing was required.

A more moderated approach may not have come at a political cost, because the government would still have been acting significantly (and arguably more appropriately), yet the response would have required considerably fewer resources. However, there seems to be a presumption in the *Hine Review* that the more aggressive approach still offered good value for money. This view appears to be based on the assumption that the severe threat is realized, but this will not do, because when assessing value for money, the less than certain chance that the severe threat will be realized has to be factored in. Fortunately, pandemics are quite rare, but unfortunately, this means that it is not possible to estimate accurately the chance that the severe threat will occur. This is partly why the government responded as if the severe threat would materialize. However, if an informed guess, on the basis of past experience, can be made on the chance of the severe threat being realized – say, 25 per cent – then the government would need to respond four times to reap the benefits of tackling a severe threat once. Therefore, the cost side would have to be multiplied by four, and even then this would not account for the broader unintended consequences associated with fear, desensitization, etc. It is of course possible that a 'worst case' response to every pandemic does indeed represent a good use of resources, and it may in any case be the type of response that most policymakers and the general public want to see, but both of these considerations require more analysis and public discourse. A more sobering thought, however, is that even the most aggressive response might well be ineffective against the inevitable catastrophic pandemics that lie ahead.

References

Ariely, D. (2008). *Predictably Irrational: The Hidden Forces that Shape Our Decisions*. New York: HarperCollins.

Beck, U. (1992). *Risk Society: Towards a New Modernity*. London: Sage.

Bernasconi, M. and Loomes, G. (1992). Failures of the Reduction Principle in an Ellsberg-Type Problem. *Theory and Decision* 32: 77–100.

Cabinet Office/Department of Health (2007). *A National Framework for Responding to an Influenza Pandemic*. London: Department of Health.

Curley, S. P. and Yates, F. J. (1989). An Empirical Evaluation of Descriptive Models of Ambiguity Reactions in Choice Situations. *Journal of Mathematical Psychology* 33: 397–427.

Department of Health (2002). *Getting Ahead of the Curve: A Strategy for Combating Infectious Diseases*. London: Department of Health.

Einhorn, H. J. and Hogarth, R. M. (1986). Decision Making Under Ambiguity. *Journal of Business* 59: S225–S250.

Ellsberg, D. (1961). Risk, Ambiguity and the Savage Axioms. *Quarterly Journal of Economics* 75: 643–69.

Epstein, H. (2011). Flu Warning: Beware the Drug Companies! *New York Review of Books*, 11 May.

Ferguson, N. M., Cummings, D. A. T., Fraser, C., Cajka, J. C., Cooley, P. C. and Burke, D. S. (2006). Strategies for Mitigating an Influenza Pandemic. *Nature* 442: 448–52.

Henry, C. (2006). *Decision-Making Under Scientific, Political and Economic Uncertainty*. Laboratoire d'Econométrie Cahier No. DDX-06-12. Paris: Ecole Polytechnique.

Henry, C. and Henry, M. (2002). *Formalization and Applications of the Precautionary Principle. Laboratoire d'Econométrie Cahier No. 2002-008.* Paris: Ecole Polytechnique.

Hine, D. (2010). *An Independent Review of the UK Response to the 2009 Influenza Pandemic [Hine Review].* London: The Cabinet Office.

Holland Jones, J. and Salathe, M. (2009). Early Assessment of Anxiety and Behavioral Response to Novel Swine-Origin Influenza A (H1N1). *PLoS One* 4: e8032.

Klein, R. (2000). The Politics of Risk: The Case of BSE. *BMJ* 321: 1091–2.

Loomes, G. C. and Sugden, R. (1982). Regret Theory: An Alternative Theory of Rational Choice under Uncertainty. *Economic Journal* 92: 805–24.

O'Riordan, T. and Jordan, A. (1995). The Precautionary Principle in Contemporary Environmental Politics. *Environmental Values* 4: 191–212.

Oxford, J., Lambkin-Williams, R. and Mann, A. (2007). The Threat of Avian Influenza H5N1: 'do we have the tools for the job?' *Antiviral Chemistry and Chemotherapy* 18: 71–4.

Phillips, N. (chairman) (2000). *The BSE Inquiry Vol. 1: Findings and Conclusions [Phillips Report].* London: Stationery Office.

Rubin, G. J., Amlot, R., Page, L. and Wessely, S. (2009). Public Perceptions, Anxiety, and Behaviour Change in Relation to the Swine Flu Outbreak: Cross Sectional Telephone Survey. *BMJ* 339: b2651.

Sunstein, C. R. (2005). *Laws of Fear: Beyond the Precautionary Principle.* Cambridge University Press.

The Guardian (2001). A catalogue of failures that discredits the whole system: there must be an inquiry into the foot and mouth saga. 16 May.

2010 (Swine) flu response was £1.2 billion well spent, review finds. 1 July.

The Independent (2010). WHO flu experts reject charges of business influence in pandemic. 15 April.

(2010). Governments accused of panicking over swine flu. 22 April.

(2010). A little knowledge: how research scientists were caught out by swine flu. 3 May.

1.1 | *A response to Oliver*

CHRISTOPHER EXETER

Francis Daniels Moore, the American surgeon and pioneer of numerous medical advances, commented in his 1959 textbook *Metabolic Care of the Surgical Patient*: 'The fundamental act of medical care is assumption of responsibility' (Moore, 1959). These ten words could summarize the UK government's response to the 2009 outbreak of H1N1, more commonly known as 'swine flu', and on which Adam Oliver's chapter concentrates.

Swine flu was not a virus unknown to clinicians in 2009. There had been previous outbreaks. The 1918 flu pandemic in humans was associated with H1N1. In February 1976 a US army recruit stationed at Fort Dix, New Jersey reported feeling tired and weak. He died the following day of H1N1 influenza. A number of his colleagues were hospitalized, and around 200 cases were reported. However, awareness of symptoms revealed that another strain of swine flu had emerged in continental United States. A decision was taken to undertake a mass vaccination; one that remains controversial still today. Further outbreaks followed: in 1988 a case of zoonosis occurred, where a woman contracted swine flu and subsequently died following a visit to a county fair. Other visitors were also suspected of contracting the infection. There was a further known episode in the Philippines in 2007.

In April 2009 the second flu pandemic involving the H1N1 virus emerged in the Veracruz region of Mexico, on the country's Gulf of Mexico coast, and had been spreading amongst the population for a number of months prior to being officially classified as an epidemic. The number of cases rose, and the epidemic quickly became a pandemic. However, by November 2009 there was a decline in the number of reported cases of H1N1 influenza, and by spring 2010 the fall was so sharp that on 10 August 2010 the Director-General of the World Health Organization, Margaret Chan, announced the pandemic was at an end.

The response varied from country to country and, as Oliver states, the UK initially tried to buy time by containing the virus. As school-children were amongst the first affected, this involved issuing antivirals to affected children and temporarily closing schools. This was followed by a series of other measures including the stockpiling of antivirals, a mass public health campaign, and culminated with the introduction of the National Flu Pandemic Service, a telephone and online diagnosis and treatment facility, in July 2010.

Understanding the aetiology of the infection is important when considering the consequential response by the UK government, which Oliver discusses, and therefore whether this provides any indications for the future. In particular, as Oliver states, the question is whether the UK government's response was the result of ambiguity aversion: which put simply is whether people would rather choose an option with fewer unknown elements than with many unknown elements.

Ambiguity aversion can be seen as an individual's rational response towards the probability of a future outcome, whether this is positive or negative for the public, clinicians or government. With swine flu, not only were individuals faced with the risk of being infected but they perceived a very real threat of severe complications, or worse still death, arising from infection.

Returning to Francis Daniels Moore and his view that 'the fundamental act of medical care is assumption of responsibility', then when coupled with ambiguity aversion we can begin to put some context around why pressure, for example, was being placed on primary and ambulatory health care services from people suffering with non-threatening symptoms compared with those similarly seen in seasonal flu outbreaks.

As Oliver indicates, from July 2009 people living in England who believed they had contracted the infection were encouraged to contact the National Flu Pandemic Service either online or by phone and if confirmed were provided with a unique reference number to obtain antivirals via a friend or 'flu buddy', as they came to be known in the vernacular. Oliver also states that the resulting policy response can be seen through the lens of the precautionary principle: given the potentially serious complications or implications of not having a proper response to the outbreak that the public could understand, then 'some notion of the precautionary principle was necessary'.

This approach can also be seen in the way the English administration responded to the outbreak in comparison with the Scottish and Welsh administrations. The Chief Spokesperson was the then Chief Medical Officer, Professor Sir Liam Donaldson, who came to public prominence during this time with his situation briefings, advice for patients, and the Department of Health and NHS's plans to deal with the pandemic.

Oliver contends that the nature of the English administration's response may be linked to 'institutional memory' when 'Sir Liam's predecessors, Sir Donald Acheson and Sir Kenneth Calman, were publicly criticized' for the way they handled the bovine spongiform encephalopathy/variant Creutzfeldt-Jakob disease scare during the 1980s, and more recently the catastrophic response to the foot and mouth disease outbreak in 2001. This may well be the case, but there may potentially be other reasons.

Firstly, whilst foot and mouth disease is zoonotic, the risk to humans is slight, crossing from one species to another with difficulty, and the public broadly understood this to be the case. However, what the public saw was a chaotic response from the government that resulted in both distressed and non-infected animals often being needlessly slaughtered. Does government learn from the chaos of its past mistakes? The history of the UK public administration suggests that it rarely if ever does, and therefore it is debatable whether government was learning from the past and applying it to the swine flu outbreak.

The second and more probable reason rests with attitudes and behaviours of early twenty-first century life, and this breaks down into two explanatory subsets.

The first was that this was a symptom of the way government is run today: the UK, and in particular the English administration, is characterized as one of governing by reaction or panic, events are viewed or more appropriately distorted through the lens of 'national security' and it cannot be dismissed that this was the case with the H1N1 outbreak. Britain has never subscribed to Abraham Lincoln's principle of 'government of the people, by the people, for the people' (1863).

The second of these relates to global life today. People are much more mobile, travel is part of life whether for work or leisure, life today thrives on being well connected – with the incidence of isolation being much lower. This then raises the question of what can be done today to contain serious infection.

It is worth noting that at the same time as cases of swine flu were on the rise, China was dealing with an outbreak of pneumonic plague in its western province of Qinghai. Whilst related to bubonic plague, pneumonic plague is much deadlier, attacking the lungs, and is spread by the air, usually via coughing. China responded by quarantining 10,000 people in an area of 1,000 square miles. This is clearly an extreme response, and only totalitarian or heavily surveillanced countries could get away with such behaviour. Of course, how countries manage infections spreading across populations is a valid question, but returning to ambiguity aversion, the question of what level of response is appropriate needs to be borne in mind, and it is definitely not a solution in itself.

Epstein et al. (2007) considered the issue of containing the spread of pandemic flu by restricting international air travel. Their findings, in the context of the US, suggest that domestic air travel restrictions are unlikely to have much of an impact, as it would merely be replaced by ground transportation. If applied internationally, there may be a small delay in pandemic spread if other disease control measures are implemented. However, they warn that if travel restrictions are applied alone without other measures, epidemics may in fact worsen by delaying the outbreak of pandemic flu into high flu seasons.

A similar theme was picked up by Finnie et al. (2012), in a 120-year literature review to understand the impact of influenza on enclosed societies. They showed that rapid intervention in terms of correct diagnosis, prescribing antiviral drugs and the implementation of control measures such as restricting movement were necessary components of pandemic planning.

In part the English response saw this: people were told to stay at home, to restrict contact with others if possible, and diagnosis was moved from laboratory or clinician-confirmed to self-diagnosis via the National Flu Pandemic Service. But were these merely common-sense measures and was an opportunity lost? People with seasonal flu are routinely advised to remain home-based, they would naturally want to limit contact with others, and this returns us to the question of whether government learns from experience. The National Flu Pandemic Service if operationalized into an effective, general and low-level online diagnostic and advisory service would help patients, and improve the productivity of the NHS. Not only would a service be readily available in case of future outbreaks, saving time and money, but it would also create an element of normality to the public thereby reducing the risk of ambiguity aversion for both the public and the government.

Oliver's central argument is that whilst government 'had to act in the face of the swine flu pandemic', he nevertheless asks 'did it act too much?' This is important, as it will inform how future administrations handle pandemics. There is no doubt the government had to do something, but was it proportionate to the risk? Franklin D. Roosevelt's inaugural address as President of the United States in 1933 contains the immortal phrase 'The only thing we have to fear is fear itself', but read the full sentence and the words contain a powerful resonance with how governments behave today: '... nameless, unreasoning, unjustified terror which paralyzes needed efforts to convert retreat into advance'. We see this all the time: whether it is the 'threat' of terrorism and needless security arrangements (we are still far more likely to die crossing the street than be killed in a plane attacked by terrorists), the overreaction to peaceful protests, or the empowering nature of the Internet to individuals and groups which 'threatens' government authority, the need to control and mitigate risk seems to be the mantra of government. This is the total antithesis to Abraham Lincoln's vision. Estimates are crude, but in the opening weeks of the swine flu outbreak one had a greater probability of winning the lottery than even catching the infection. Therefore, it seems reasonable to agree with Oliver's central thesis that the UK government was too ambiguity averse in its response to swine flu. It neither took proper account of the evidence nor learnt from the past.

Following the experience of the 2009 pandemic people may well view advice from clinicians and politicians with scepticism, which could cause delay in future diagnosis and treatment. Given the ever-plunging trust that the public now has in politicians, it would seem sensible for administrations to ensure a senior clinician remains the chief spokesperson. It may well be that in a future pandemic, people will still default to ambiguity aversion. Significant resources in terms of time and money will be deployed, or more accurately reinvented. An ability to learn from the past or for administrations to be more systematic and strategic continues to elude Westminster and Whitehall, so we cannot expect significant change in that direction. Maybe it is as simple as Francis Daniels Moore suggested and that medical care does indeed rest on the assumption of responsibility, which is ultimately what the public expects.

References

Epstein, J. M., Goedecke, D. M., Yu, F., Wagener, D. K. and Bobashev, G. V. (2007). Controlling Pandemic Flu: The Value of International Air Travel Restrictions. *PLoS One* 2(5): e401.

Finnie, T. J. R., Hall, I. M. and Leach, S. (2012). Behaviour and Control of Influenza in Institutions and Small Societies. *Journal of the Royal Society of Medicine* 105: 66–73.

Lincoln, A. (19 November 1863). *The Gettysburg Address*. Gettysburg, Pennsylvania.

Moore, F. D. (1959). *Metabolic Care of the Surgical Patient*. Philadelphia: W. B. Saunders.

2 | Models of governance of public services: empirical and behavioural analysis of 'econs' and 'humans'

GWYN BEVAN AND BARBARA FASOLO

This chapter develops Le Grand's argument about the need to recognize that those who choose to work in public services are not wholly 'knights' (Le Grand, 2003) driven by *altruism*, but are a mix of 'knights' (altruistic) and 'knaves' (selfish). He argued that *choice and competition* between schools and hospitals through quasi markets in which money follows the pupil or patient is the primary policy instrument to combat government failure. This is because quasi markets appeal to both knightly and knavish motives. They create pressure to improve services to respond to threats to market shares, providers' incomes and hence jobs (Le Grand, 2007). The reason why we disagree with Le Grand in his proposed remedy to his diagnosis is that the choice and competition model assumes that people as users and providers of public services act as 'econs', as described by Thaler and Sunstein (2008), i.e. behave as in conventional microeconomics. We know that 'humans' behave differently, as has been demonstrated by carefully designed psychological experiments. Thus, although, if asked, people will say they desire more choice and believe that the greater the choice the better, there is ample evidence that in health care, just as in more mundane consumer choices (Iyengar and Lepper, 2000), users do not behave like econs and do not use information on provider performance to switch from those that are poor to those that are good. Instead of the choice and competition model, we see scope for developing the more psychologically plausible model of governance based on users and providers as 'humans', where users do not use public information on provider performance to switch between providers, but providers respond to threats to their *reputation* via public reporting of rankings of performance (Hibbard et al., 2003).

In this first section we present the four alternative models of governance: altruism, hierarchy and targets, reputation, and choice and competition.

- *Altruism* assumes providers are 'humans' and are internally motivated to perform well. To do better, they need more resources or
  information. This model does not require external incentives, has
  low monitoring costs and is popular with professionals (Le Grand,
  2007). In the National Health Services (NHSs) of the UK this was
  the traditional model and was associated with a system where failure
  was rewarded and success ignored (Bevan, 2010).
- *Hierarchy and targets* assumes providers are 'econs' and respond to
  rewards for success and sanctions for failures. This model imposes
  external incentives by strong performance management, has monitoring costs and is unpopular with professionals (Bevan and Hood,
  2006; Le Grand, 2007).
- *Reputation* assumes providers are 'humans' and respond to
  threats to their reputation. A reputation model is a system of
  performance measurement that satisfies criteria specified by
  Hibbard et al. (2003): a ranking system, published and widely
  disseminated, easily understood by the public (so that they can
  see which providers are performing well and poorly) and
  followed up by future reports (that show whether performance
  has improved or not). This model 'names and shames' providers
  that perform poorly, has monitoring costs and is unpopular with
  professionals.
- *Choice and competition* assumes users and providers are 'econs' and
  that users choose better performing providers, whereas providers
  respond to the consequences of these choices on market shares. This
  model creates external incentives by a quasi-market system in which
  there is choice of providers and money follows the pupil or patient. It
  is difficult to design effective quasi markets as they require good
  information, supply-side flexibility and freedom to manage. Quasi
  markets have high transaction costs, but are popular with governments, because pressure on poor performance comes from an 'invisible hand' (Le Grand, 2007). They promise to have more potential to
  respond to users' needs than centrally driven systems of hierarchy
  and targets and reputation.

The next section of our chapter reports empirical evidence of the
impacts of these different models using a rich set of contrasting
examples described below. These examples show that the applicability
of each model importantly depends on the accountability structure

embedded in the organization, and that often, in practice, the models other than altruism may be applied in various combinations.

- *US hospitals* are not generally directly accountable to government and have to generate their incomes from market shares in a system in which there is enough excess capacity for hospitals to compete. These hospitals may be governed by altruism, reputation or choice and competition.
- *The four NHSs of the UK* are accountable to ministers in each country, and hence all four models of governance are applicable. From 1997, all governments abandoned the model of competition (the 'internal market') in favour of altruism. From 2000, the government in England abandoned altruism and introduced governance by hierarchy and targets and reputation (through 'star rating'): hierarchy and targets, as chief executives of 'zero-rated' organizations were at risk of being sacked; and reputation, as 'star ratings' were published annually in national and local media. From 2006, the government in England added policies based on choice and competition. The governments of the devolved countries (Scotland, Wales and Northern Ireland) continued with policies based on altruism.
- *Secondary schools in the UK* are either run by elected local councils or are independent. British schools are not under direct central government control: the Secretary of State for Education is not empowered to sack a headteacher of a 'failing' school. This means that ministers cannot apply hierarchy and targets and the alternatives are hence altruism, reputation, or choice and competition. The government in England has continued to govern through choice and competition (with quasi markets) and reputation (by publishing league tables for examination results for 16-year-olds) since 1994. The government in Wales uses quasi markets only, having stopped publishing league tables in 2001. The government in Scotland relies on altruism: there has never been a quasi market and publishing league tables was stopped in 2002.

We find that: reputation and hierarchy and targets were effective drivers of improvement for hospitals and ambulance services in the UK; reputation was effective for hospitals in the US and schools in the UK; and that neither altruism nor choice and competition were as effective as the other models. This raises the familiar challenge to economics: if the reputation model works in practice, can we show

how it works in theory? The third section draws on behavioural economics to explain the psychological mechanisms behind each model. We conclude by considering the paradox: why do governments in the UK prefer to use models based on altruism or choice and competition when practice and theory suggest that these are relatively ineffective?

Effectiveness of the four models of governance: three case studies

1. *US hospitals*

In their systematic review of evaluations of public reports of hospital performance, Fung et al. (2008) found that the impacts of publishing performance varied, and concluded that the choice and competition model was sometimes effective. Hibbard (2008) questioned this conclusion as she argued that the effect of report cards could be due, not to choice and competition, but rather to reputation citing evidence from a controlled experiment (Hibbard et al., 2003, 2005). This experiment was designed to examine the impacts of reporting on quality of care across three sets of hospitals: public-report, where the report was disseminated widely to the public; private-report, where the report was supplied to managers only; and no-report, where no information was made available publicly or privately. Hibbard et al. found that the public-report set made significantly greater efforts to improve quality than the other two sets, and that threats to reputation and not market shares[1] were the key driver of performance. Private reporting, which relied on altruism, proved to be a weak driver of change. This finding is supported by evidence from the most studied system of public reporting (Fung et al., 2008; Marshall et al., 2000), namely the Cardiac Surgery Reporting System (CSRS) of the New York State Department of Health. CSRS satisfies Hibbard's criteria, with one qualification: hospital performance was not ranked but 'outliers' (with mortality rates statistically significantly higher or lower than the mean) were

---

[1] Later analysis showed that these managers were correct: 'There were no significant changes in market share among the hospitals in the public report from the pre to the post period ... no shifts away from low-rated hospitals and no shifts toward higher-rated hospitals in overall discharges or in obstetric or cardiac care cases during any of the examined post-report time periods' (Hibbard et al., 2005).

identified. One of the paradoxes of this system, which questions the efficacy of the model of choice and competition, was that neither users nor providers acted as 'econs'. Users continued to go to those hospitals that CSRS showed had significantly high risk-adjusted surgical mortality rates. Although poor performance had no effect on providers' market shares, they did respond to threats to their reputations: 'When a hospital is publicized as having the worst mortality in the state, not only do physicians and hospital administrators pay attention, but there also is a greater likelihood that the resources necessary to correct the problem will be forthcoming' (Chassin, 1996, p. 88). The outcome was that New York State had 'the most rapid rate of decline (of risk-adjusted mortality rates) of any state with below-average mortality' (Chassin, 2002).[2]

2. *The four NHSs of the UK*

The evidence from the US suggests that the reputation model has greater impacts than those of altruism and choice and competition. But this evidence is limited: it is from one exercise across a small number of hospitals in Wisconsin and cardiac surgery in New York State. The NHSs in the four UK countries following devolution offer evidence of the impacts of the four different models on a massive scale. Research into the choice and competition model has failed to find evidence of powerful direct effects and econometric studies have estimated its impacts to be limited.[3] In contrast, as we now report, the effects of the policies based on hierarchy and targets and reputation models were direct and the impacts dramatic. We start by presenting evidence from 'star ratings', which were applied in England from 2000 to 2005. The revolutionary idea of the annual 'star rating' of NHS providers was that success would be rewarded and failure would result in sanctions. This was emphasized with the threat of the sack for

---

[2] There are issues of gaming in response to CSRS and this claim is disputed (Dranove et al., 2003).

[3] We are aware of recent econometric studies (Cooper et al., 2011; Gaynor et al., 2010) that have identified improvements in quality, with a common measure being mortality rates from acute myocardial infarction (AMI) in areas where competition has increased. We are puzzled by these findings, given that other studies showed that patients rarely exercised choice between hospitals, and that even if they had done so, this would be for elective care, whereas AMI mortality is a measure of the quality of emergency care (see Bevan and Skellern, 2011).

failure, to make clear to those who worked in the English NHS the sharp break from policies of the past. Once this was well understood, and the power of the reputation model became clear, there appears to have been less emphasis on sacking chief executives. So although the 'star rating' system combined the models of hierarchy and targets with reputation, over time, the model shifted from hierarchy and targets to reputation.

This is a good 'natural experiment' to compare the impacts of different models between the NHS in England and the NHSs in the devolved countries because:

- Each country had similar systems of health care, received a sustained massive influx of 'growth money', and pursued similar targets for reducing hospital waiting times and reducing ambulance response times to calls for life-threatening emergencies.
- England sought improvement through hierarchy and targets and reputation.
- The devolved countries sought improvement through altruism.

We consider the period from 1997 to 2005, which offers two different kinds of comparisons:

- A 'before and after' comparison for England of altruism (1997–2000) vs 'star ratings' for acute hospital trusts (2000–2005), and ambulance trusts (2002–2005) (akin to a 'within-subject' study in experimental psychology).
- A comparison over the period of 'star rating' between hierarchy and targets and reputation in England vs altruism in the devolved countries (akin to a 'between-subject' study).

Figure 2.1 shows the transformation in performance of the English NHS in terms of the reduction of numbers with long waits for hospital admission following the introduction of 'star ratings' in 2000. The targets in star ratings became more demanding over time and were that no one would be waiting more than 12 months by April 2003 and more than 9 months by April 2004. These targets were achieved. Figure 2.2 shows comparative performance across the four countries of the percentages of those waiting more than 12 months for inpatient elective hospital admission between 2000 and 2003: only in England did this percentage fall from what it had been in 2000 when each country's NHS began to experience substantial real growth in

Numbers waiting for elective hospital admission ('000s)

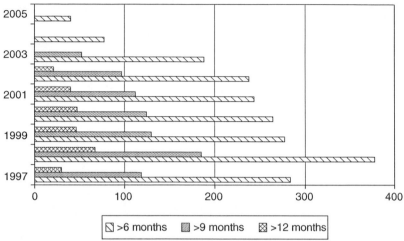

Figure 2.1 Numbers waiting more than 6, 9 and 12 months for elective hospital admission in England from 1997 to 2005

% patients waiting for elective hospital admission > 12 months

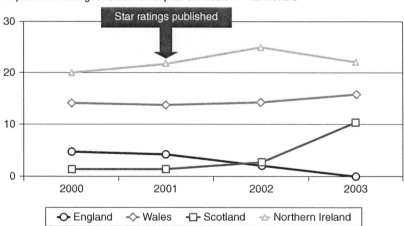

Figure 2.2 Percentage of patients on waiting lists for hospital admission waiting more than 12 months in England, Wales, Scotland and Northern Ireland from 2000 to 2003
Source: National Health Service Waiting Lists by Region: Regional Trends 35, 36, 37 and 38 (www.statistics.gov.uk).

No/'000 waiting > 6 months for elective hospital admission

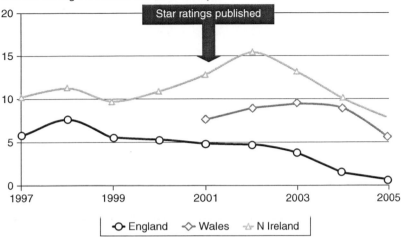

Figure 2.3 Numbers per thousand waiting more than 6 months for elective hospital admission in England, Wales and Northern Ireland from 1997 to 2005 *Source*: Bevan (2009).

resources. Figure 2.3 gives numbers per thousand waiting more than 6 months for inpatient admission and shows how the improvement in performance for reducing this number for Wales (and Northern Ireland) lagged behind that for England.[4] Figure 2.4 gives numbers per thousand waiting more than 3 months to be referred to a specialist, and shows that whereas in England this ratio was also reduced, in Wales (and Northern Ireland) these ratios increased. Hospital performance influenced the targets each country set their NHSs.

The comparison between England and Wales is best in terms of a 'natural experiment' as these countries were most similar in policies and organization prior to devolution and although spend per capita in Wales exceeded that of England, the degree of excess was less than that for Northern Ireland and Scotland. Besley et al. (2009) undertook a

---

[4] After 2003, the definitions of those on waiting lists changed in Scotland to exclude from their statistics up to a third of those who were waiting for admissions and the data for Scotland are not comparable with other countries. But by using comparable data for the time patients waited after being discharged, Propper et al. (2008, 2010) undertook a rigorous econometric analysis of Scotland and England and showed that performance in Scotland was worse than in England.

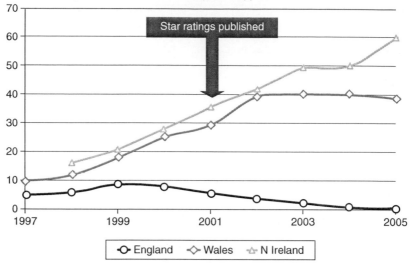

Figure 2.4 Numbers per thousand waiting more than 3 months for GP referral to a specialist in England, Wales and Northern Ireland from 1997 to 2005
Source: Bevan (2009).

rigorous econometric analysis comparing data on waits for inpatient admission in England and Wales, and found that, given their starting positions in 2000, the performance in Wales was worse than in England. The stark differences between these targets as set for England and Wales was highlighted by the Auditor General for Wales (2005) and are summarized in Table 2.1. This shows that by December 2005, at the end of the period of star ratings in England, to achieve the targets for specialist referral and hospital admission, hospitals in England would have to complete both within nine months, but within Wales would have been allowed *three years*.

Hospitals are an exemplar of the complexities of multi-tasking, as identified in the landmark paper by Holmstrom and Milgrom (1991); hence evidence on performance on waiting times is problematic as these are inadequate measures of their overall performance.[5] The next

---

[5] This objection is qualified to some extent by the way in which 'star ratings' were based on a set of other indicators in a 'balanced scorecard' (see Bevan and Hood, 2006), and that, for their first three years, 'star ratings' of acute hospitals also included assessments of their implementation of clinical governance (Bevan and

Table **2.1** *Targets for waiting times in England and Wales*

Service	England (2004 and 2005)	Wales (end March 2005)
First outpatient appointment	March 2004: 17 weeks December 2005: 13 weeks	18 months
Inpatient/day case treatment	March 2004: 9 months December 2005: 6 months	18 months*
Potential longest overall waiting time within current national target for outpatients and inpatient/ day cases	March 2004: 13 months December 2005: 9 months	36 months

¹ With a guarantee of an offer of alternative treatment for waits over 12 months by 31 March 2005.
Source: Auditor General for Wales, 2005, p. 16 (www.wao.gov.uk/reportsandpubli cations/2005.asp).

example from the NHS is not vulnerable to that objection: for ambulance services their overriding priority ought to be to respond as quickly as possible to what appear to be life-threatening emergency calls. Hence, if these organizations were driven by altruism, they would aim to do this without any need for external incentives.

The governments in England, Wales and Scotland set a target for their ambulance services of meeting 75 per cent of Category A calls within 8 minutes: in England and Wales in 2001, and in Scotland by 2007–8. Figure 2.5 shows the distribution of performance for ambulance services in England before and after the introduction of their 'star ratings' in 2002 (one year after they had been introduced for acute hospital trusts) in terms of the percentage of Category A calls met within 8 minutes. In 2001, only one service met that target, with many services responding to less than 50 per cent of Category A calls within 8 minutes. After the introduction of 'star ratings' all services improved and, in 2003, each service either achieved or was close to achieving

Cornwell, 2006). Furthermore, the public's principal and consistent complaint about the NHS in the 1990s and early 2000s was its long waiting times. Moreover, as Connolly et al. (2011) point out, there is no evidence of better performance by hospitals in the devolved countries in comparison with England on other dimensions of quality.

% ambulance response times to life-threatening emergencies < 8 minutes
(target 75%)

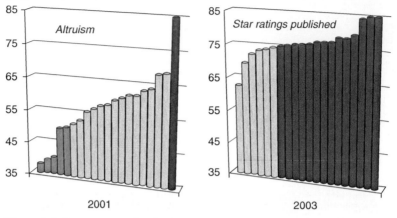

Figure 2.5 Percentages of ambulance responses within 8 minutes to Category A calls by ambulance services in England in 2001 and 2003
Source: Bevan and Hamblin (2009).

% ambulance response times to life-threatening emergencies < 8 minutes

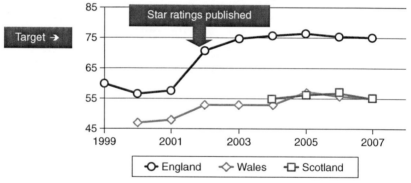

Figure 2.6 National average percentages of ambulance responses within 8 minutes to Category A calls for England, Wales and Scotland from 1999 to 2007
Source: Bevan and Hamblin (2009).

that target. Figure 2.6 compares national performance in terms of the percentage of Category A calls met within 8 minutes across England, Wales and Scotland. This shows the striking difference between countries for those waiting for an ambulance to respond to what may be a life-threatening emergency: in England about one in four can expect to wait longer than 8 minutes, but in Wales and Scotland this proportion is almost one in two. Bevan and Hamblin (2009) contrast responses by the governments in England and Wales to failure by their ambulance services to meet the Category A 8-minute target. In England, that failure resulted in public censure and sackings of chief executives of ambulance services. In Wales, the failure resulted in the government setting successively less demanding 'milestone' targets: from April 2004, the target was reduced to 65 per cent (the threshold for a service in England to have been zero rated); from April 2005 to 60 per cent.

3. Secondary schools in the UK

The models of school governance in England in many ways fore-shadowed the models applied later to the NHS (see Table 2.2). These included the introduction of quasi markets in which 'money followed the pupil (or patient)', introduction of national standards, the creation of new inspectorates to inspect all organizations over a four-year period and the publication of comparative performance on a national basis. As these policies were introduced prior to devolution, they also broadly applied to Wales.[6] Scotland has always had a distinctively different educational system with markedly different policies. Teelken (2000) reviews differences between England and Scotland highlighting the comparative lack of diversity of schools in Scotland and the absence of a national curriculum, and a weak quasi market. Table 2.3 summarizes key differences for schools' policies across the three countries. For our purposes, the key differences are in the publication of school league tables of examination performance for secondary schools at age 16 (the normal school leaving age):

- In England, the government has published this information every year from 1994.
- In Wales, the government published this information every year from 1994 until 2001 but not thereafter.
- In Scotland, the government published this information every year from 1998 to 2002 only.

---

[6] Although Wales, unlike England, did not publish league tables of test results for primary schools.

Table 2.2 *Similarities in policies for schools and hospitals in England in the 1980s and 1990s*

	Hospitals in England	Schools in England
Quasi markets	From 1991 to 1997: 'money followed the patient' and hospitals were separated from health authority control	From 1988: 'money followed the pupil' and allowed schools to opt out of local authority control
National standards	From 1997: National Institute of Clinical Excellence (NICE) developed guidelines for cost-effective care and appointed 'Czars' to devise standards for priority services (such as cancer and coronary heart disease) through national service	From 1996 national curriculum (Education Act, 1996, Chapter 56, sections 358–63) frameworks
Creation of new inspectorates to inspect all organizations over a four-year period	1999–2004: Commission for Health Improvement (CHI)	From 1992: the Office for Standards in Education (OFSTED)
Publication of comparative performance ranked on a national basis	2001–2005: annual 'star ratings'	From 1994: annual league tables for secondary schools (see e.g. Department for Education, 1994–2011)

The government's league tables for England, published in 2009, give school performance by each local authority over four years (from 2006 to 2009) for the percentage of pupils at the end of Key Stage 4 (i.e. taking GCSE between ages 14 and 16) achieving five or more grades above C, and the averages for the local authority, and England. This is designed to offer information by local authority and hence for choice and competition. The *Daily Telegraph* ranks school performance by

Table 2.3 *Comparisons of policies for schools in England, Wales and Scotland*

	England	Wales	Scotland
Opting out	From 1988		From 1989 but with limited effects as compared with England
Local management	From 1988 to governing bodies		From 1993 to headteachers
Quasi markets	From 1988		Choice in principle but weak marketization as compared with England
National curriculum	From 1988		None
Inspections with reports published	From 1992 by OFSTED	From 1992 by OFSTED and then from 1998 by IESTYN*	By Her Majesty's Inspectorate of Education (which dates back to 1840) which from 1998 was made an Executive Agency of the Scottish government
School league tables published ranking performance	From 1994	From 1994 to 2001	From 1998 to 2002

* IESTYN is Her Majesty's Inspectorate for Education and Training in Wales.

county.[7] Such school league tables satisfy Hibbard's four criteria[8] and do indeed have reputational effects.

[7] www.telegraph.co.uk/education/leaguetables/6974678/GCSE-league-tables-Key-stage-4.html.
[8] These tables are a ranking system (although this is not done by the government), the information is published and widely disseminated, it is easily understood by the public who can see which schools are performing well and poorly, and it is published annually.

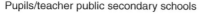

Pupils/teacher public secondary schools

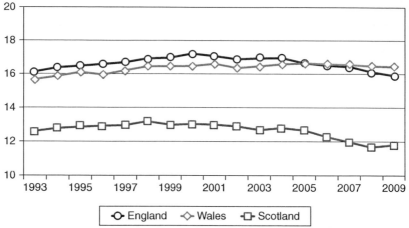

Figure 2.7 Pupil–teacher ratios in secondary schools in England, Wales and Scotland from 1993 to 2008

Figure 2.7 shows how throughout this period, the ratios of pupils to teachers have been similar in England and Wales (in 2004, an average secondary school teacher in each country would have had about 17 pupils), although this ratio has recently fallen in England but remained constant in Wales; and Scotland has throughout had a much more generous ratio (in 2004, an average secondary school teacher would have had about 13 pupils). Figure 2.8 shows examination performance in terms of five good grades at age 16 improving in all three countries from 1994 to 2002. In 1994, Scotland had the best performance (48%), England next (43%) and Wales the worst (39%). In 2002, Scotland had improved and still had the best performance (60%), England and Wales were similar (50%). After 2002, perform-ance in Scotland slightly deteriorated and although performance improved in both England and Wales the gap between them re-emerged. In 2008, England had the best performance (64%) and Wales had similar performance to Scotland (58%).

Burgess et al. (2010) have undertaken a rigorous econometric analy-sis of the natural experiment between Wales and England and found 'systematic, significant and robust evidence that abolishing school league tables markedly reduced school effectiveness in Wales' (Burgess et al., 2010, p. 2). They estimated the relative impacts of the policy in

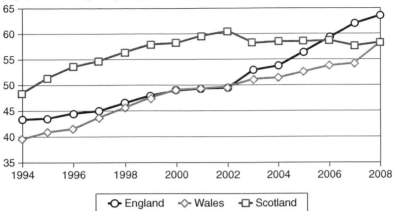

% pupils achieving > 5 good grades at age 16

Figure 2.8 Examination performance in terms of five good grades at age 16 in England, Wales and Scotland from 1994 to 2008
Note: Data are missing for 1998, 2001 and 2005; these have been estimated as the mean values for adjacent years.

Wales to have been a fall of nearly two GCSE grades per student per year, and for Welsh schools to achieve English levels of performance they would need Welsh class sizes to be about 30 per cent smaller than in England. This effect could be due to reputation, or to choice and competition; however, these same authors also point out that the different impact of policies does 'not vary significantly by the level of local competition' (Burgess et al., 2010, p. 22) and because there is generally a relatively low level of potential choice in Wales the matched English schools are located in largely rural areas. Hence, they conclude that 'It appears unlikely, therefore, that market-based accountability via parental choice is the main driver behind our results' (Burgess et al., 2010, p. 23). We take this as evidence that the explanation for the difference in performance between England and Wales is due to the reputation model.

Discussion: behavioural analysis of the mechanisms behind the four models of governance

In this section we point to behavioural research which sheds light on the mechanisms whereby each of the four models can 'work'.

We consider in order, altruism, hierarchy and targets, reputation, and choice and competition (which turns out to be especially problematic).

1. Altruism: the problem of inadequate feedback

For the purpose of this behavioural analysis, we reframe the 'altruism' model as 'the private provision of a report to the provider' (Hibbard et al., 2003). Why does private reporting improve performance? The answer is that private reporting is feedback and our human brain has evolved to learn and make good use of feedback. This is why 'giving feedback' is one of the nudges described by Thaler and Sunstein (2008). Private feedback can improve performance because it *offers information about own performance*, and because it *increases salience of the criteria* used to measure performance. Because human attention is bounded by cognitive and motivational limitations, tools that attract attention and increase salience of important criteria are helpful when trying to change human behaviour. But the evidence we have presented suggests that such private reporting is, as argued by Berwick et al. (2003), *insufficient feedback*. It could be made more effective if it were to include information about how to improve performance and were followed by a goal-setting plan (Kluger and DeNisi, 1998). Even with these additions, however, such feedback will often lack the necessary high-powered incentives to counteract inertia and generate the necessary drive to improve delivery of services.

2. Hierarchy and targets: the power of reference points and looming losses

We reframe the hierarchy and targets model as setting targets for providers with serious sanctions for failure and rewards for success. Prospect theory (Kahneman and Tversky, 1979) explains why high-powered incentives to improve the delivery of services are triggered by setting targets so that failure results in losses. The basic explanation is a strong 'stability bias' that anchors people to reference points (e.g. Samuelson and Zeckhauser, 1988) and 'loss aversion': people feel losses more keenly than they do gains (Tversky and Kahneman, 1991). Hence, the sanctions for failure are more powerful than rewards for success.

3. Reputation: *the power of spotlight and moral emotions*

We reframe the reputation model as 'the provision to providers *and to the public* of regular reports that rank performance in ways that are easy *for the public* to understand'. A system designed to satisfy these criteria (Hibbard et al., 2003) has been shown to have had the necessary high-powered incentives to improve the delivery of services. From our evidence it looks to be the most effective of all the models considered, at least in the short term. Why does reputation work? We offer two interpretations.

The first is the most discussed in the literature and revolves around the role of the *public* as the key trigger of change. If the public is aware of the existence of published performance data, and these data are a straightforward ranking of providers, this ranking sticks in the mind (Hibbard et al., 2005). Even if users do not exercise choice, and market share is not itself affected, a poor ranking has an effect as published data make accountability relationships salient (e.g. Tetlock, 1983). It is through this that poorly ranked providers are pressured to change and do change. Accountability encourages individuals to exert additional effort, so improves performance in tasks where additional effort helps, as for some decision errors (Simonson and Nye, 1992). In this interpretation, the reputation model exploits the same behavioural mechanism as loss aversion under hierarchy and targets.

We offer a second, more novel, interpretation which assumes no role of the public and only works via the mind of the provider from the shame, embarrassment and guilt as sequelae of being in the 'spotlight' (as shown by Thaler and Sunstein, 2008). There are a couple of psychological reasons why spotlight works. Slovic and Västfjäll's chapter describes one explanation: 'affect'. Just like making a donation to a charity makes one 'feel good' ('warm glow', Kahneman and Knetsch, 1992), receiving a low rank makes us 'feel awful'. In this interpretation providers are not just 'econs' responding to incentives, but 'humans' who juggle – alongside economic considerations – their own emotions and ego (Higgins, 1997; Kluger and DeNisi, 1998).

People generally like to think of themselves as moral and honest (e.g. Mazar and Ariely, 2006), so why do providers need a public report to trigger quality-improving exercises that they should have been doing all along? An answer in the most recent behavioural research is that just like judgements of probability, risk and value, moral judgements are also guided (or misguided) by the automatic and implicit 'system 1' of reasoning. As a consequence, we tend to use suboptimal heuristics (moral heuristics, Sunstein, 2005) with predictable errors. On the upside, by mere virtue of being predictable, these errors can be corrected too by appropriate 'moral design' (Gigerenzer, 2010). We argue that public reports could act as a particular instance of 'moral design', reminding public servants of why they chose to work in the public sector to start with. We have mentioned how public reports have the potential of shaking the public's trust in the institution. Indeed, one of the most powerful moral heuristics ingrained in our minds is 'do not betray', which triggers the even more powerful reaction of 'punish betrayal'. Reputation could work out of fear of having betrayed the public's trust and provides an urgent reason for acting before the public reacts and 'punishes' this betrayal. This also means that systems that inflict reputational damage on failing organizations may be seen as objectionable. The problem is, however, that shocks of this kind are an integral part of generating the high-powered incentives necessary for improvement.

4. *Choice and competition: the problem of inadequate choice architecture*

Behavioural research suggests that there are two fundamental reasons why the choice model might not have worked as well as expected. The first reason is inadequate implementation of the choice model. The second reason is more potent and involves inadequate architecture: the choice model makes the strong assumption that the public want to choose in situations where they cannot or do not want to exercise choice. Behavioural research provides a firm set of evidence-based guidelines on when provision of choice is expected to translate into exercise of choice, social welfare and subjective satisfaction (Botti and Iyengar, 2006), and none of them are met for health care. Some of these guidelines pertain again to format and amount of information, but the most important we review here concern the chooser and the context of choice:

- Individuals have articulated and stable preferences before the information is seen and the decision is made (Chernev, 2003).
- Different individuals have different preferences and needs and options vary in the degree to which they meet these different tastes and needs.

- People have the knowledge and expertise, or the willingness and time, to exert the effort to learn the relevant information, to make the choice (Loewenstein, 1999).
- The choice is not among options with unpleasant outcomes and does not require tradeoffs that cause psychological pain (Botti and Iyengar, 2004).

Applying these guidelines to school or hospital governance yields an interesting contrast[9] and suggests that even if the choice model were well designed, it probably could only be effective for school choice. Choice for hospitals remains a tricky context for applying a choice model, even when the choice is simplified or 'nudges' are used (such as opt-out defaults, feedback, etc.). In the health context, people prefer 'surrogate choice' (i.e. choice by an adviser) to choice by themselves and to no-choice, which suggests that a softer choice model could be via the interplay of an 'adviser'.

Conclusion: policy, practice and theory

We have presented strong evidence that systems that are designed to inflict reputational damage, by satisfying Hibbard's four criteria (Hibbard et al., 2003), have had powerful impacts in improving performance in what has been measured: for hospitals in the US,

[9] In the case of secondary school choice, the choosers are parents who, by the time their children reach the age of 16, have a good idea of the type of educational setting they deem more suitable for their children (e.g. academic or sport-oriented); children are different in their needs and tastes and – in most urban areas – there is a variety of school offerings that can cater to different needs and tastes; parents are typically involved in the decision and have multiple occasions for learning about the schools' quality; and finally the choice revolves around giving opportunities for growth and future success of one's offspring. In the case of hospital choice, the choosers are patients whose preferences for what is important to them are constructed in the process of choosing and are heavily influenced by the order in which information is presented; patients with a similar problem all have the same basic need to get the problem cured in the best possible manner and as soon as possible; patients perceive there is little variety among hospitals and feel it is almost unethical to expect that there is variety across hospitals; people do not have the medical knowledge or expertise and – being unwell – also little time or willingness to learn about the choice; and finally the choice is among cures or places where there is a risk of dying, contracting serious infections and experiencing complications as well as the virtual certainty of experiencing discomfort, pain, separation from loved ones and interruption of normal daily routines (Boyce et al., 2010).

schools in the UK, and, alongside hierarchy and targets, for hospitals and ambulances in the UK. We have argued that an explanation for the power of the reputation model comes from seeing both users and providers of public services as 'humans' rather than 'econs'. In England the policy preference for the NHS is choice and competition in a quasi market (Secretary of State for Health, 2010), which is paradoxical as recent evaluations of the policy introduced into the NHS have found only weak evidence for choice and competition in quasi markets being a sound lever for improvement (Audit Commission and Healthcare Commission, 2008; Brereton and Vasoodaven, 2010; Cooper et al., 2011; Dixon et al., 2010; Gaynor et al., 2010). In England the policy preference for schools is both choice and competition and reputation (via published league tables). The other UK countries have abandoned school league tables, did not introduce analogues to 'star ratings' for their NHSs and are basing their policies on the assumption that those who are responsible for delivering services are driven by altruism.

Why do governments favour policies based on markets or altruism when these do not appear to be as effective as hierarchy and targets and reputation either in practice or in theory? This looks like a case of producer capture: the producers who suffer from 'naming and shaming' and hierarchy and targets persuade those to whom they provide services and the press that such systems are iniquitous and unfair, so they become unpopular with the public. Ministers in England may be better able to 'name and shame' poorly performing providers than ministers in the smaller countries because of the greater 'relational distance' in England (Hood, 2007).[10] But even in England, hospitals seem to have been able to capture the government, which continues to 'name and shame' 'failing' schools, but not until recently 'failing' hospitals. This is paradoxical, because as we have argued, the choice and competition model appears to be more effective for schools than for hospitals. The explanation seems to be that providers of health care are more powerful than teachers and, as ever, politics trumps whatever evidence and theory might suggest.

---

[10] Burgess et al. (2010, p. 6) point out that the rationale for the Welsh Assembly government stopping the publication of school league tables was that they 'do not have the support of either the teaching profession or members of the public' and was part of a policy of 'greater trust in producer determined solutions'.

References

Audit Commission and Healthcare Commission (2008). *Is the Treatment Working?* London: Audit Commission (http://archive.audit-commission .gov.uk/auditcommission/sitecollectiondocuments/AuditCommission Reports/NationalStudies/IstheTreatmentWorking.pdf).

Auditor General for Wales (2005). *NHS Waiting Times in Wales. Volume 1 – The Scale of the Problem.* Cardiff: The Stationery Office (www.wao.gov .uk/reportsandpublications/2005.asp).

Berwick, D. M., James, B. and Coye, M. J. (2003). Connections Between Quality Measurement and Improvement. *Medical Care* 41(1, suppl.): I-30–I-38.

Besley, T. J., Bevan, G. and Burchardi, K. B. (2009). *Naming and Shaming: The Impacts of Different Regimes on Hospital Waiting Times in England and Wales.* Discussion Paper No. 7306. London: Centre for Economic Policy Research.

Bevan, G. (2009). Have Targets Done More Harm Than Good in the English NHS? No. *BMJ* 338: a3129.

(2010). Approaches and Impacts of Different Systems of Assessing Hospital Performance. *Journal of Comparative Policy Analysis* 12(1/2): 33–56.

Bevan, G. and Cornwell, J. (2006). Structure and Logic of Regulation and Governance of Quality of Health Care: Was OFSTED a Model for the Commission for Health Improvement? *Health Economics, Policy and Law* 1(4): 343–70.

Bevan, G. and Hamblin, R. (2009). Hitting and Missing Targets by Ambulance Services for Emergency Calls: Impacts of Different Systems of Performance Measurement Within the UK. *Journal of the Royal Statistical Society (A)* 172(1): 1–30 (www3.interscience.wiley.com/cgi-bin/ fulltext/120848267/PDFSTART).

Bevan, G. and Hood, C. (2006). What's Measured is What Matters: Targets and Gaming in the English Public Health Care System. *Public Administration* 84(3): 517–38.

Bevan, G. and Skellern, M. (2011). Does Competition Between Hospitals Improve Clinical Quality? A Review of Evidence from Two Eras of Competition in the English NHS. *BMJ* 343: d6470.

Botti, S. and Iyengar, S. S. (2004). The Psychological Pleasure and Pain of Choosing: When People Prefer Choosing at the Cost of Subsequent Satisfaction. *Journal of Personality and Social Psychology* 87(3): 312–26.

(2006). The Dark Side of Choice: When Choice Impairs Social Welfare. *American Marketing Association* 25(1): 24–38.

Boyce, T., Dixon, A., Fasolo, B. and Reutskaja, E. (2010). *Choosing a High-Quality Hospital: The Role of Nudges, Scorecard Design and Information*. London: The King's Fund (www.kingsfund.org.uk/publications/choosing_a.html).

Brereton, L. and Vasoodaven, V. (2010). *The Impact of the NHS Market*. London: Civitas (www.civitas.org.uk/nhs/download/Civitas_Literature Review_NHS_market_Feb10.pdf).

Burgess, S., Wilson, D. and Worth, J. (2010). *A Natural Experiment in School Accountability: The Impact of School Performance Information on Pupil Progress and Sorting*. Working Paper No. 10/246. Bristol: The Centre for Market and Public Organisation.

Chassin, M. R. (1996). Improving the Quality of Health Care: What Strategy Works? *Bulletin of the New York Academy of Medicine* 73(1): 81–91 (www.ncbi.nlm.nih.gov/pmc/articles/PMC2359372/pdf/bullnyacadmed 01031–0089.pdf).

(2002). Achieving and Sustaining Improved Quality: Lessons from New York State and Cardiac Surgery. *Health Affairs* 21(4): 40–51.

Chernev, A. (2003). When More is Less and Less is More: The Role of Ideal Point Availability and Assortment in Consumer Choice. *Journal of Consumer Research* 30(2): 170–83.

Connolly, S., Bevan, G. and Mays, N. (2011). *Funding and Performance of Healthcare Systems in the Four Countries of the UK before and after Devolution*. Revised Edition. London: The Nuffield Trust.

Cooper, Z., Gibbons, S., Jones, S. and McGuire, A. (2011). Does Hospital Competition Save Lives? Evidence from the English NHS Patient Choice Reforms. *Economic Journal* 121: F228–F260.

Department for Education (1994–2011). Performance Tables (www.education .gov.uk/schools/performance/archive/index.shtml).

Dixon, A., Robertson, R., Appleby, J., Burge, P., Devlin, N. and Magee, H. (2010). *Patient Choice: How Patients Choose and How Providers Respond*. London: King's Fund.

Dranove, D. K., McClellan, D. and Satterthwaite, M. (2003). Is More Information Better? The Effects of 'Report Cards' on Health Care Providers. *Journal of Political Economy* 111: 555–8.

Fung, C. H., Lim, Y.-W., Mattke, S., Damberg, C. and Shekelle, P. G. (2008). Systematic Review: The Evidence that Publishing Patient Care Performance Data Improves Quality of Care. *Annals of Internal Medicine* 148: 111–23.

Gaynor, M. S., Propper, C. and Moreno-Serra, R. (2010). *Death by Market Power: Reform, Competition and Patient Outcomes in the National Health Service*. Working Paper No. w16164. Cambridge: NBER.

Gigerenzer, G. (2010). Moral Satisficing: Rethinking Moral Behavior as Bounded Rationality. *Topics in Cognitive Science* 2: 528–54.

Hibbard, J. H. (2008). What Can We Say about the Impact of Public Reporting? Inconsistent Execution Yields Variable Results. *Annals of Internal Medicine* 148: 160–1.

Hibbard, J. H., Stockard, J. and Tusler, M. (2003). Does Publicizing Hospital Performance Stimulate Quality Improvement Efforts? *Health Affairs* 22(2): 84–94.

(2005). Hospital Performance Reports: Impact on Quality, Market Share, and Reputation. *Health Affairs* 24(4): 1150–60.

Higgins, E. T. (1997). Beyond Pleasure and Pain. *American Psychologist* 52: 1280–300.

Holmstrom, B. and Milgrom, P. (1991). Multi-Task Principal-Agent Analyses: Linear Contracts, Asset Ownership and Job Design. *Journal of Law, Economics and Organisation* 7: 24–52.

Hood, C. (2007). Public Service Management by Numbers: Why Does it Vary? Where Has it Come From? What are the Gaps and the Puzzles? *Public Money and Management* 27(2): 95–102.

Iyengar, S. S. and Lepper, M. (2000). When Choice is Demotivating: Can One Desire Too Much of a Good Thing? *Journal of Personality and Social Psychology* 79: 995–1006.

Kahneman, D. and Knetsch, J. L. (1992). Valuing Public Goods: The Purchase of Moral Satisfaction. *Journal of Environmental Economics and Management* 22: 57–70.

Kahneman, D. and Tversky, A. (1979). Prospect Theory: An Analysis of Decision under Risk. *Econometrica* 47: 263–91.

Kluger, A. N. and DeNisi, A. (1998). Feedback Interventions: Toward the Understanding of a Double-Edged Sword. *Current Directions in Psychological Science* 7(3): 67–72.

Le Grand, J. (2003). *Motivation, Agency and Public Policy: Of Knights and Knaves, Pawns and Queens*. Oxford University Press.

(2007). *The Other Invisible Hand: Delivering Public Services Through Choice and Competition*. Princeton University Press.

Loewenstein, G. (1999). Is More Choice Always Better? *Social Security Brief* 7: 1–7.

Marshall, M. N., Shekelle, P. G., Leatherman, S. and Brook, R. H. (2000). The Public Release of Performance Data: What Do We Expect to Gain? A Review of the Evidence. *Journal of the American Medical Association* 283(14): 1866–74.

Mazar, N. and Ariely, D. (2006). Dishonesty in Everyday Life and its Policy Implications. *Journal of Public Policy and Marketing* 25(1): 117–26.

Propper, C., Sutton, M., Whitnall, C. and Windmeijer, F. (2008). Did 'Targets and Terror' Reduce Waiting Times in England for Hospital

Care? *The B.E. Journal of Economic Analysis and Policy* 8(2): article 5
(www.bepress.com/bejeap/vol8/iss2/art5).

(2010). Incentives and Targets in Hospital Care: Evidence from a Natural
Experiment. *Journal of Public Economics* 94(3–4): 318–35.

Samuelson, W. and Zeckhauser, R. (1988). Status Quo Bias in Decision
Making. *Journal of Risk and Uncertainty* 1: 7–59.

Secretary of State for Health (2010). *Equity and Excellence: Liberating the
NHS.* Cm 7881. London: Department of Health (www.dh.gov.uk/en/
Publicationsandstatistics/Publications/PublicationsPolicyAndGuidance/
DH_117353).

Simonson, T. and Nye, P. (1992). The Effect of Accountability on Susceptibility to Decision Errors. *Organizational Behavior and Human Decision
Processes* 51(3): 416–66.

Sunstein, C. R. (2005). Moral Heuristics. *Behavioral and Brain Sciences*
28(4): 531–42.

Teelken, C. (2000). Market Forces in Education: A Comparative Perspective
in England and Scotland. *Scottish Educational Review* 32(1): 142–55.

Tetlock, P. E. (1983). Accountability and Complexity in Thought. *Journal of
Personality and Social Psychology: Attitudes and Social Cognition* 45:
74–83.

Thaler, R. H. and Sunstein, C. R. (2008). *Nudge: Improving Decisions about
Health, Wealth and Happiness.* New Haven: Yale University Press.

Tversky, A. and Kahneman, D. (1991). Loss Aversion in Riskless Choice:
A Reference-Dependent Model. *Quarterly Journal of Economics* 106:
1039–61.

2.1 | *A response to Bevan and Fasolo*

CHARITINI STAVROPOULOU

Introduction

Gwyn Bevan and Barbara Fasolo discuss four models of governance of public services, namely altruism, hierarchy and targets, reputation, and choice and competition. They specifically look at two areas of policy, health care and education, to examine their overall effectiveness. They provide theoretical justification for why some models work while others may not, and they use three, carefully chosen, case studies to discuss their arguments. The UK presents a very interesting case to examine, as it seems that its four governments (England, Wales, Scotland and Northern Ireland) have experimented with all four models of governance in health care and education. The US health care system also merits attention, as it is more of a free market. Bevan and Fasolo illustrate that reputational damage has perhaps the strongest impact on improving performance, particularly among hospitals in the US and schools in the UK, followed by hierarchy and targets, among hospitals and ambulances in the UK. They conclude by challenging the fact that governments in the UK seem to insist more on policies based on markets and altruism when in fact, according to the authors, these are the models that have shown the weakest impact on improving performances.

In this comment, I extend further the discussion on the theoretical arguments that the authors provide and I discuss the challenges of evaluating the empirical evidence. I conclude with some further thoughts on the instability of public policies in the UK that do not seem to last long enough to be evaluated.

On the theoretical explanation

Most theoretical models of neoclassical economics on agents' motivation assume selfish behaviour and impersonal transactions. The theory on choice and competition, for instance, assumes that providers

63

compete with each other in order to attract more service users. It predicts that when firms compete in a price-regulated market, then quality improves and so does consumer welfare, although the impact on social welfare is less clear (Gaynor, 2006). At the opposite extreme of self-interested behaviour lies the theory of altruism, which assumes that individuals are motivated by moral values rather than financial incentives. Le Grand (2003), in his work on knights and knaves, argues that people can be of both natures, i.e. both altruistic and selfish, and he suggests that quasi-market policies would capture both, and therefore are the most effective.

Bevan and Fasolo provide a new theoretical thinking on the mechanisms of the four models of public policy they discuss. At the heart of their theoretical argument lies the distinction between 'econs' and 'humans'. The former term refers to agents behaving as in neoclassical economics, i.e. they make rational choices based on the information they have, while the latter describes agents who are likely to behave on the basis of cognitive factors and moral values. Of the four models of governance of public service presented in the chapter, two, i.e. altruism and reputation, assume that providers are 'human', while the other two, i.e. targets and choice and competition, assume that providers are 'econs'.

Most theoretical attempts in health economics use perfect principal–agency models to describe physician–patient interaction and therefore focus mainly on understanding the behaviour of the agent. What is interesting about the arguments of Bevan and Fasolo is that they try to understand the more personal mechanisms that underlie the relationship between the agent and the principal. This seems particularly vital in the context of health care and education, where transactions become less impersonal and determine, to a large extent, the behaviour of the individuals.

On the empirical evidence

In practice, disentangling the effects of reputation, choice or any other policy model is important from a normative perspective, as proposed government interventions in principal–agency settings depend crucially on proper measurement of these effects. Yet, disentangling and measuring the effect of policies is not always a straightforward process.

Let us consider, for example, the two main models of public governance presented by the authors: reputation and choice. The authors claim, following Hibbard et al. (2003), that the reputation model can be reframed as the 'provision to providers and to the public of regular reports in ways that are easy for the public to understand'. If this is the case, then the similarity with the choice and competition model is quite apparent. For choice and competition to work, the provision of clear and easily accessible information is also essential. This often makes the distinction between the effects of the two policies rather blurred. For example, do league tables of schools or a ranking of hospitals inform individuals to make better choices or do they aim at improving the provider's performance through reputation effects? Clearly, it could be that they actually serve both purposes.

If choice cannot be exercised, then the answer is clearer and any improvement in performance and outcomes could be attributed to reputation effects. In this respect the authors provide solid examples, such as the 'star rating' system in acute hospital trusts in England from 2000 to 2005, which involved annual publication of hospital perform-ances in the national and local media. They show that the introduction of the 'star rating' system reduced significantly waiting times for hos-pital admissions in England when during the same period waiting times increased in Wales, Scotland and Northern Ireland. Given that during this period patients in England could not choose their hospital, the improvement in the performance of the hospitals was attributed, by the authors, to reputation effects.

However, when choice and competition policies are in place, then the provision of information, i.e. ratings of hospitals, certainly serves the purpose of allowing the service users to choose, but it may still impose reputation effects. Indeed, Bevan and Fasolo point out that even if competition is in place but choice is not really exercised, poorly ranked providers may be pressured to change. In this case it is often difficult to distinguish the effect of reputation from that of choice. An interesting insight, in that respect, is given by Ma and McGuire (1998) in a study that explored the reasons that led to a decrease in the cost of care in mental health hospitals in the US. The authors illustrate that reputation effects were shown to be the main determinant of the significant drop in the costs of mental health care and substance abuse care, even when there were no financial gains (Ma and McGuire, 1998). It is worth noting though that, as the authors claim, the reputation effect is just a hypothesis, and there can be many other reasons explaining the change in the provider behaviour. This claim in a sense confirms what is argued in this commentary, i.e. that distinguishing and measuring the effects of policy models is not a straightforward task.

Moving on from the choice and competition model, the distinction between reputation and targets effects is not clear either. As ranking depends on a number of criteria that the providers need to meet to score higher, the similarity of the two policy models becomes again quite evident. Looking at the example of 'star rating' among hospitals in England between 2000 and 2005, rating was based on a number of targets set by the Department of Health. It becomes therefore a bit difficult to judge the extent to which the improvement in the hospitals' performance was down to reputation effects or targets. Or indeed, both.

Another issue of evaluating policies is often related to the unanticipated consequences they have. For instance, the unintended consequences of reporting quality have been highlighted by a number of authors. Casalino et al. (2007) summarize the reasons why reporting quality may increase inequalities not only because minority groups are less likely to use these reports but also because patients that are perceived as more likely to lower the scores may be avoided by doctors. Similar results have been claimed for 'report cards' in the US. Dranove et al. (2003) looked at Medicare patients and found that the publication of cards made providers select patients that improved their scores, leading, at least in the short run, to decreased patient outcomes. This raises questions regarding the social welfare consequences that some of these policies may have.

On the policy implications

Bevan and Fasolo present evidence that suggests that the four models of public policy they discuss imply different results under different circumstances and settings. For example, they suggest that reputation effects work best for hospitals in the US and schools in the UK, while hierarchy and targets work better for hospitals and ambulances in the UK. They consequently criticise the UK government for using policies that have been shown to be relatively ineffective, such as altruism and competition, and they question their rationale to do so. But what is also striking is the instability of government policies. Indeed, some of the UK policies discussed in their chapter have been implemented and then abandoned within only a few years, in many cases by the same government.

This implies that there was not enough time to consider the effectiveness of a particular policy, simply because it was abandoned before coherent conclusions could be drawn. For example, the 'name and shame' policy in the English NHS hospitals showed at least some evidence that it did improve hospital performance. Yet it was replaced, at least in terms of government rhetoric, within five years.

If this is the case, the question is not why governments use policies where there is no evidence supporting their effectiveness. The real issue is why governments, specifically in the UK, do not allow enough time for the policies they implement to be tested over time. An obvious answer to the question is that governments change and so do the political views of policy-makers. Yet this offers only part of the explanation as often policies change even within the same government. Using the case studies examined by the authors, both the 'star rating' scheme for hospitals in England, a policy assuming providers act as 'humans', and choice and competition, that assumes individuals act like 'econs', were introduced, and in the former case, later downplayed, by the Labour government.

A plausible explanation for the instability of policies, a phenomenon which has been observed not only in British politics but in most Western European countries after the 1980s, is the stronger role that interest groups have developed in politics over the years (Richardson, 2000). Bevan and Fasolo highlight the importance of interest groups, in particular among health care providers in the UK, who, as they claim, influence politics more than theory or empirical evidence do.

Conclusions

To conclude, it has been argued in this commentary that choosing the right model of public policy is a challenging task for three main reasons. First, because, as Bevan and Fasolo have shown, policies may have different results in different settings. Second, as has been illustrated in this commentary, disentangling and measuring the effects of a policy is not always a straightforward task. And third, because it seems that Western governments do not allow much stability in the implementation of public policies, and as a result it is hard to empirically test the effectiveness of these policies in the long term.

Yet, behavioural approaches promise a better understanding of the underlying mechanisms of a number of policies, by challenging assumptions of selfish behaviour and impersonal transactions in settings, such as health care and education, where these assumptions seem often unrealistic. They can also offer interesting methodological insights through the use of laboratory experiments. Given that appropriate natural experiments are not always easy to devise, laboratory experiments provide controlled environments where behaviours can be tested and different models can be compared.

References

Casalino, L. P., Elster, A., Eisenberg, A., Lewis, E., Montgomery, J. and Ramos, D. (2007). Will Pay-for-Performance and Quality Reporting Affect Health Care Disparities? *Health Affairs* 26(3): w405–w414.

Dranove, D., Kessler, D., McClellan, M. and Satterthwaite, M. (2003). Is More Information Better? The Effects of 'Report Cards' on Health Care Providers. *Journal of Political Economy* 111: 555–88.

Gaynor, M. (2006). Competition and Quality in Health Care Markets? *Foundations and Trends in Microeconomics* 2(6): 441–508.

Hibbard, J. H., Stockard, J. and Tusler, M. (2003). Does Publicizing Hospital Performance Stimulate Quality Improvement Efforts? *Health Affairs* 22(2): 84–94.

Le Grand, J. (2003). *Motivation, Agency and Public Policy: Of Knights and Knaves, Pawns and Queens.* Oxford University Press.

Ma, C. A. and McGuire, T. G. (1998). Costs and Incentives in a Behavioral Health Carve-Out. *Health Affairs* 17(2): 53–69.

Richardson, J. (2000). Government, Interest Groups and Policy Change. *Political Studies* 48: 1006–25.

3 From irresponsible knaves to responsible knights for just 5p: behavioural public policy and the environment

KATE DISNEY, JULIAN LE GRAND
AND GILES ATKINSON

Introduction

How should individuals be encouraged to change their behaviour in order to reduce their impact on the environment? How can they be persuaded to curb the waste they make, to decrease the air and water pollution they generate, to throw away less waste or to reduce their carbon footprint? Should government policy-makers rely upon people's sense of social responsibility or their feelings of public duty to behave appropriately? Should governments simply supply individuals and households with information about the environmental cost of their activities? Explicitly appeal to a sense of public duty through exhortation and entreaty? Or should they go in a different direction, give up on notions of social responsibility and public duty, and instead try to regulate in some way those activities with an adverse impact on the environment? If so, in what way? Through imposing bans or other forms of legal restrictions on those activities – or through creating a financial incentive to reduce the activities by imposing a charge or tax on them, or on the waste they generate?

The answer to these questions will in part depend upon the answers to a further set of questions concerning the structure of individual motivation. Should individuals be regarded as essentially public-spirited with respect to the environment, committed to promoting the welfare of their fellow citizens and the wider society through economizing on the damage they do: socially responsible 'knights', in terms of a metaphor one of us has used elsewhere (Le Grand, 2006)? In which case, the provision of the relevant information, perhaps coupled with some exhortation to remind people of their social duty, should be sufficient to change their environmentally damaging behaviour. Or should people be treated as primarily self-interested agents, indifferent to those negatively affected by their waste products and only responsive to incentives that directly affect (either positively or negatively) their own personal interests: not knights, but something closer to those whom David Hume (among others) termed 'knaves'?[1] In which case, the government will need to use policy methods that appeal to people's sense of self-interest (or self-preservation), such as charges, taxation, subsidies or direct regulation.

More fundamentally, what if (as we know intuitively has to be the case) most individuals possess actually a mix of self-interested and altruistic motivations: a mixture of knight and knave? Do measures that rely upon one set of motivations risk driving out the other? In particular, if governments rely upon incentive measures that appear to assume that individuals are knaves, such as charging, taxing or regulation, does this damage more knightly motivations, and thus actually 'crowd out' pro-environmental behaviour? Or could the use of these policy measures actually reinforce knightly motivations in some way, thus 'crowding in' such behaviour?

Another set of questions concerns the durability of behaviour change induced by government policy. Will people simply respond positively to a particular environmental measure while it is in force, but revert to their previous environmentally damaging behaviour if it is removed? Even if it is not removed, will its impact remain at its initial level or will its effects gradually wear off, with individuals reverting to their original behaviour? Again this will depend on the psychological processes involved in individuals' reactions to the policy concerned, the extent to which the behaviour is simply a response to an external incentive or is one that is actually internalized by the individual in some way.

All of these issues are part of a larger debate arising from recent developments in behavioural economics and psychology. In particular, following the pioneering work of Richard Titmuss (1971), economists Bruno Frey (1997, 1999) and one of the present authors (Le Grand, 2006) have explored the question as to whether the introduction of, particularly, financial incentives 'crowd out' or 'crowd in' altruistic or knightly behaviour in a variety of different contexts, including blood donation, voluntary work and the payment of medical professionals. In psychology, the development of what is termed self-determination

---

[1] See Le Grand (2006: Ch. 2) for extensive discussion of the knaves metaphor and its usage by Hume, Mandeville and others.

theory (SDT) has examined the psychological processes by which external factors (including financial and other incentives) might crowd out socially desirable behaviour, or alternatively, are internalized and become intrinsic motivational factors, thus crowding in that behaviour.

This chapter is an attempt to shed a little light on these issues. It draws on some of the results of an empirical investigation of a natural experiment involving a specific financial incentive: the imposition of a charge on plastic bags by a major British retailer, Marks and Spencer (M&S). Specifically, it tries to answer the following questions. First, did the plastic bag charge at M&S crowd in or crowd out motivation for pro-environmental individual behaviour, specifically for a reduction in the use of plastic bags? Second, if either phenomenon occurred, what was going on psychologically for this to happen? In particular, can self-determination theory give us insight into the psychological processes that influence crowding out or crowding in when charges are levied on certain kinds of behaviour, and, if so, can it give some indication of the durability of any behaviour change that may have occurred?

It is important to add at this point that, as noted by Frey (2001), there is often a presumption that charging in an environmental context will lead to the crowding out of pro-environmental behaviour. The worry stems partly from the work of Titmuss and of Frey himself referred to above concerning the deleterious impact of introducing financial incentives on altruistic behaviour of various kinds (including blood donation and voluntary work). However, these incentives were mostly positive ones, involving financial rewards rather than penalties. Of more direct relevance to the charging issue is the famous study of an Israeli nursery school (Gneezy and Rustichini, 2000). The frequent tardiness of parents collecting their children stimulated a nursery in Israel to introduce a fine for the late collection of children. The fine, however, resulted in an increase in the frequency of parents collecting their children late. The authors suggest that the fine removed the parents' guilt and feeling of moral obligation regarding picking their children up late and allowed them to feel that they had purchased a commodity. Of more concern is that this moral obligation failed to reappear after the removal of the fine; rather, the incidence of parental lateness remained stable at the higher level.

So this chapter can be viewed in part as an attempt to see if these kind of consequences might occur in charging for environmentally damaging behaviour – in this case, for the use of plastic bags. The chapter begins with a brief exposition of self-determination theory. It then summarizes some of the recent events concerning the debate over plastic bags, describes the M&S study and draws out the relevant results. There is a brief concluding section.

Self-determination theory

Self-determination theory was developed by psychologists Richard Ryan and Edward Deci. It is a theory both of the factors that motivate individual behaviour and of what economists might term the satisfaction or utility that people get from that behaviour. With respect to the factors that motivate behaviour, the theory distinguishes between autonomous actions and those that are perceived to be controlled or influenced by factors external to the self. Autonomous actions occur when people do something because they find it intrinsically interesting, enjoyable or important. Controlled actions occur when individuals are motivated to perform them by some form of external pressure. This could take the form of direct rewards or punishments, such as financial payments or the threat of losing one's job; or they could be more subtle influences, such as the esteem of one's peers, the pressure of relatives and friends, or even internalized feelings of guilt or moral obligation. With respect to satisfaction, Deci and Ryan argue that autonomous actions or behaviour deliver the highest degree of satisfaction or utility. Controlled action may be just as highly motivated as autonomous activity, but evidence indicates that the quality of the experience and performance is not as good in general when people are controlled as when they are autonomous (Deci and Ryan, 2000).

Deci and Ryan go on to distinguish between two kinds of controlled motivation (which they also, somewhat confusingly, term extrinsic motivation), according to the degree of control involved. At the extreme of heavy control is 'external regulation': when behaviour is motivated entirely by direct rewards or penalties. At the other extreme is 'introjected regulation', when social or other external factors engender a sense of pride or self-worth for individuals acting in accordance with an internalized 'introjected' value or standard, or guilt or shame when they do not.

They also distinguish between two kinds of autonomous motivation, one of which they regard as a form of intrinsic motivation and the other extrinsic. The intrinsic motivation is the kind of autonomous motivation already referred to: that arising from the intrinsic enjoyment or interest in the task being undertaken. The extrinsic motivation is where there is a strong 'identification' with an external value or standard: when the individual identifies with the value or standard, internalizes it as part of their own morality, and regards the behaviour concerned as an essential part of their identity. This is to be distinguished from the introjected regulation described in the previous paragraph, which it otherwise rather resembles, in that with identified motivation individuals do not feel pride if they do something socially approved of, or shame if they do not; rather, the activity concerned is simply part of their identity and they will carry on with it, regardless of changes in the outside environment.

Deci and Ryan also discuss the factors that might affect the degree of control and hence the kind of motivation that people might experience. Contextual support to decision-making and situations where motivators provide a convincing rationale for undertaking a certain kind of behaviour can reduce the element of perceived control and enhance feelings of autonomy, leading to introjected or even identified motivation. Conversely, threat of punishment, deadlines, formal or overbearing means of communication can make individuals feel controlled and less autonomous. In consequence, as noted above, the quality (and indeed quantity) of their relevant actions might diminish.

These concepts can be used to describe some of the psychological processes involved in the phenomena of crowding in and crowding out of altruistic or knightly behaviour by external stimuli such as financial rewards or penalties. An external stimulus may crowd in altruistic behaviour (that is, induce more altruistic behaviour than if the stimulus was not present) if it is perceived as supporting or reinforcing; the stimulus may crowd out (or reduce) altruistic behaviour, as compared with that if the stimulus were not present, if it is perceived as controlling.

The concepts of introjected and identified motivation are principally relevant to the phenomenon of crowding in. They do not determine the amount of crowding in that occurs, but rather they influence the sustainability of any crowding in once the external stimulus is withdrawn. If the internalization that has occurred is of the introjected kind, then the removal of the external stimulus will reduce or eliminate the behaviour concerned if the societal approval is no longer there.

But if the internalization is of the identified kind, then the change in behaviour will remain, even if the social pressures are withdrawn, for the internalization will then have successfully promoted people's sense of autonomy and reduced their feelings of social control.

SDT also provides clues as to the external stimuli that are likely to increase people's sense of autonomy, and thus the extent to which they identify with the policy. According to the theory, the policies concerned are more likely to promote autonomy, be successfully internalized and lead to sustainable crowding in, if they have a meaningful rationale, if they are perceived as fair, and if they give choice and support to the individual (De Young, 1996; Deci and Ryan, 2000; Vallerand and Reid, 1984). More specifically, if a particular external stimulus provokes people into trying a new behaviour, then this is likely to increase perceived self-efficacy and competence, which would mediate the behavioural change initiated by the incentive (Bandura, 1977; de Charms, 1968). This would mean that the motivation was initially derived from the presence of the incentive but then became internalized, making the behaviour change more likely to persist, even if the incentive were to be removed. Reversing this argument, Thøgersen (2005) argues that perceived helplessness or a lack of self-efficacy and competence is a crucial problem in motivating people to behave environmentally. Empowerment affects 'how hard he or she will strive to solve environmental and ethical problems through his or her own behavioural effort' (Thøgersen, 2005, p. 146), so increasing competence increases the likelihood of sustainable consumption. Perceived helplessness is implicit in amotivation – a complete loss of motivation to act and a feeling of apathy (i.e. the opposite of empowerment) – and has been shown to be negatively correlated with environmentally friendly behaviour (Pelletier et al., 1999). We return to this below.

Insights into the usefulness of SDT in understanding the impact of charging on individual behaviour can be obtained from some of the empirical evidence on the phenomenon. The Israeli nursery study has already been mentioned, where the introduction of a fine on lateness appeared to crowd out parents' willingness to pick up their children on time (Gneezy and Rustichini, 2000). The researchers speculate that this arose because the fine removed parents' sense of moral obligation: what one might term introjected *de*-regulation. In a study of public transport, the experience of travelling by bus due to an incentive (a free bus pass) failed to increase the number of people who decided to leave their car at home when the incentive was removed (Thøgersen and Møller, 2004). In this case, although people were willing to give public transport a go when the opportunity arose (as it was free), trying public transport may have just reinforced beliefs in its inconvenience, and hence weakened people's belief in the underlying rationale for the policy.

Of more direct relevance to environmental charging policy, a study on the pricing of waste collection in Denmark strongly indicated that crowding in occurred (Thøgersen, 1994, 2003). The monetary incentive appeared to encourage attempts to master pro-environmental behaviours (in this case, recycling and composting), and success at this increased competence, which in turn increased self-determination and motivation. This was reinforced by a comparison between a sample that paid for their waste collection depending on its weight and one that paid a fixed charge. The former had higher perceived self-efficacy and stronger internalized norms than the latter (Thøgersen, 2003).

Charging and plastic bags

Plastic bags have become a symbol of our wasteful lifestyle and are accused of causing environmental harm. They have stimulated a plethora of campaigns and websites trying to 'Ban the Bag' and have motivated governments around the world to take action. Ireland brought attention to both the plastic bag problem and the use of market instruments to change behaviour when they introduced a Plastic Bag Levy (PBL) in 2002. This reduced plastic bag consumption by approximately 90 per cent almost overnight and reduced plastic bag litter to 0.3 per cent of litter pollution nationally compared with 5 per cent before the levy (Litter Monitoring Body, 2003).

It is clear that the levy has not only changed consumer behaviour in relation to disposable plastic bags, it has also raised national consciousness about the role each one of us can and must play if we are to tackle collectively the problems of litter and waste management. (Irish Environment Minister talking to the BBC, 2002)

As the above quote demonstrates, the levy seems to have had a wider effect on general environmental consciousness than just changing plastic bag consumption. If true, this would mean that financial incentives may be an effective way of making society more sustainable, beyond that predicted by economic theory alone. Unfortunately, the evidence of these wider impacts is only anecdotal and it is not a universally held view. Australia, Scotland and the UK more broadly have all previously reviewed the possibility of introducing a levy on plastic bags but have all dismissed it in favour of voluntary agreements, threatening further legislation only if these voluntary targets are not met (Defra, 2006; Environment Australia, 2002; National Plastic Bags Working Group, 2002; Scottish Government, 2008). When asked why Tesco were not going to charge for bags, Terry Leahy, the Chief Executive claimed that:

It would make a bigger immediate difference but it wouldn't buy-in customers, it would be imposing a price on them and when you look at the wider challenges we face in the environment they can't just be met by tax or regulation or pricing. (BBC, 2006)

In November 2007 the London Local Authorities (Shopping Bag) Bill was submitted to the Houses of Parliament, attempting to allow the London councils to force stores to charge for plastic bags. Gordon Brown stated that if supermarkets did not make significant progress in reaching a 25 per cent reduction in plastic bags by the end of 2008, then this policy would be extended nationally (Brogan, 2008). The *Daily Mail* started a national Ban the Bag campaign and plastic bags became front-page news for some time, leading supermarkets to experiment with a variety of policies to reduce their plastic bag use. By early 2009, however, the London Bill had been dismissed without hearing and the front page had been taken over by the credit crunch. There is little talk about plastic bags at all now and certainly no talk about a national plastic bag levy. Individual stores have each taken their own approach to tackling their plastic bag problem including charging, rewarding with points or vouchers, hiding plastic bags or simply reminding customers. One of these is M&S, whose charging scheme is the focus of our study.

Charging: a natural experiment

The M&S plastic bag charge enabled a natural experiment to be conducted by allowing a survey via questionnaire *ex ante* – to assess behaviour and motivation when plastic bags were freely available – and also *ex post*, to assess behaviour and motivation after the implementation of the charge using a between-subjects design in order to prevent the recall effect. A questionnaire was used that was developed following an in-depth literature review, taking guidance from previous studies (for example, Fiorillo, 2007; Pelletier et al., 1998).

Participants were stopped directly after paying for their goods at the checkout. Their use of bags on the shopping trip in question was recorded as well as their habitual bag use at M&S, other food stores, other non-food stores and, in the case of the *ex post* sample, the participants' habitual plastic bag use before the introduction of the charge.

As people were not expected to know their exact bag consumption, the question and answer format was as follows: How often do you reuse bags at M&S? 1: Never, 2: Rarely, 3: Sometimes, 4: Almost always or always, 5: Don't know. This allowed people to be categorized by their stated bag use habits. This was followed by questions in a similar format concerning bag use at other stores and by a list of 15 questions that targeted an individual's motivation level or other possible reasons that one may or may not wish to bring one's own bag to a supermarket. Finally, some demographic questions were included, both to use as controls and so that these factors could be investigated to see if they affected the way the charge was interpreted and influenced the likelihood of crowding in or crowding out. The demographic factors included age, sex, income and level of education.

The *ex ante* survey was conducted between 6 April and 5 May 2008 immediately prior to the introduction of the 5p charge at M&S (denoted time 0). Throughout this time M&S were giving away a Bag for Life (BfL) for free (normally worth 20p) with each food purchase in order to encourage the use of BfLs after the charge and to increase acceptance of the policy. Checkout staff were also meant to inform customers of the forthcoming introduction of the charge. A total of 404 interviews were completed in this stage, in three different locations: Covent Garden, Swindon and Brighton.

The *ex post* survey was conducted between mid-October and early December 2008. As the charge was introduced on 6 May, this gave approximately six months to allow people to adjust to the charge. This was considered to be enough time to allow any implementation effect to have receded and/or for a habit to have formed.

It was intended that the *ex ante* and *ex post* samples would be similar in demographic and social composition and the questionnaires were thus conducted in the same locations at similar times of the day.

In total, 547 interviews were carried out *ex post* (denoted time 1) in four locations: Covent Garden, Swindon, Brighton and Angel. In the *ex post* survey, it became apparent that the charge had not been implemented properly in the Covent Garden M&S which is why the alternative London location of Angel was also chosen. To ensure that this did not distort the results, all tests were run both on the entire sample and a sample including only Brighton and Swindon. They were generally the same but any significant differences are noted throughout.

A methodological point concerns the empirical identification of crowding in or crowding out. It is often difficult to assess whether a particular external stimulus has led to crowding in, crowding out or neither. This is because all three phenomena may lead to changes in behaviours that, though different in magnitude, are in the same direction. For instance, consider the introduction of a price charge for plastic bags that were previously free. If there is neither crowding out or crowding in, then standard economic theory would predict a drop in demand for plastic bags (or an increase in plastic bag reuse). If there is crowding in, then we would also expect a drop in demand for plastic bags, but of an amount more than that if there had been no crowding in. If there is crowding out, there could also still be a drop in demand for plastic bags, but of an amount that is less than the amount that economic theory would predict. Only if the crowding out is so extreme that people feel so controlled by the imposition of a price that it actually makes them use *more* plastic bags than they did before, will we observe behaviour in a different direction, that is, the price charge results in an increase in demand.

This creates problems for trying to identify crowding in or crowding out from simply observing a fall in demand for new plastic bags following the introduction of the charge (or an increase in the reuse of plastic bags), since, as we have just explained, such a fall in demand (or increase in reuse) is consistent with crowding in, non-extreme crowding out or neither. Hence it is necessary to look at other behaviours relating to the environment following the charge's introduction to try to identify the existence or otherwise of these phenomena.

We do not report here on all of the results of this study, but simply concentrate on those that are of relevance to the concerns of this chapter: did the charge crowd in or crowd out behaviour, and, if it did either of these, how durable is any change likely to be?

Did the charge crowd in or crowd out motivation?

We would expect the introduction of a charge on plastic bags to increase the reuse of such bags in M&S. And indeed it did, with 16.8 per cent stating in the *ex ante* survey that they would reuse bags and 37.8 per cent in the *ex post* survey.

However, for the reasons explained above, this on its own cannot tell us whether there was crowding in, crowding out or neither, since an increase in reuse is consistent with all three types of phenomena. For that, it is necessary to turn to other results from the survey. In particular, we examine whether there were changes in other forms of pro-environmental behaviour that could be attributed to the charge.

In the *ex post* survey individuals were asked whether they were more or less likely to reuse bags at non-M&S food stores since the introduction of the M&S charge, and a dummy variable (dofs) was created and set equal to 1 for those who were more likely to do so, 0 otherwise. Thirty-eight per cent answered that they were more likely to reuse at other food stores since the introduction of the M&S charge with 0.73 per cent saying that they were less likely, and the remainder claiming that there had been no change in their behaviour. Since those who were more likely to reuse at other stores (where no charge was levied) were clearly motivated by factors other than cost, this would suggest a crowding in of motivation.

The same was done for their likelihood to reuse bags in other non-food stores after the charge (dos), but here only 10.4 per cent of the sample said that they were more likely to reuse bags. Getting people to use their own bags in non-food stores has been shown to be quite difficult (Dee and Barclay, 2005) and there has been very little public discussion about plastic bags other than those given out by supermarkets. The 10.4 per cent who took the initiative and started to reuse at non-food stores must have more fully internalized the behaviour of bringing their own bag, which means that the charge at M&S had crowded in their motivation significantly.

A dummy variable was also created which was set equal to 1 for those that started to reuse bags more frequently at M&S itself after the charge. Using a logit regression, dofs was regressed on reuse_more and a vector of control variables.[2] This showed that those who reused

---

[2] All regression results are available from Katedisney@hotmail.com.

bags more at M&S after the introduction of the charge were also significantly more likely to start reusing bags at other food stores that did not charge. This confirms that their motivation must have been crowded in. When running the same regression with dos (bag use at non-food stores) the relationship is no longer significant, though it is still heading in the expected direction. In the Brighton and Swindon sample, individuals who started to bring their own bags to M&S more after the charge was introduced were 129.6% more likely to take their own bag to other food stores (0.1% level) but this dropped to 50.6% in the entire sample (1% level).

Did the M&S strategy win the hearts and minds of the shoppers?

As stated above, in order to obtain more insight into the psychological effects underlying the phenomenon, a number of questions were used to try to elicit people's motives and attitudes towards plastic bags, the environment, science and society. The relevant ones are discussed in more detail here.

First, individuals were asked whether they agreed or disagreed with the statement *'People (society, friends or family) would criticize me if I used a bag'* and a dummy variable (dcriticize) was created and set equal to 1 for those who agreed with this statement. Running a logit regression of dcriticize on a dummy variable (time) set equal to 0 for the *ex ante* sample and 1 for the *ex post* sample shows that after the introduction of the charge, people were 40.5% less likely to agree with this statement (1% level).[3]

This is somewhat unexpected. Between the two rounds of interviews many supermarkets increased efforts to discourage plastic bag use, so we might have expected the social norm to shift towards plastic bag reuse if it changed at all, and for the use (and the effectiveness) of social sanctions to have thus increased. The fact that it has shifted away from this in our sample may demonstrate that the charge at M&S has crowded out motivation for bag reuse and shifted the mode of thinking away from a social obligation towards a financial one, but this would be inconsistent with the increase in bag reuse in other stores where there is no charge. An alternative, more convincing explanation is that plastic bag reuse has been internalized to such an extent that

---

[3] This is for the entire sample but the corresponding figure for the Brighton and Swindon only sample is 44.4% less likely to agree.

it is no longer simply a social norm, but has become a moral norm: people no longer require the pressure of social sanctions. This would suggest the crowding in is the result of *identification* with the norm for bringing one's own bag.

The latter hypothesis seems more likely as throughout the time of the *ex ante* survey there was significant media attention on plastic bag consumption, yet bag reuse was fairly low. Throughout this time people may have been aware that they 'should' reuse bags and that society, the government and the media were highly critical of those who did not. By the time of the second round of questionnaires plastic bags were no longer a public focus as the credit crunch dominated media attention, so social criticism for using plastic bags will have been seen to have been much reduced, and bag reuse became much more of a personal matter. The literature also demonstrates that feeling pressured to do something, for example by society, is often an ineffective motivator (Reich and Robertson, 1979); just as it failed to encourage bag reuse before the charge in the majority, the reduction in social pressure seems not to have harmed efforts to encourage bag reuse *ex post*. If the social norm had been replaced by only a financial norm – rather than by the development of a moral norm – then one would have expected bag reuse at other stores where there was no financial incentive to remain unchanged.

The idea that the crowding in is explained by actual identification with the moral norm is supported by some of the other statements in the questionnaire where a significant change was noted: that of trust amongst individuals. Both *ex ante* and *ex post*, individuals were asked to strongly agree to strongly disagree (1–4) with the following state-ment, *'People will only use less plastic bags if they have a financial incentive'*. This variable was labelled trust and a dummy (dtrust) was created, as this was thought to measure the trust that participants had in society specifically to bring their own bags, but also to behave environmentally responsibly in general, without coercion. It is well known that, if it is believed that others will cooperate, then individuals are more willing to cooperate themselves (Sustainable Development Commission, 2006). Before the charge, 69% of participants strongly or partly agreed that people would only use fewer plastic bags if there was a financial incentive. This dropped to 52% in the *ex post* sample. Running a logit regression of dtrust on time and a vector of demographic variables shows that the *ex post* sample were 56.9% (0.1% level) less likely to agree with the statement or, equivalently,

56.9% more likely to trust that their fellow shoppers would reuse bags without the need for financial incentives.[4] This is a rather dramatic shift in social beliefs; if this trend spilled over to other social behaviours, it could rebut the idea that charging for environmental goods creates a society of selfish individuals with no social awareness.

Social sanctions are a form of external punishment that are often used when there is no other means (for example, governmental) of enforcing a regulation. Often we endorse our own behaviours by using internal punishments or rewards, such as guilt or the so-called 'warm glow effect'. Although in this case the behaviour requires no external intervention, it is still dependent on a punishment/reward of some sort; while self-determination theory would admit that the motivation is more internalized than those behaviours solely motivated for the sake of external rewards, it is not fully internalized. In the M&S case study, in the *ex ante* survey 25% stated that they strongly agreed with the statement that they felt guilty if they took a plastic bag with a further 40% agreeing. In the *ex post* survey, however, the number strongly feeling guilty fell to 10% and those agreeing were 38%. As was the case with the criticism statement discussed above and interpreted as a social norm, this may be interpreted in at least two ways. Making the 5p payment to charity for the bag may free people from the burden of their guilt. There is no doubt that in many cases this is true. Many of these shoppers would be reluctant to bring their own bag regardless of what you charged because they consider the inconvenience cost so high. It is not inefficient to have a few bags being used if payments are being made to offset the environmental cost. Besides, there are always times when one forgets a bag or needs to make a spontaneous shop and does not happen to have one handy. The question really is: does this freedom from guilt mean that people are inclined to bring their own bag less than they would have before the charge, and do they feel less environmental responsibility in general because of this? We would argue that predominantly this was not the case, for largely the same reasons as with the social norm above. But then why would individuals reuse bags where there was no charge in place if they had no social pressure and no internal pressure such as

[4] This figure is for the entire sample but the corresponding figure for the Brighton and Swindon sample only is that the *ex post* sample were 50.2% more likely to trust that their fellow shoppers would reuse bags without coercion.

guilt? This is important because introjected individuals – those display-ing behaviour based on the threat of feelings of personal guilt – are highly unstable and much more likely to find an excuse to switch back to the easier behaviour than individuals who have fully integrated the behaviour (Koestner et al., 2001). Introjected individuals may be willing to participate in easy behaviours but as soon as the tasks become more difficult they are more inclined to search for a way out than individuals with more internalized motivations. Introjected individuals are still better than those that are purely externally motivated because they should still continue to bring their own bag even where there is not a financial incentive, whereas an externally motivated person would not. It is when behaviour change becomes more difficult and requires more learning and persistence that the shift from introjection to identifi-cation may become more important. So, the fact that participants in this experiment were 53.7%[5] (0.1% level) less likely to feel guilty after the introduction of the charge could be a very good thing indeed.

Why was the M&S policy a success?

Overall, it is apparent that the M&S environmental policy successfully crowded in pro-environmental behaviour. Moreover, the crowding in appears to have quite deep psychological roots, with some signs that the policy was internalized to the extent of it becoming a moral norm. Knaves were turned into knights – at least to some extent.

Self-determination theory is quite clear about the frailty of the process of internalization in humans, describing the process as innate but easily thwarted (Deci et al., 1994). A review of the policy at M&S may hint at why it was so successful at not only reducing plastic bag consumption in their stores (which economists could happily explain), but also why people started to reuse bags elsewhere and apparently started to trust each other more. Put another way, why did the policy succeed in creating such a high level of internalization?

According to SDT, autonomy is the key to self-determination, but the promotion of autonomy has specific requirements. First, there must be a meaningful rationale for the policy. In this case, the reason for charging for bags was made clear through information campaigns; the *ex ante*

---

[5] This is for the entire sample; the corresponding figure for the sample with just Brighton and Swindon is 59.3%.

survey showed that 77 per cent of people before the charge was introduced agreed that the M&S charge was necessary to help the environment. Second, the policy should be perceived as fair. In this case the participants at M&S were asked whether they thought it was fair to charge 5p for a plastic bag; before the charge was introduced, 85 per cent believed that it was, thus increasing the likelihood of internalization from the policy.

Third and perhaps most importantly, SDT predicts that policies that give choice and support to individuals, rather than those that force them to change their behaviour, are more likely to promote autonomy and thus be successfully internalized. Charging, in this respect, is likely to be helpful. People were given the choice to reuse a bag or to buy a bag if they needed, and they were also given free bags for life before the policy was implemented, further increasing the apparent fairness of the policy and reducing its cost to the individual. But what was often more important was the way that the price acted as a signal or a reminder: 49 per cent of people after the charge stated that the charge had made them remember to bring their own bag more. Numerous people wanted to bring their own bag and had tried many times but they had failed due to their own poor memory. It seems that most people wanted the 5p charge largely to remind themselves, with the added benefit that they could also see that they were not wasting their time, as they could see that everyone else was joining in the effort since reusing bags is a visible public act. It is significant that people did feel able to adapt to the regulation and were given one month to get used to it without penalty. By the end of the month many people seemed to have realized that they preferred using their own stronger bags anyway, and they did not need convincing any further, perhaps just reminding.

In summary, the M&S regulation supported a policy that most people believed in (reducing plastic bag consumption), that was regarded as fair, that gave a choice about the relevant behaviour rather than people being forced into it, and that made people feel that they were supported. It is perhaps therefore not surprising that the available evidence suggests that the policy was successfully internalized.

Conclusion

We may summarize our principal conclusions as follows. The introduction of a 5p charge for plastic bags by M&S led to increased reuse of bags, not only at M&S, but also at other food stores. This suggests some crowding in of the relevant 'knightly' behaviour. Moreover, the evidence suggests that the psychological process associated with the crowding in was what has been termed identification, that is, the behaviour has become a part of the moral identity of the individuals concerned, and was not simply a response to social pressure. Knaves had become knights – at least for a small area of behaviour. In turn, this seems to be the result of the charge having a well-understood rationale, being considered fair, giving people choice and supporting them in their choice or reminding them of its desirability. All of these contributed to people's sense of autonomy and hence their identification with the policy.

The small scale of this study obviously limits its generalizability. Further, the environmental problems that we face are increasingly complex, and will not be as easy to solve as stuffing a plastic bag in your handbag or pocket. People will need to be motivated to learn to do things differently on a much larger canvas, and to persist in these new behaviours if they are to be effective in combating more serious problems than plastic waste disposal, such as climate change. But nonetheless there may be useful lessons to be learned from natural experiments such as the one reported here. To deal with environmental problems at whatever level, we must find policies that not only make it economically sensible to behave responsibly with respect to the environment, but that also enhance our fundamental motivations for doing so. The results of this small study suggest that charging for environmental 'bads' in some contexts may be just such a policy.

References

Bandura, A. (1977). Self-Efficacy: Toward a Unifying Theory of Behavioral Change. *Psychology Review* 84(2): 191–215.

BBC (2002). Irish bag tax hailed success. BBC News (http://news.bbc.co.uk/1/hi/world/europe/2205419.stm#, accessed 10 November 2007).

(2006). Chief Executive of Tesco on how the scheme will work. BBC News (http://news.bbc.co.uk/1/hi/business/5244708.stm, accessed 4 August 2006).

Brogan, B. (2008). Gordon Brown gives supermarkets one year to start charging for plastic bags ... or else. *Daily Mail* (www.dailymail.co.uk/news/article-522765/Gordon-Brown-gives-supermarkets-year-start-charging-plastic-bags—else.html, accessed 29 February 2008).

de Charms, R. (1968). *Personal Causation: The Internal Affective Determinants of Behavior*. New York: Academic Press.

De Young, R. (1996). Some Psychological Aspects of Reduced Consumption Behavior: The Role of Intrinsic Satisfaction and Competence Motivation. *Environment and Behavior* 28(3): 358–409.

Deci, E. L., Eghrari, H., Patrick, B. and Leone, D. (1994). Facilitating Internalization: The Self-Determination Theory Perspective. *Journal of Personality* 62(1): 120–42.

Deci, E. L. and Ryan, R. (2000). The 'What' and 'Why' of Goal Pursuits: Human Needs and the Self-Determination of Behavior. *Psychological Inquiry* 11(4): 227–68.

Dee, J. and Barclay, V. (2005). *Plastic Check-Out Bag Use in Non-Supermarket Retail Outlets*. Australian Government: Department of Environment, Waste, Heritage and the Arts (www.environment.gov .au/archive/settlements/publications/waste/plastic-bags/planet-ark/pubs/ planet-ark.pdf, accessed November 2007).

Defra (2006). *Local Environmental Quality: Plastic Bags* (www.defra .gov.uk/environment/localenv/litter/bags/index.htm, accessed 30 March 2007).

Environment Australia (2002). *Plastic Shopping Bags – Analysis of Levies and Environmental Impacts: Final Report*. Prepared in association with RMIT Centre for Design and Eunomia Research and Consulting Ltd (www.environment.gov.au/settlements/publications/waste/plastic-bags/ pubs/analysis.pdf, accessed 5 November 2007).

Fiorillo, D. (2007). *Do Monetary Rewards Undermine Intrinsic Motivations of Volunteers? Some Empirical Evidence for Italian Volunteers*. Munich Personal RePEc Archive (http://mpra.ub.uni-muenchen.de/7783/1/ MPRA_paper_7783.pdf, accessed April 2008).

Frey, B. S. (1997). Integration into Economics. In B. S. Frey (ed.), *Not Just for the Money: An Economic Theory of Personal Motivation*. Cheltenham: Edward Elgar.

  (1999). Morality and Rationality in Environmental Policy. *Journal of Consumer Policy* 22: 395–417.

  (2001). *Inspiring Economics: Human Motivation in Political Economy*. Cheltenham: Edward Elgar.

Gneezy, U. and Rustichini, A. (2000). A Fine is a Price. *The Journal of Legal Studies* 29(1): 1–17.

Koestner, R., Houlfort, N., Paquet, S. and Knight, C. (2001). On the Risks of Recycling Because of Guilt: An Examination of the Consequences of Introjection. *Journal of Applied Social Psychology* 31(12): 2545–60.

Le Grand, J. (2006). *Motivation, Agency, and Public Policy: Of Knights and Knaves, Pawns and Queens*. Oxford University Press.

Litter Monitoring Body (2003). *The National Litter Pollution Monitoring System – System Result* (www.litter.ie/docs/DoEHLG%20System% 27s%20Results%20Report%20Final%202002.pdf, accessed November 2011).

National Plastic Bags Working Group (2002). *Plastic Shopping Bags in Australia: Report to the National Packaging Covenant Council* (www .environment.gov.au/settlements/publications/waste/plastic-bags/pubs/ report-2002.pdf, accessed November 2007).

Pelletier, L. G., Dion, S., Tuson, K. and Green-Demers, I. (1999). Why Do People Fail to Adopt Environmental Protective Behaviors? Toward a Taxonomy of Environmental Amotivation. *Journal of Applied Social Psychology* 29(12): 2481–504.

Pelletier, L. G., Tuson, K. M., Green-Demers, I., Noels, K. and Beaton, A. M. (1998). Why Are You Doing Things for the Environment? The Motivation Toward the Environment Scale (MTES). *Journal of Applied Social Psychology* 28(5): 437–68.

Reich, J. W. and Robertson, J. L. (1979). Reactance and Norm Appeal in Anti-Littering Messages. *Journal of Applied Psychology* 9(1): 91–101.

Scottish Government (2008). Calls to end 'plastic bag culture'. The Scottish Government: News (www.scotland.gov.uk/News/Releases/2008/02/ 28115506, accessed 21 May 2008).

Sustainable Development Commission (2006). *I Will if You Will: Towards Sustainable Consumption*. Sustainable Development Commission and National Consumer Council.

Thøgersen, J. (1994). Monetary Incentives and Environmental Concern: Effects of a Differentiated Garbage Fee. *Journal of Consumer Policy* 17(4): 407–42.

  (2003). Monetary Incentives and Recycling: Behavioural and Psychological Reactions to a Performance-Dependent Garbage Fee. *Journal of Consumer Policy* 26(2): 197–228.

  (2005). How May Consumer Policy Empower Consumers for Sustainable Lifestyles? *Journal of Consumer Policy* 28(2): 143–77.

Thøgersen, J. and Møller, B. (2004). Breaking Car-Use Habits: The Effectiveness of Economic Incentives. 3rd International Conference on Traffic & Transport Psychology, ICTTP, Nottingham, 5–9 September.

Titmuss, R. (1971). *The Gift Relationship: From Human Blood to Social Policy*. London: Allen & Unwin.

Vallerand, R. J. and Reid, G. (1984). On the Causal Effects of Perceived Competence on Intrinsic Motivation: A Test of Cognitive Evaluation Theory. *Journal of Sport and Exercise Psychology* 6(1): 94–102.

3.1 | *A response to Disney, Le Grand and Atkinson*

RICHARD COOKSON

Introduction

What happens when supermarkets introduce a small charge for plastic bags? Answer: people start bringing their own bags. This happened nationally in the Republic of Ireland in 2002, where a plastic bag levy reportedly reduced usage by 90 per cent, and more recently in Wales, where similarly large reductions have been reported following the introduction of a single use carrier bag charge in October 2009 (Leonard, 2012). As Disney, Le Grand and Atkinson (henceforth DLA) show in their uncontrolled before/after study, this also happened at four Marks & Spencer supermarkets in London in 2008.

In and of itself, this finding may seem unremarkable – or even rather obvious – and of limited policy importance. The production and disposal of plastic bags wastes energy and creates nuisance in terms of landfill and litter. However, it poses a much smaller threat to human lives and livelihoods than other more important environmental hazards. Sceptically minded readers might therefore suspect politicians of using action on plastic bags as an environmental policy 'gimmick' designed to appeal to environmentally conscious middle-class voters while avoiding the difficult and unpopular actions necessary to tackle more important environmental challenges.

What makes DLA's chapter interesting, however, is its survey evidence about the moral psychology of supermarket customers and its broader discussion of how financial incentives and moral motivations can work in tandem to help tackle more important environmental and public policy problems.

Motivation crowding in

The basic idea explored by DLA is that giving people a financial incentive to behave in accordance with a particular norm can sometimes also increase their non-financial moral motivation to do so. In this 'win–win' scenario, people come to believe that their new behavioural habit is morally right, and become motivated to follow it irrespective of any payment. In other words, money can sometimes teach morality. This is a new twist on an old Aristotelian idea. According to Aristotle, people learn appropriate moral motivations – or 'virtues' – though training and practice, especially in childhood but also in adulthood. The new twist is that moral training may sometimes involve financial rewards and penalties.

This idea is interesting and controversial because it is diametrically opposed to the well-known behavioural economic theory of 'motivation crowding out' developed by Bruno Frey (Frey and Oberholzer-Gee, 1997) and applied to public policy issues by Julian Le Grand (Le Grand, 2006). Motivation crowding out occurs when giving people external rewards and punishments to behave in accordance with a particular norm tends to reduce or 'crowd out' their internal motivation to do so. Or, in Le Grand's colourful terminology, paying people to change their behaviour can turn them from 'knights' into 'knaves'. In this 'win–lose' situation, people come to believe that behaving in accordance with the norm is no longer worth doing for its own sake but is now only worth doing to gain rewards or avoid punishments.

In refining the opposite idea of 'motivation crowding in' – i.e. the case in which financial incentives turn people from 'knaves' into 'knights' – DLA draw on 'self-determination theory' developed by the psychologists Richard Ryan and Edward Deci (Deci and Ryan, 2000). This theory distinguishes two different non-financial motivations for conforming with a behavioural norm: (i) autonomous moral motivation derived from identification with the norm, and (ii) controlled social motivation derived from social pressure to conform with the norm. According to DLA, paying people to change their habits can sometimes increase their autonomous moral motivations to behave in accordance with the new habit.

Survey evidence

The interesting questions that DLA seek to address are therefore: (1) in this particular case, did the financial punishment for plastic bag use lead to 'crowding in' of autonomous moral motivations to reuse one's own plastic bags, and (2) in general, under what circumstances will systems of external rewards and punishments designed to change the behaviour of members of the public lead to 'crowding in' of autonomous moral motivation?

DLA's answer to the first question is 'yes', and their answer to the second question is that 'crowding in' of autonomous moral motivation is likely to occur when the following three conditions are satisfied:

(1) The system is perceived by a majority of the public as justified by a meaningful rationale.
(2) The system is perceived by a majority of the public as fair.
(3) The system is perceived by a majority of the public as providing choice and support to the individual, rather than forcing behaviour change.

DLA provide survey evidence that conditions (1) and (2) were met for a large majority of their sample of customers at the four Marks & Spencer stores. They also provide survey evidence tangentially supportive of (3): that 49 per cent of respondents felt that the charge helped them remember to bring their own bags.

However, I want to focus on DLA's answer to the first question. Did supermarket customers at their Marks & Spencer's study sites really undergo motivation 'crowding in' – or was it just the money? DLA provide four pieces of evidence that it was not just the money:

(1) In their *ex post* sample of customers, recruited several months after the charge had been imposed, 38 per cent answered that they were now more likely to reuse bags at other food stores. Furthermore, those who said they now reused their own bags more – i.e. had responded to the change in financial and/or moral motivation – were substantially more likely to say this than others. DLA interpret this as evidence of a change in moral motivation, since other food stores did not impose a charge.
(2) Compared with respondents in the *ex ante* sample of customers, recruited before the charge was imposed, respondents in the *ex post* sample were 56.9 per cent less likely to agree that *'People will only use less plastic bags if they have a financial incentive'*. DLA interpret this as a 'dramatic shift in social beliefs' towards the view that people are morally motivated to use plastic bags less.
(3) Respondents in the *ex post* sample were 40 per cent less likely to agree that *'People (society, friends or family) would criticize me if I used a*

bag' than respondents in the *ex ante* sample. DLA interpret this as evidence that the relevant non-financial motivations must involve internal moral pressure rather than external social pressure.

(4) Respondents in the *ex post* sample were less likely to say they feel guilty if they use a plastic bag. DLA again interpret this as evidence that the relevant non-financial motivations must involve internal moral pressure rather than external social pressure.

A different interpretation

However, each piece of evidence can be interpreted differently, in line with the view that it was just the money after all. Both (1) and (2) may be due to a change in effort costs rather than a change in moral motivation. Getting into the habit of bringing your own bags is a low-effort behaviour change which brings minor benefits – in particular, one can bring larger, stronger bags. Once one has got into the habit for one supermarket with the help of financial incentives, it may then take little or no effort to maintain the habit and extend it to other supermarkets. So the *ex post* effort costs of habit maintenance and extension may be much less than the *ex ante* effort costs of habit formation. This may explain why many of the people who got into the habit of reusing their bags at Marks & Spencer said they would now do the same in other supermarkets, rather than any change in autonomous moral motivation. It may also explain why many people felt that financial incentives were no longer necessary to encourage people to reuse bags less. Furthermore, (3) can be interpreted as evidence of a reduction in external social pressure – a form of motivation 'crowding out' rather than 'crowding in' – that was counterbalanced by the stronger effect of financial incentives. DLA point out that 'feeling pressured to do something, for example by society, is often an ineffective motivator'. But on the other hand, there is good evidence that external social pressure can sometimes be a highly effective motivator, at least in the case of giving to charity (DellaVigna et al., 2012). So the role of social pressure in this case is not clear. Finally, (4) can be interpreted as direct evidence of 'crowding out' of internal moral motivation. According to philosopher Bernard Williams, 'guilt' refers to internal moral pressure whereas 'shame' refers to external social pressure (Williams, 2008).

All in all, the evidence provided by DLA is consistent with the view that in this case the money mattered far more than any non-financial motivation, whether of the autonomous moral kind or of the controlled social kind. Furthermore, it is also consistent with the view that there may have been 'crowding out' of non-financial motivations, rather than 'crowding in'.

Surprise, surprise – more research is needed

What is needed are empirical tests of 'motivation crowding in' theory that rely less on self-reported attitudes – which are always subject to multiple interpretations – and more on tangible differences in behaviour predicted by 'crowding in' and 'crowding out' theory respectively. It would also be useful to gather some evidence that distinguishes more carefully between autonomous moral motivation (i.e. 'guilt') and controlled social pressure (i.e. 'shame'). It should not be too difficult to come up with suitable psychology experiments, since controlled social pressure requires that other people can see or know about your actions, whereas autonomous moral motivation applies even if your actions are unknown to the rest of the world: it requires only your own moral conscience. Until such tests are performed and further evidence accumulates, the idea that a small financial penalty can sometimes turn people from irresponsible 'knaves' into responsible 'knights' is probably best regarded as a philosophically interesting curiosity rather than a well-established phenomenon that can be used to guide public policy.[1]

References

Deci, E. and Ryan, R. (2000). The 'What' and 'Why' of Goal Pursuits: Human Needs and the Self-Determination Theory Perspective. *Journal of Personality* 62(1): 120–42.

DellaVigna, S., List, J. and Malmeindier, U. (2012). Testing for Altruism and Social Pressure in Charitable Giving. *Quarterly Journal of Economics* 127(1): 1–56.

Frey, B. and Oberholzer-Gee, F. (1997). The Cost of Price Incentives: An Empirical Analysis of Motivation Crowding Out. *American Economic Review* 87: 746–55.

---

[1] I would like to thank Chris Belshaw for helpful discussion about the philosophy of plastic bags.

Le Grand, J. (2006). *Motivation, Agency and Public Policy: Of Knights and Knaves, Pawns and Queens.* Oxford University Press.

Leonard, K. (2012). Carrier bag charge: supermarkets say use in Wales cut up to 90%. BBC News Wales, 4 April (www.bbc.co.uk/news/uk-wales -17595142).

Williams, B. (2008). *Shame and Necessity.* Berkeley: University of California Press.

4 | *The more who die, the less we care: psychic numbing and genocide*

PAUL SLOVIC AND DANIEL VÄSTFJÄLL

A defining element of catastrophes is the magnitude of their harmful consequences. To help society prevent or mitigate damage from catastrophes, immense effort and technological sophistication are often employed to assess and communicate the size and scope of potential or actual losses.[1] This effort assumes that people can understand the resulting numbers and act on them appropriately.

However, recent behavioural research casts doubt on this fundamental assumption. Many people do *not* understand large numbers. Indeed, large numbers have been found to lack meaning and to be underweighted in decisions unless they convey *affect* (feeling). As a result, there is a paradox that rational models of decision-making fail to represent. On the one hand, we respond strongly to aid a single individual in need. On the other hand, we often fail to prevent mass tragedies – such as genocide – or take appropriate measures to reduce potential losses from natural disasters. This might seem irrational but we think this occurs, in part, because as numbers get larger and larger, we become insensitive; numbers fail to trigger the emotion or feeling necessary to motivate action.

We shall address this problem of insensitivity to mass tragedy by identifying certain circumstances in which it compromises the rationality of our actions and by pointing briefly to strategies that might lessen or overcome this problem.

---

[1] Portions of this chapter appeared earlier in Slovic (2007, 2010) and Slovic and Västfjäll (2010). This material is based upon work supported by the Hewlett Foundation, and by the National Science Foundation under Grant #SES-0649509. Support for this chapter was also provided by the US National Science Foundation under Grants #SES-1024808 and #SES-1227729. Any opinions, findings and conclusions or recommendations expressed in this material are those of the authors and do not necessarily reflect the views of the Hewlett Foundation or the National Science Foundation.

Background and theory: the importance of affect

Risk management in the modern world relies upon two forms of thinking. *Risk as feelings* refers to our instinctive and intuitive reactions to danger. *Risk as analysis* brings logic, reason, quantification and deliberation to bear on hazard management. Compared to analysis, reliance on feelings tends to be a quicker, easier and more efficient way to navigate in a complex, uncertain and dangerous world. Hence, it is essential to rational behaviour. Yet it sometimes misleads us. In such circumstances we need to ensure that reason and analysis also are employed.

Although the visceral emotion of fear certainly plays a role in risk as feelings, we shall focus here on the 'faint whisper of emotion' called *affect*. As used here, *affect* refers to specific feelings of 'goodness' or 'badness' experienced with or without conscious awareness. Positive and negative feelings occur rapidly and automatically; note how quickly you sense the feelings associated with the word *joy* or the word *hate*. A large research literature in psychology documents the importance of affect in (1) conveying meaning upon information and (2) motivating behaviour. Without affect, information lacks meaning and will not be used in judgement and decision-making.

Facing catastrophic loss of life

Risk as feelings is clearly rational, employing imagery and affect in remarkably accurate and efficient ways; but this way of responding to risk has a darker, non-rational side. Affect may misguide us in important ways. Particularly problematic is the difficulty of comprehending the meaning of catastrophic losses of life when relying on feelings. Research reviewed below shows that disaster statistics, no matter how large the numbers, lack emotion or feeling. As a result, they fail to convey the true meaning of such calamities and they fail to motivate proper action to prevent them.

The psychological factors underlying insensitivity to large-scale losses of human lives apply to catastrophic harm resulting from human malevolence, natural disasters and technological accidents. In particular, the psychological account described here can explain, in part, our failure to respond to the diffuse and seemingly distant threat posed by global warming as well as the threat posed by the presence of nuclear weaponry. Similar insensitivity may also underlie our failure to respond adequately to problems of famine, poverty and disease afflicting large numbers of people around the world and even in our own backyard.

The Darfur genocide

Since February 2003, hundreds of thousands of people in the Darfur region of western Sudan, Africa, have been murdered by government-supported militias, and millions have been forced to flee their burned-out villages for the dubious safety of refugee camps. This has been well documented. And yet the world looks away. The events in Darfur are the latest in a long list of mass murders since the Second World War to which powerful nations and their citizens have responded with indifference. In her Pulitzer Prize-winning book *A Problem from Hell: America and the Age of Genocide*, Samantha Power documents in meticulous detail many of the numerous genocides that occurred during the past century. In every instance, American response was inadequate. She concludes: 'No U.S. president has ever made genocide prevention a priority, and no U.S. president has ever suffered politically for his indifference to its occurrence. It is thus no coincidence that genocide rages on' (Power, 2003, p. xxi).

The United Nations General Assembly adopted the Convention on the Prevention and Punishment of the Crime of Genocide in 1948 in the hope that 'never again' would there be such odious crimes against humanity as occurred during the Holocaust of the Second World War. Eventually, some 140 states would ratify the Genocide Convention, yet it has never been invoked to prevent a potential attack or halt an ongoing massacre. Darfur has shone a particularly harsh light on the failures to intervene in genocide. As Richard Just has observed, 'we are awash in information about Darfur ... [N]o genocide has ever been so thoroughly documented while it was taking place ... but the genocide continues. We document what we do not stop. The truth does not set anybody free ... [H]ow could we have known so much and done so little?' (Just, 2008, pp. 36, 38).

Affect, analysis and the value of human lives

This brings us to a crucial question: how *should* we value the saving of human lives? An analytic answer would look to basic principles or fundamental values for guidance. For example, Article 1 of the UN

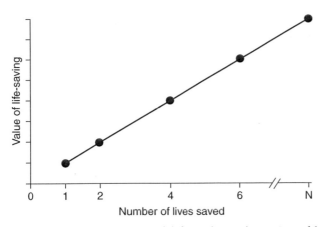

Figure 4.1 A normative model for valuing the saving of human lives: every human life is of equal value
Source: Slovic (2007).

Universal Declaration of Human Rights asserts that '[a]ll human beings are born free and equal in dignity and rights'.[2] We might infer from this the conclusion that every human life is of equal value. If so, then – applying a rational calculation – the value of saving N lives is N times the value of saving one life, as represented by the linear function in Figure 4.1.

An argument can also be made for judging large losses of life to be disproportionately more serious because they threaten the social fabric and viability of a group or community (see Figure 4.2). Debate can be had at the margins over whether one should assign greater value to younger people versus the elderly, or whether governments have a duty to give more weight to the lives of their own people, and so on, but a perspective approximating the equality of human lives is rather uncontroversial.

How *do* we actually value human lives? Research provides evidence in support of two descriptive models linked to affect and intuitive thinking that reflect values for life-saving profoundly different from those depicted in the normative (rational) models shown in Figures 4.1 and 4.2. Both of these descriptive models demonstrate responses that are insensitive to large losses of human life, consistent with apathy towards genocide.

[2] Full text available at: www.un.org/en/documents/udhr/.

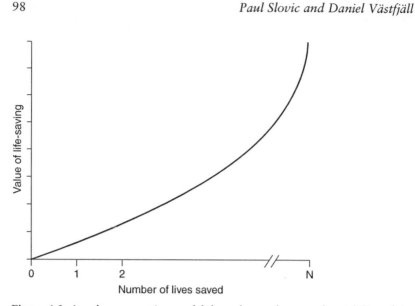

Figure 4.2 Another normative model: large losses threaten the viability of the group or society
Source: Slovic (2007).

The psychophysical model

There is considerable evidence that our affective responses and the resulting value we place on saving human lives follow the same sort of 'psychophysical function' that characterizes our diminished sensitivity to changes in a wide range of perceptual and cognitive entities – brightness, loudness, heaviness and wealth – as their underlying magnitudes increase.

As psychophysical research indicates, constant increases in the magnitude of a stimulus typically evoke smaller and smaller changes in response. Applying this principle to the valuing of human life suggests that a form of *psychophysical numbing* may result from our inability to appreciate losses of life as they become larger. The function in Figure 4.3 represents a value structure in which the importance of saving one life is great when it is the first, or only, life saved but diminishes as the total number of lives at risk increases. Thus, psychologically, the importance of saving one life pales against the background of a larger threat: we may not 'feel' much difference, nor value the difference, between saving 87 lives and saving 88.

Fetherstonhaugh et al. (1997) demonstrated this potential for psychophysical numbing in the context of evaluating people's willingness to fund various life-saving interventions. In a study involving a

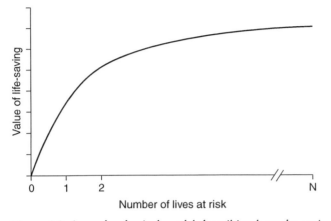

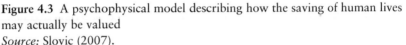

Number of lives at risk

Figure 4.3 A psychophysical model describing how the saving of human lives may actually be valued
Source: Slovic (2007).

hypothetical grant-funding agency, respondents were asked to indicate the number of lives a medical research institute would have to save to merit receipt of a $10 million grant. Nearly two-thirds of the respondents raised their minimum benefit requirements to warrant funding when there was a larger at-risk population, with a median value of 9,000 lives needing to be saved when 15,000 were at risk (implicitly valuing each life saved at $1,111), compared to a median of 100,000 lives needing to be saved out of 290,000 at risk (implicitly valuing each life saved at $100). Thus, respondents saw saving 9,000 lives in the smaller population as more valuable than saving more than ten times as many lives in the larger population. The same study also found that people were less willing to send aid that would save 4,500 lives in Rwandan refugee camps as the size of the camps' at-risk population increased.

In recent years, vivid images of natural disasters in South Asia and the American Gulf Coast, and stories of individual victims there, brought to us through relentless, courageous and intimate news coverage, unleashed an outpouring of compassion and humanitarian aid from all over the world. Perhaps there is hope here that vivid, personalized media coverage featuring victims could also motivate intervention to halt the killing.

Perhaps. Research demonstrates that people are much more willing to aid identified individuals than unidentified or statistical victims.

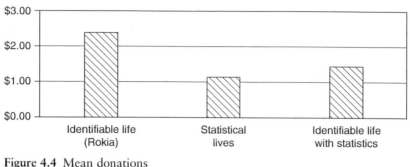

Figure 4.4 Mean donations
Source: Small et al. (2007).

But a cautionary note comes from a study in which Small et al. (2007) gave people who had just participated in a paid psychological experiment the opportunity to contribute up to $5 of their earnings to the charity, Save the Children. In one condition, respondents were asked to donate money to feed an identified victim, a seven-year-old African girl named Rokia, of whom they were shown a picture. They contributed more than twice the amount given by a second group who were asked to donate to the same organization working to save millions of Africans (statistical lives) from hunger. Respondents in a third group were asked to donate to Rokia, but were also shown the larger statistical problem (millions in need) shown to the second group. Unfortunately, coupling the large-scale statistical realities with Rokia's story significantly *reduced* contributions to Rokia (see Figure 4.4).

Why did this occur? Perhaps the presence of statistics reduced the attention to Rokia that was essential for establishing the emotional connection necessary to motivate donations. Alternatively, recognition of the millions who would not be helped by one's small donation may have produced negative feelings that inhibited donations. Note the similarity here at the individual level to the failure to help 4,500 people in the larger refugee camp. The rationality of these responses can be questioned. We should not be deterred from helping one person, or 4,500, just because there are many others we cannot save.

In sum, research on psychophysical numbing is important because it demonstrates that feelings necessary for motivating life-saving actions are not congruent with the normative/rational models in Figures 4.1 and 4.2. The non-linearity displayed in Figure 4.3 is consistent with the devaluing of incremental loss of life against the background of a large tragedy. It can thus explain why we don't feel any different upon learning that the death toll in Darfur is closer to 400,000 than to 200,000. What it does not fully explain, however, is apathy towards genocide, inasmuch as it implies that the response to initial loss of life will be strong and maintained, albeit with diminished sensitivity, as the losses increase. Evidence for a second descriptive model, better suited to explain apathy towards large losses of lives, follows.

The collapse of compassion

American writer Annie Dillard (1999) reads in her newspaper the headline 'Head Spinning Numbers Cause Mind to Go Slack'. She writes of 'compassion fatigue' and asks, 'At what number do other individuals blur for me?'[3]

An answer to Dillard's question is beginning to emerge from behavioural research. Studies by social psychologists find that a single individual, unlike a group, is viewed as a psychologically coherent unit. This leads to more extensive processing of information and stronger impressions about individuals than about groups. Consistent with this, a study in Israel found that people tend to feel more distress and compassion and to provide more aid when considering a single victim than when considering a group of eight victims (Kogut and Ritov, 2005). A follow-up study in Sweden found that people felt less compassion and donated less aid towards a pair of victims than to either individual alone (Västfjäll et al., 2010). Perhaps the blurring that Annie Dillard asked about begins for groups as small as two people.

The insensitivity to life-saving portrayed by the psychophysical-numbing model is unsettling. But the studies just described suggest an even more disturbing psychological tendency. Our capacity to feel is limited. To the extent that valuation of life-saving depends on feelings driven by attention or imagery, it might follow the function shown in Figure 4.5, where the emotion or affective feeling is greatest at $N = 1$ but begins to decline at $N = 2$ and collapses at some higher value of N that becomes simply 'a statistic'. Whereas Robert J. Lifton (1967) coined the term *psychic numbing* to describe the 'turning off' of

---

[3] 'She struggles to think straight about the great losses that the world ignores: "More than two million children die a year from diarrhea and eight hundred thousand from measles. Do we blink? Stalin starved seven million Ukrainians in one year, Pol Pot killed two million Cambodians ..."' (Dillard, 1999, pp. 130–1).

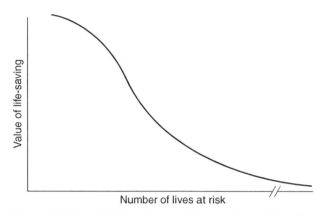

Figure 4.5 A model depicting psychic numbing – the collapse of compassion –
when valuing the saving of lives
Source: Slovic (2007).

feeling that enabled rescue workers to function during the horrific
aftermath of the Hiroshima bombing, Figure 4.5 depicts a form of
psychic numbing that is not beneficial. Rather, it leads to apathy and
inaction, consistent with what is seen repeatedly in response to mass
murder and genocide.

The failure of moral intuition

Thoughtful deliberation takes effort. Fortunately, evolution has
equipped us with sophisticated cognitive and perceptual mechanisms
that can guide us through our daily lives efficiently, with minimal need
for 'deep thinking'.

Consider how we typically deal with risk. Long before we had
invented probability theory, risk assessment and decision analysis,
there were such faculties as intuition, instinct and gut feeling, honed
by experience, to tell us whether an animal was safe to approach or
water was safe to drink. As life became more complex and humans
gained more control over their environment, analytic ways of thinking
evolved to boost the rationality of our experiential reactions. Beyond
the question of how water looks and tastes, we now can look to
toxicology and analytic chemistry to tell us whether it is safe to drink.
But we can still use our feelings as well, an easier path.

As with risk, the natural and easy way to deal with moral issues is
to rely on our intuitions: 'How bad is it?' Well, how bad does it feel?

We can also apply reason and logical analysis to determine right and wrong, as our legal system attempts to do. But, as Jonathan Haidt, a psychologist at the University of Virginia, has demonstrated, moral *intuition* comes first and usually dominates moral *judgement* unless we make an effort to critique and, if necessary, override our intuitive feelings (Haidt, 2001).

Unfortunately, moral intuition fails us in the face of genocide and other disasters that threaten human lives and the environment on a large scale. We cannot trust it. It depends upon attention and feelings that may be hard to arouse and sustain over time for large numbers of victims, not to mention numbers as small as two. Left to its own devices, moral intuition will likely favour individual victims and sensational stories that are close to home and easy to imagine. Our sizeable capacity to care for others may be demotivated by negative feelings resulting from thinking about those we cannot help. Or it may be overridden by pressing personal and local interests. Compassion for others has been characterized by social psychologist Daniel Batson as 'a fragile flower, easily crushed by self-concern' (Batson et al., 1983, p. 718). Faced with genocide and other mass tragedies, we cannot rely on our intuitions alone to guide us to act properly.

What to do?

Behavioural research, supported by common observation and the record of repeated failures to arouse citizens and leaders to halt the scourge of genocide and to prevent thousands from perishing in natural disasters, sends a strong and important message. Our moral intuitions often fail us. They seduce us into calmly turning away from massive losses of human lives, when we should be driven by outrage to act. This is no small weakness in our moral compass.

Educating moral intuitions. A natural response to the growing awareness of our insensitivity to problems of scale is to consider ways to educate moral intuitions. But how can we modify our gut instincts to better understand and respond to problems large in scope? This is not an easy question to answer, but we can speculate about possible ways forward.

One way of infusing intuition with greater feeling is by changing the way we frame information. The affective system primarily deals with the here and now and with concrete images. We speculate that reframing a large-scale problem may be a way of increasing affect, attention and action. For instance, '800,000 killed in the last 100 days' can be broken down and reframed as '1 life lost every 11 seconds'. The latter represents a situation where the singularity effect (the increased response to one individual in the collapsed model described above) is located in time. Both the one life lost and the near-time horizon of 'every 11 seconds' induce accessible images and thus are likely to create more affect and different information processing (Trope and Liberman, 2003).

More generally, if statistics represent 'human beings with the tears dried off', tears and feeling can be increased by highlighting the images that lie beneath the numbers. For example, organizers of a rally designed to get the US Congress to do something about 38,000 deaths a year from handguns piled 38,000 pairs of shoes in a mound in front of the Capitol (Associated Press, 1994). Students at a middle school in Tennessee, struggling to comprehend the magnitude of the Holocaust, collected six million paper clips as a centrepiece for a memorial (Schroeder and Schroeder-Hildebrand, 2004). Flags were 'planted' on the lawn of the University of Oregon campus to represent the thousands of American and Iraqi war dead (see Figure 4.6). In this light it is instructive to reflect on the characterization by Holocaust survivor Abel Hertzberg: 'There were not six million Jews murdered: there was one murder, six million times.'

When it comes to eliciting compassion, psychological experiments demonstrate that the identified individual victim, with a face and a name, has no peer, providing the face is not juxtaposed with the statistics of the larger need (Small et al., 2007). But we know this as well from personal experience and media coverage of heroic efforts to save individual lives. The world watched tensely as rescuers worked for several days to rescue 18-month-old Jessica McClure, who had fallen 22 feet into a narrow abandoned well shaft. Charities such as Save the Children have long recognized that it is better to endow a donor with a single, named child to support than to ask for contributions to the bigger cause.

The face need not even be human to motivate powerful intervention. A dog stranded aboard a tanker adrift in the Pacific was the subject of one of the most costly animal rescue efforts ever (Vendantam, 2010). Hearing this, columnist Nicholas Kristof (2007) recalled cynically that a single hawk, Pale Male, evicted from his nest in Manhattan, aroused

Figure 4.6 Flags depicting American and Iraqi war dead
Source: Slovic and Västfjäll (2010). Reprinted by permission of the publisher (Taylor & Francis, www.tandf.co.uk/journals).

more indignation than two million homeless Sudanese. He observed that what was needed to galvanize the American public and their leaders to respond to the genocide in Darfur was a suffering puppy with big eyes and floppy ears: 'If President Bush and the global public alike are unmoved by the slaughter of hundreds of thousands of fellow humans, maybe our last, best hope is that we can be galvanized by a puppy in distress' (Kristof, 2007).

Further to this last point, Paul Farmer (2005) has written eloquently about the power of images, narratives and first-person testimony to overcome our 'failure of imagination' in contemplating the fate of distant, suffering people. Such documentation can, he asserts, render abstract struggles personal and help make human rights violations 'real' to those unlikely to suffer them. Who hasn't gained a deeper understanding of the Holocaust from reading Elie Wiesel's *Night* or *The Diary of Anne Frank*? Fiction, too, can create empathy and meaning. Barbara Kingsolver conveyed this rather elegantly:

The power of fiction is to create empathy . . . A newspaper could tell you that one hundred people, say, in an airplane, or in Israel, or in Iraq, have died today. And you can think to yourself, 'How very sad', then turn the page and see how the Wildcats fared. But a novel could take just one of those hundred lives and show you exactly how it felt to be that person ... You could taste that person's breakfast, and love her family, and sort through her worries as your own, and know that a death in that household will be the end of the only life that someone will ever have. As important as yours. As important as mine. (Kingsolver, 1995, p. 231)

If the power of the narrative and the personal story can be used to enhance the understanding of large numbers, we should think about how to use this to educate children about numbers. We teach children about the mechanics of operations such as addition, division, etc., but we do not teach them how to 'feel the meaning' behind numbers that represent real-life entities such as people and endangered species. Research in numerical cognition suggests that we have an 'intuitive number sense' (Dehaene, 1997) that allows us to represent and manipulate numerical quantities non-symbolically (Peters et al., 2008). This number sense provides the conceptual basis for mapping numerical symbols onto their meaning (e.g. Dehaene, 2001) and is present even in infants (Libertus and Brannon, 2009). Yet, people fail to assign meaning to large numbers. The number sense initially develops to deal with precise representation of small numbers, while large quantities are only approximate representations (Feigenson et al., 2004). The development of a non-verbal number sense, with the ability to approximate larger magnitudes, appears to depend on the input a child receives (Clements and Sarama, 2007). Thus, children have the tools for understanding large numbers, but are not given sufficient knowledge on how to apply these tools to appropriately deal with real-world numbers. We believe that development of methods designed to help children 'feel the meaning' of numbers might be an important way to combat scope insensitivity and psychic numbing. Maybe the intuitive number sense can be more tightly coupled with our moral senses by educating children about the affective meaning of numbers.

From moral intuition to moral judgement. If strategies to educate intuition and overcome psychic numbing are successful, there will be an upsurge of emotion that needs to be channelled into effective action by national governments. Here is where moral intuitions need to be bolstered by moral judgement to design laws and institutions that commit states to respond to mass tragedies rather than being silent witnesses. And if education of intuition proceeds slowly or not at all, maintaining the current level of psychic numbing, recognition of the deficiencies of moral intuition points even more strongly to the need for institutionalized mechanisms to protect human rights. The Convention on the Prevention and Punishment of the Crime of Genocide (UN General Assembly, 1948) and the United Nations were supposed to do this but they have repeatedly failed. Efforts to address this with new treaties such as 'responsibility to protect' (UN General Assembly, 2005) are urgently needed.

Recognizing that international actors will resist laws that pre-commit them to act to prevent or stop genocide, Slovic et al. (2012) have proposed a 'softer' solution based on the intrinsic reasonableness of moral judgements applied to the value of human life. Specifically, officials should be required to publicly deliberate and reason about actions to take in response to genocide and other mass atrocities. Just as we expect government to proffer reasons to justify intervention, we should expect and require public justification for decisions not to intervene to save human lives. This merging of intuition and deliberation may be achieved through the reporting requirements of a deliberation-forcing regime that would likely ramp up pressure on governments to take action.

The stakes are high. Failure to overcome the numbing to which our moral intuitions are susceptible may force us to witness passively another century of genocide and mass abuses of innocent people, as in the previous century.

References

Associated Press (1994). 38,000 shoes stand for loss in lethal year. *The Register-Guard*, 21 September: 6A.

Batson, C. D., O'Quin, K., Fultz, J., Vanderplas, M. and Isen, A. (1983). Self-Reported Distress and Empathy and Egoistic versus Altruistic Motivation for Helping. *Journal of Personality and Social Psychology* 45: 706–18.

Clements, D. H. and Sarama, J. (2007). Early Childhood Mathematics Learning. In J. F. K. Lester (ed.), *Second Handbook of Research on Mathematics Teaching and Learning*. New York: Information Age, pp. 461–555.

Dehaene, S. (1997). *The Number Sense: How the Mind Creates Mathematics*. New York: Oxford University Press.

(2001). Précis of The Number Sense. *Mind and Language* 16: 16–36.

Dillard, A. (1999). *For the Time Being*. New York: Alfred A. Knopf.

Farmer, P. (2005). *Never Again? Reflections on Human Values and Human Rights*. Tanner Lectures on Human Values, Salt Lake City, Utah (www .tannerlectures.utah.edu/lectures/documents/Farmer_2006.pdf).

Feigenson, L., Dehaene, S. and Spelke, E. (2004). Core Systems of Number. *Trends in Cognitive Sciences* 8: 307–14.

Fetherstonhaugh, D., Slovic, P., Johnson, S. M. and Friedrich, J. (1997). Insensitivity to the Value of Human Life: A Study of Psychophysical Numbing. *Journal of Risk and Uncertainty* 14: 283–300.

Haidt, J. (2001). The Emotional Dog and its Rational Tail: A Social Intuitionist Approach to Moral Judgment. *Psychological Review* 108: 814–34.

Just, R. (2008). The Truth Will Not Set You Free: Everything We Know about Darfur and Everything We're Not Doing about It. *New Republic*, August: 36–47.

Kingsolver, B. (1995). *High Tide in Tucson*. New York: HarperCollins.

Kogut, T. and Ritov, I. (2005). The 'Identified Victim' Effect: An Identified Group, or Just a Single Individual? *Journal of Behavioral Decision Making* 18: 157–67.

Kristof, N. D. (2007). Save the Darfur puppy. *New York Times*, 10 May.

Libertus, M. E. and Brannon, E. M. (2009). Behavioral and Neural Basis for Number Sense in Infancy. *Current Directions in Psychological Science* 18: 346–51.

Lifton, R. J. (1967). *Death in Life: Survivors of Hiroshima*. New York: Random House.

Peters, E., Slovic, P., Västfjäll, D. and Mertz, C. K. (2008). Intuitive Numbers Guide Decisions. *Judgment and Decision Making* 3: 619–35.

Power, S. (2003). *A Problem from Hell: America and the Age of Genocide*. New York: Harper Perennial.

Schroeder, P. and Schroeder-Hildebrand, D. (2004). *Six Million Paper Clips: The Making of a Children's Holocaust Museum*. Minneapolis, MN: Kar-Ben.

Slovic, P. (2007). 'If I look at the mass I will never act': Psychic Numbing and Genocide. *Judgment and Decision Making* 2: 79–95.

(2010). The More Who Die, the Less We Care. In E. Michel-Kerjan and P. Slovic (eds.), *The Irrational Economist: Making Decisions in a Dangerous World*. New York: Public Affairs Press, pp. 30–40.

Slovic, P. and Västfjäll, D. (2010). Affect, Moral Intuition, and Risk. *Psychological Inquiry: An International Journal for the Advancement of Psychological Theory* 21: 387–98.

Slovic, P., Zionts, D., Woods, A. K., Goodman, R. and Jinks, D. (2013). Psychic Numbing and Mass Atrocity. In E. Shafir (ed.), *The Behavioral Foundations of Public Policy*. Princeton University Press, pp. 126–42.

Small, D. A., Loewenstein, G. and Slovic, P. (2007). Sympathy and Callousness: The Impact of Deliberative Thought on Donations to Identifiable and Statistical Victims. *Organizational Behavior and Human Decision Processes* 102: 143–53.

Trope, Y. and Liberman, N. (2003). Temporal Construal. *Psychological Review* 110: 403–21.

UN General Assembly (1948). Convention on the Prevention and Punishment of the Crime of Genocide (www.un.org/millennium/law/iv-1.htm).

(2005). Resolution adopted by the General Assembly: 60/1. 2005 World Summit Outcome (http://unpan1.un.org/intradoc/groups/public/documents/un/unpan021752.pdf).

Västfjäll, D., Peters, E. and Slovic, P. (2010). *Compassion Fatigue: Donations and Affect are Greatest for a Single Child in Need* (manuscript in preparation).

Vedantam, S. (2010). *The Hidden Brain: How Our Unconscious Minds Elect Presidents, Control Markets, Wage Wars, and Save Our Lives.* New York: Spiegel & Grau.

4.1 | A response to Slovic and Västfjäll

JONATHAN WOLFF

There is no denying the importance of the issues raised in Paul Slovic and Daniel Västfjäll's chapter. Anything that helps us understand why it is we human beings are sluggish in our response to huge-scale human tragedy, and can help us to do better in future, is surely to be welcomed. The chapter combines a moral claim – that we have a very strong and significant moral duty to respond to large-scale human tragedies – a psychological explanation of why we do not, and a proposal for bringing moral duty and psychology into closer harmony. My response will fall into two stages; the first, briefly, to discuss the claimed basis of the moral claim, and the second to discuss the psychological questions, which are especially important in practical terms. To improve the world we often need both a diagnosis of its ills and a cure for them. If the diagnosis is incorrect, then it is a matter of chance whether the proposed cure will work.

The moral background to the argument is covered very quickly. The salient suggestion is this:

Article 1 of the UN Universal Declaration of Human Rights asserts that '[a]ll human beings are born free and equal in dignity and rights'. We might infer from this the conclusion that every human life is of equal value. If so, then – applying a rational calculation – the value of saving N lives is N times the value of saving one life, as represented by the linear function in Figure 4.1.

The authors go on to register some potential modifications: they conjecture that mass killings are even more ethically troublesome than provided for by this formula because they can lead to social breakdown. They also consider various weighting factors. But they move on quickly and do not engage with the philosophical literature.

This is understandable in the circumstances, but I just want to register that the issue is much more problematic than it may appear. For example, there has been an extensive discussion of whether, in cases where I could save a larger or greater number, there really is a duty to save the greater number, even when all else is equal (Anscombe, 1967; Munoz-Dardé, 2005; Otsuka, 2004; Taurek, 1977). Less controversially, we might wonder whether the Nazi Holocaust really would have been only half as bad or wrong if the number of Jews who died had been three million rather than six million. But whatever one thinks of that example, it seems very unlikely that anyone would agree that a young person should be denied life-saving surgery so that his organs could be harvested to save four others (Foot, 1967). Yet if the value of saving lives is a linear function of the number of lives saved, why not?

I raise these issues not because they are unanswerable or because they will have any significant consequences for the main argument of the chapter, but simply to bring out the point that the moral background is more complex than apparently assumed here. But really the case that there is a duty to intervene to save many lives if possible does not depend on any particular moral theory, so now I will turn to the main contentions of the chapter.

The authors are especially concerned about numbers and 'affect'. The problem, as they see it, is captured in the following:

On the one hand, we respond strongly to aid a single individual in need. On the other hand, we often fail to prevent mass tragedies – such as genocide – or take appropriate measures to reduce potential losses from natural disasters. This might seem irrational but we think this occurs, in part, because as numbers get larger and larger, we become insensitive; numbers fail to trigger the emotion or feeling necessary to motivate action.

But not all is so negative, there are some hopeful signs too:

In recent years, vivid images of natural disasters in South Asia and the American Gulf Coast, and stories of individual victims there, brought to us through relentless, courageous and intimate news coverage, unleashed an outpouring of compassion and humanitarian aid from all over the world. Perhaps there is hope here that vivid, personalized media coverage featuring victims could also motivate intervention to halt the killing.

It would seem hard to deny that there is a numbing effect of large numbers, and evidence for this is cited to good effect in the chapter. And there may be some encouraging signs that humanitarian aid can be forthcoming even in the face of large-scale tragedy. Yet in the cases under discussion there are several contrasts at issue:

1. Small numbers versus large numbers.
2. Prevention versus cure.

3. Identified lives versus statistical lives.
4. Man-made disasters versus natural disasters.
5. Situations with a 'cut-off point' versus situations without apparent limit.
6. The certainty of being able to bring about an effect, versus causal uncertainty.
7. Actions that cost money versus actions that risk lives.

All of these distinctions could lead to differences in response. The chapter concentrates primarily on the first. It also discusses our failure to take preventative measures for large-scale disasters. But could our failure to take preventative measures be partly explained by a more general lack of interest in prevention? It is very hard to get people to take threats to their own health seriously, while it is very easy to get them to become concerned about their illnesses. Hence there could be another factor here. However, the authors also discuss our response to ongoing situations as well as prevention, and so perhaps we should put this to one side.

The distinction between our response to threats to statistical lives and our response to threats to those identified is well documented, for example in safety and health care resource allocation, societies often use cost–benefit analysis with regard to the saving of statistical lives, but to do so seems inhuman in the case of identified lives. Perhaps, however, it may be that this distinction is very closely related to the phenomenon of large and small numbers. The salient point about small numbers is that the people are, or could be, identified. Large number cases yield not exactly statistical lives, but anonymous lives, which could well have lesser psychological impact.

Is there a difference in our response to man-made and to natural disasters? We tend to think of famines and environmental factors as natural, and wars and so on as human made, although it is easily argued that most natural disasters could have been avoided if different decisions had been made and acted on, as Amartya Sen has argued in the example of famines (Sen, 1981), so perhaps this distinction is not as critical as it may have seemed. In any case, it is unclear whether there is a general distinction about our psychological response to natural and to man-made disasters: the arguments could go both ways. So I will also leave this to one side.

But the next distinction – between situations with a cut-off point and those without – seems vital. Consider again the response to the tsunami.

The event had happened and was over. Many people died, yet for the survivors it was reasonably clear what had to be done, and that it would be possible to do this. Contrast this with the case of Darfur, where there was surely a sense of desperation. What could we do to bring it to an end? This sense of impotence may well impede motivation to act.

The next distinction is closely related to this one. A cut-off point gives us something like certainty, anything else uncertainty. Consider again the effective charity campaigns that send us leaflets suggesting that giving a small amount of money will provide enough for a child's eye operation, or to keep a family alive for a year, or to buy a goat. These are all presented as facts that will happen, implicitly, with certainty, and as is now well known there is a bias in our reasoning in favour of achieving certainty (Kahneman and Tversky, 1979). Suppose a charity identified an individual and suggested that our donation would fund an operation with a 50 per cent chance of success. Would that change the pattern of donation? Again, in the case of the tsunami there is something like certainty, whereas for Darfur it was much less clear what was needed. If we sent money, would it be spent on food, or simply used to arm one side in the civil war? Could food aid hinder other activities, or even deliver a public relations victory to the wrong side? Would military intervention inflame the situation? And if we kept everyone alive this year, what would happen next year? Arguably, the most important obstacle was not the numbing effect of large numbers, but again the sense of impotence in the face of a complex situation that none of us could master either in thought or in action. We didn't know how to make the situation better in any sustainable way.

Finally, it is surprising that the authors spend relatively little time considering forms of intervention. Almost all the examples concern individual donor behaviour. Yet my sending money to Oxfam – however much I sent – would not have prevented genocide in Darfur. The only thing that could help would be substantial and sustained military action. This risks lives. And mine would not be one of the lives at risk. Now I am not arguing that it is never morally correct to risk lives in order to save lives. The issue remains psychological at this point. One reason why we might be inclined to do nothing is not (merely) the numbing effect of large numbers, but the immense sacrifice that we might be asking others to make in order to help. If we put this together with the previous points – we don't know how to bring the situation to an end and we don't know whether our intervention will make things better rather than worse – it is far less surprising that we sit on our hands rather than acting in the face of threatened genocide.

Nevertheless, the authors may still be right that our best approach to improving the situation in the future is to highlight the 'small number' cases in the big numbers. If this has the effect they hope, then it may make us try to overcome the other problems: to figure out how to bring things to an end, and to intervene at the lowest possible risk. As it is, the numbing effect of large numbers may well prevent us even from seeking solutions to the other difficulties.

References

Anscombe, G. E. M. (1967). Who is Wronged? *Oxford Review* 5: 16–17.

Foot, P. (1967). The Problem of Abortion and the Doctrine of Double Effect. *Oxford Review* 5: 5–15.

Kahneman, D. and Tversky, A. (1979). Prospect Theory: An Analysis of Decision under Risk. *Econometrica* 47: 263–92.

Munoz-Dardé, V. (2005). The Distribution of Numbers and the Comprehensiveness of Reasons. *Proceedings of the Aristotelian Society* 105: 191–217.

Otsuka, M. (2004). Skepticism about Saving the Greater Number. *Philosophy and Public Affairs* 32: 413–26.

Sen, A. (1981). *Poverty and Famines*. Oxford University Press.

Taurek, J. (1977). Should the Numbers Count? *Philosophy and Public Affairs* 6: 293–316.

5 | Healthy habits: some thoughts on the role of public policy in healthful eating and exercise under limited rationality

MATTHEW RABIN

'Nothing so needs reforming as other people's habits.'

– Mark Twain

'The diminutive chain of habit is scarcely heavy enough to be felt till it is too strong to be broken.'

– simplification of Samuel Johnson quote used in nineteenth-century temperance literature

'The child is the Father of the Man.'

– William Wordsworth

'The second half of a man's life is made up of nothing but the habits he has acquired during the first half.'

– Fyodor Dostoevsky

'Men's natures are alike; it is their habits that separate them.'

– Confucius

'My problem lies in reconciling my gross habits with my net income.'

– Errol Flynn

Introduction

In this chapter, I explore some possible policy implications concerning habitual activities relating to health – such as eating and exercise – that have (for good reason) become the subject of social and policy debate. I do so from the perspective of economic theory, empirical evidence and with a focus on the implications of some recent research in behavioural economics.

I emphasize several themes. First, I outline a simple economic perspective on habitual behaviour. Although it also accords with common sense, reasonable psychology and empirical evidence, there is some tendency by social scientists and policy-makers to neglect this perspective.

Second, as somebody who doubts the full rationality of many forms of habitual behaviour, I discuss two basic errors that may lead people to engage in too many bad habits and too few good habits. One is widely discussed in psychology, behavioural economics and the popular media: the human propensity to over-pursue immediate gratification. Those forming habits simply care too much about current pleasures compared to what they themselves want in the long run. The other error has received less attention, and is less appreciated by behavioural economists and others, yet is likely to be crucial in the context of habit formation: people tend to underestimate (or at least under-attend to) the habitual nature of many activities. There is good psychology to suggest this is so. Furthermore, there is some evidence, and a very important logic, demonstrating that this under-appreciation of the power of habits may be a tremendously costly error that policy-makers may want to consider.

Third, I emphasize the extreme lack of evidence on the degree to which eating and exercise are habit forming, and on the degree to which people may behave irrationally in the face of this habit formation. Although I am not (anywhere remotely close to) an expert in empirical research in this area, I believe it is fair to say that there is remarkably little evidence on how important the habits formed by children, adolescents and young adults are in determining later behaviour and preferences. It seems obvious, and almost surely true to some extent, that the role of habits is important. But it seems immensely important to know just how important. Even more importantly, do we have reason to believe that mature individuals, and children and their guardians, fail to take fully into account the role of habits in their lives? Here too I think the psychological theory and lay impressions are on target. But whether people systematically err in their acquisition of any particular bad or good habit is rarely carefully established, even by those proposing policies that would seem predicated on the existence of such an error.

Finally, of course, if we believe that it is likely that many people are making these errors, and that these errors are both inherently unlikely to be meliorated by market incentives and are conducive to being addressed by policy, then we might want to study or implement policy interventions. I briefly discuss examples of possible interventions based on the errors posited.

In the next section I discuss the most straightforward economist's conceptualization of what it means for activities to be habit forming, doing so within the utility framework. It is also my view of the most useful way to think about it. But while rational-choice economics assumes people behave 100 per cent rationally in the face of habit formation, in the following section I outline two specific types of errors (self-control problems and misprediction of preferences) that seem likely to lead people to over-indulge in bad habits, and in the subsequent section I discuss more directly just how these errors affect habitual behaviours. I then discuss my thoughts on the policy implications we might draw, and conclude in the final section with a brief review of empirical evidence – which is essentially a call for economists and policy-makers to gather much more evidence.

My policy perspective in this chapter is that we should want to intervene in people's eating, exercising and other behaviours insofar as it helps individuals achieve their own goals. This means I will not discuss either the social benefits of healthful behaviour, nor be judgemental about others' tastes. Although it is presumably better for society at large if people are healthier, I leave that public policy goal as outside the scope of this chapter.[1] My focus is on whether there is self-harm from activities. I am also uninterested in deciding whether some behaviours are good or bad based on my tastes or aesthetics. Mark Twain's quote above that 'Nothing so needs reforming as other people's habits' strikes a chord as a permanently relevant ironic comment on policy debates in the domains we are considering. From the point of view of this chapter, it is important that we find out if people are fatter than they want to be, exercise less than they want, smoke or drink more than they want, etc. – not what 'we' want. Indeed, the two

---

[1] Economists are famously willing to make the point that bad health need not be costly to society. Indeed, it is my understanding that the current best estimate is that society benefits *financially* from tobacco-induced lung cancer. Speaking like an economist: if it kills people relatively cheaply and with relatively good timing – late in people's working lives but early in their social-security and medicare collecting lives (in the US case) – it can be beneficial. Even if one buys into this calculus, I am not sure of the state-of-the-art estimates for obesity, but suspect they are likely to be different.

errors I review are 'Twain-proof': 'we' are the same as 'they' for these errors. It is not my assumption that only readers who avoid the habits discussed will deem them worthy of regulating, but those of us who succumb to them as well.[2]

Preferences and habits

How might we think about habitual behaviour? As an economist who believes in the profound insight of utility theory for disciplined theoretical, empirical and policy work on this topic, I will articulate a natural way for economists (behavioural or not) to think about habitual behaviour. As argued below, positing the usefulness of modelling behaviour in terms of people having well-defined 'utility' for different outcomes which they are more or less trying to optimize is a very separate thing from saying that people *succeed* in that optimization. My perspective is, in fact, that the formal language of 'preferences' is an efficient way to understand errors: without being clear about what people's goals are, it is hard to be clear about when it is right to say that somebody has made an error.[3]

The most basic notion of what it might mean for a good or an activity to be habit forming, as modelled over the years, most famously in Becker and Murphy's (1988) notion of addiction, is that of intertemporal complementarities in the utility from consumption: an activity is habit forming if the *marginal* utility a person gets today from

---

[2] This is in contrast to other types of errors policy-makers and economists might study (such as over-trading in stocks) where we might be confident that 'we' don't make the same errors as the population at large.

[3] In contrast to the utility-based notion of habit explored in this chapter, some psychological, neurobiological and economics approaches view habitual behaviours more as 'unthinking' and not subject to optimization at all. Absent-mindedly reaching for cashews from a bowl on a coffee table, or lighting up a cigarette with friends at a bar without even thinking about it, can certainly in common parlance be considered a habit. An 'addict' in some domain may be somebody who reacts to a cue by not optimizing in any sense. Indeed, research in both psychology (such as Baumeister et al., 1994) and economics (see Bernheim and Rangel, 2004) has emphasized some of the sundry ways that certain addictive or habitual behaviour can be seen as variants of loss of volition. These issues are of course very real and potentially very important. But they concern basically understanding the daily behaviour of those already addicted. They do not address the 'Dostoevskian' point of asking how changes in the current environment may change what becomes habitual in the future, which is a major theme I emphasize below.

consuming the good today is higher when she has consumed more of it in the past. Habits can be either 'good', where the more you do of the activity the happier you are in the future, or 'bad' – the more you do it, the less happy you are in the future. A good habit like exercise exhibits this shift – even if a certain exercise level starts out very unpleasant or even impossible (if you are out of shape, you may not be able to walk to work or climb four flights of stairs), the more you do it the less unpleasant it becomes; it may even become a pleasant thing, or a compulsion.

Most of the focus of policy, of course, is on bad habits. The key insight of the utility approach is that the notion that the marginal utility is higher when a person has consumed more in the past is perfectly consistent with the possibility that past consumption lowers utility *levels*. The essence of harmful habits is that current consumption decreases your future well-being while causing you to desire those products more in the future. O'Donoghue and Rabin (1999b, 2000b) lay out a simplified, binary-choice form of the Becker et al. (1991) model of tobacco addiction, which applies equally to other types of habit forming activities. Without presenting the mathematical model here, I can outline the basic features. We assume that each day a person can either take a 'hit' or not take a hit. Our model incorporates two crucial components of harmful addictive activities. First, they involve *internalities*. The more common case is of *negative internalities*, where current consumption negatively affects future well-being.[4] Negative internalities from consuming an addictive product may include future health, career and personal problems, as well as 'tolerance' – the fact that current consumption of a product lowers the pleasure from future consumption. Habit forming activities can also generate *positive internalities* if current consumption increases the instantaneous utility from future consumption. Second, harmful addictive activities involve *habit formation*: current consumption increases the marginal utility from future consumption. In other words, past consumption is assumed to increase the marginal instantaneous utility from current consumption – e.g. smoking cigarettes at age 16 increases the *marginal* utility from smoking a cigarette at age 17. The combination of negative internalities

---

[4] Herrnstein and Prelec (1992) developed the term 'internalities' in a related context to connote (by analogy with the economics term 'externality') that consumption of a product now may impose benefits and costs on future selves.

and habit formation means that as a person consumes more and more of an addictive product, she gets less and less pleasure from this consumption, yet she may continue to consume the product because refraining becomes more and more painful.

Internalities come in many forms. Negative internalities include health problems due to over-eating or over-smoking. A person consuming cocaine or other drugs often exhibits 'tolerance' in the sense that she derives less pleasure from a given level of consumption the more she has consumed in the past. Positive internalities arise from learning and other 'investment goods', which we consume both for immediate gratification and for long-term benefits. Many cultural activities are presumed to have this property.

Activities can generate internalities without being habit forming: eating cheesecake may generate negative internalities, and going to a museum may generate positive internalities, but neither is necessarily habit forming. This is the big empirical puzzle that I think is so important for eating and exercise: although we are confident that tobacco, alcohol and other substances are very significantly habit forming, just how habit forming eating and exercise patterns are is less clear.

What do these preferences imply about behaviour? The primary assumption that economists have historically made in the context of habit formation is their standard and universally applied assumption: that people are fully rational. Before turning to potential errors people make in the next section, I first review what rationality implies about how people behave in the face of habit formation. A key prediction is that people are very much attuned to the future implications of their current behaviour. This implies that people do not engage in activities that predictably lead to damaging bad habits whose pursuit exceeds the current pleasure of the activity.

Rather than directly address the question of whether people will rationally acquire bad habits, the original theory in Becker and Murphy (1988) famously focuses on a 'steady state' analysis – looking for positive consumption levels such that a person would choose to *remain* addicted. In their empirical work, Becker et al. (1991, 1994) assume exogenous shocks in order to get people to become addicted. Although called a rational-choice model of addiction, this rather nonstandard focus in describing a behaviour whose central premise is inter-temporal tradeoffs and whose initial condition is always the same – non-addiction – might reasonably be considered a profoundly weak test of the rationality assumption. For those who think the big mistake in tobacco or alcohol addiction is to start the addiction (withdrawing from tobacco is deeply unpleasant; withdrawing from alcohol can kill you), the focus solely on 'steady-state' levels is as if one explored a rational-choice model of suicide by asking solely whether it is rational for people to stay dead once they kill themselves. Other recent researchers – see Orphanides and Zervos (1995) and Wang (2007) – followed up Becker et al.'s original research by addressing the more classical dynamic decision of whether to *become* addicted.

The early tests of whether addiction might be rational studied a particular prediction that is consistent with fully rational behaviour, but not consistent with fully myopic behaviour: that people respond to predictable changes in future prices, such as announced future tax increases. Becker et al. (1991, 1994) confirm Becker and Murphy's (1988) prediction of such future price effects. Although considered somewhat surprising that such future price elasticities were identifiable in the data – and despite scepticism that people would really know enough about future prices to react to them even if they wanted – Gruber and Köszegi (2001) and Levy (2009) in fact support the finding of such future price effects.

But as Gruber and Köszegi (2001) also point out, the existence of future price effects suggests a rejection of *complete* myopia in the face of habit formation – demonstrating that people don't engage in habit forming behaviour as if their current smoking, injecting or eating behaviour had no effects whatsoever on their future attitudes towards smoking, injecting or eating. But the fact that people are aware of such effects is predicted not only by complete rationality, it is a prediction of virtually all psychologically plausible theories of people's errors. Virtually any theory proposed by behavioural economists to modify the 100 per cent rationality model has also predicted such effects. And as theoretical and empirical research suggests – outlined in Gruber and Köszegi (2004) – the amount of irrationality consistent with the observable future price effects would lead to wildly different policy and welfare conclusions. This is an absolutely central point: notwithstanding paper titles, and notwithstanding the default assumption of economics, there are no claims I am aware of in any papers that argue that existing evidence supports the policy conclusions of a 100 per cent rational-choice model except if one a priori prefers 100 per cent as a maintained empirical hypothesis, or one prefers it as the appropriate basis for policy when evidence is not sufficient. Becker et al.'s (1991, 1994) estimates (as they themselves note in a footnote) yield future price elasticities that are small enough to be suggestive that the fully rational model is not driving behaviour. Gruber and Köszegi (2004) show that the range of assumptions about self-control problems consistent with theirs and Becker et al.'s evidence on tobacco includes optimal taxes that are much, much higher than what one would conclude under full rationality, and significantly higher than existing taxes. Levy (2009) estimates significant irrationality of both forms discussed below in tobacco consumption, suggesting very different responses than if one were to assume full rationality.

In light of these findings, I now turn to a review of the two types of errors that theoretically may matter a lot in the context of good and bad habits. I first discuss the errors broadly, and then explore their implications more directly for habit formation.

Two potential errors

The classical economics model assumes that inter-temporal preferences are *time-consistent*: a person's relative preference for well-being at an earlier date over a later date is the same no matter when she is asked. But casual observation, introspection and psychological research all overwhelmingly suggest that preferences are often *time-inconsistent*: we tend to pursue immediate gratification in a way that our 'long-run selves' do not appreciate. The most important manifestation of time inconsistency is where greater weight is placed on immediate outcomes. O'Donoghue and Rabin (1999a) label this latter tendency *present bias*.

Relative to time-consistent preferences, a person with present bias always gives extra weight to well-being *now* over any future moment, but discounts all future moments by the same discount factor. These preferences imply that at any moment a person may pursue immediate gratification more than she would have preferred if asked at any previous moment. That is, the person has a self-control problem. For example, when presented a choice between doing seven hours of an unpleasant task on 1 April versus eight hours on 15 April, if asked on 1 February virtually everyone would prefer the seven hours on 1 April. But come 1 April, given the same choice, most of us are apt to put off the work until 15 April. Irrespective of the specific choice, time consistency requires that a person make the same choice on 1 February and 1 April.

To examine inter-temporal choice given time-inconsistent preferences, researchers have converged on a simple modelling strategy: for each point in time, a person is modelled as a separate 'agent' who chooses her current behaviour to maximize her current preferences, predicting how her future selves will behave.[5] In such a framework, an important issue arises: what does a person believe about how her future selves will behave? The answer to this question depends, of course, on beliefs about future selves' preferences. Two extreme assumptions have appeared in the literature to deal with the issue of beliefs about future behaviour. *Sophisticated* people are fully aware of their future self-control problems, and therefore know exactly how their future selves will behave. *Naïve* people are fully *un*aware of their future self-control problems, and therefore believe their future selves will behave exactly as they currently would like them to behave.

Analysis of self-control problems typically involves comparisons of each of these types of people with the same long-run preferences: *time-consistent agents* are fully rational, as economists habitually assume. By systematically comparing these types of people, we are able to add insight into the role of self-control problems in habit formation, and to delineate how predictions depend on both self-control problems *per se* and on assumptions about foresight.

Although less integrated into formal economic models than self-control problems, recent research in economics has begun to focus on a second type of error that has been proposed (under different guises) by psychologists – and is of manifest relevance to habit formation. Do people rationally predict their own future tastes, and changes in those tastes? The wedge between our perceptions of what will make us happy and what does do so, and the wedge between what we think we will do and what we actually will do, are awfully big economic and social topics. Do we realize how happy more income and more work will make us? Do we have any idea what careers make us happy? Do we want kids? Are we going to get addicted if we start experimenting with this drug? Will we enjoy it? Do we fully predict and

---

[5] To see the mathematical models used by economists to study present bias, including in the context of habit formation, see for example Gruber and Köszegi (2001), Laibson (1997), Levy (2009) and O'Donoghue and Rabin (1999a, 1999b, 2000a, 2000b).

optimize with respect to the power of good and bad habits, such as exercise and eating habits?

Loewenstein et al. (2003) argue that much of the existing evidence can be summarized as a very general type of bias in prediction, which they formalize as *projection bias*: people tend to project their current tastes into the future, even in situations where those tastes change in predictable ways. In the context of habit formation, this is likely to have two very important implications: people may simply not attend to the way that current behaviour forms habits, and (more subtly, and less central to my arguments here) people may overreact to temporary fluctuations in feelings when planning future behaviour.

To see how researchers have studied misprediction across domains, think of two general categories of ways that tastes change over time: temporary fluctuations, such as cravings and random moods, and longer-term systematic changes, such as those associated with addiction, health changes and lifestyles and habits. The contention of researchers is that people under-appreciate changes in their preferences, and hence falsely project their current preferences over consumption onto their future preferences.

Several studies, for instance, lend support to the folk wisdom that shopping on an empty stomach leads people to buy too much.[6] This phenomenon can be interpreted as a manifestation of projection bias: people who are hungry act as if their future taste for food will reflect such hunger. Read and van Leeuwen (1998) provide beautiful evidence of both 'present bias' and 'projection bias' in the context of hunger. Office workers were asked to choose between healthy snacks and unhealthy snacks that they would receive in one week, either at a time when they should expect to be hungry (late in the afternoon) or satiated (immediately after lunch).[7] Half of each of these two groups was approached either immediately after lunch, while the other half of each group was approached late in the afternoon.

Table 5.1 indicates choices that subjects made a week in advance, and clearly shows that people were influenced by their current hunger as much or more than their completely predictable future hunger state. Notice that the findings of the influence of current hunger state has

---

[6] See, for example, Nisbett and Kanouse (1969) and Gilbert et al. (2002).

[7] The healthy snacks were apples and bananas, the unhealthy snacks were crisps, borrelnoten, Mars Bars and Snickers.

Table 5.1 *Percentage of subjects choosing an unhealthy snack*

		Future Hunger	
		hungry	satiated
Current hunger	hungry	78%	56%
	satiated	42%	26%

nothing to do *per se* with self-control problems – whether they 'should' or should not want healthy foods (which are the labels the authors used, but of course did not present to their subjects – who were just asked to choose among a list of items). The point is that for the choice about the exact same future situation, subjects were influenced by their current hunger. This is a surprising result given how familiar these office workers presumably are – like the 7 billion other people – with time-of-day fluctuations in hunger.

The researchers did, however, collect evidence suggesting self-control problems and time inconsistency with respect to eating: unbeknownst to the office workers, when the snacks were brought back the next week, they were allowed to change their minds. Of those who chose healthy snacks ahead of time, 44 per cent chose to switch to unhealthy items. Of those who chose unhealthy ones, only 3 per cent wanted to switch to healthy. This, in a nutshell, indicates the time inconsistency. Prospectively, people wanted to eat healthier than they wanted to eat later – at the moment of truth.

A fascinating study by Giordano et al. (2002) (also analysed in Badger et al., 2007) similarly finds an indication of both present bias and projection bias. They studied thirteen long-time adult heroin addicts who had been regularly receiving BUP – a medication that reduces craving for heroin and is used in aiding with heroin withdrawal. Addicts currently deprived of BUP like it more than those not currently deprived. Over an eight-week period, each subject was asked whether she or he would prefer each of twelve different amounts of money (ranging from $0 to $100) to a second dose after receiving an initial dose. (This second dose is still attractive to addicts.) Subjects were told (truthfully) that one of their choices, randomly selected, would be implemented. Hence, they had the incentive to choose according to their true preferences.

Half the time, subjects were asked when 'deprived' – two hours before receiving their scheduled dose for the day. In the 'satiated'

Table 5.2 *Addicts' willingness to pay for an additional heroin dose*

		When they would get the dose	
		Today	5 days from now
Current craving	Deprived	$75	$60
	Satiated	$50	$35

condition, they were asked right after receiving their dose. Half the time, subjects were asked for their willingness to pay for the additional dose today (but, again, in both cases after the initial dose, whether or not they had got that initial dose yet), and the other half were asked for getting it five days hence. In all conditions, the 'state' of craving for the dose they'd receive was identical, but the timing and the craving at the time of decision differed. They found an average willingness to pay, as a function of both their state when asked and the imminence of delivery of the dose, as shown in Table 5.2. These results also indicate a deep neglect by very experienced addicts of even very predictable changes in future craving levels.

Along with this projection bias, these results also indicate present bias: the fact that, irrespective of the craving state at the time asked, the addicts were willing to pay $15 more for a second dose on the same day than for a week later clearly indicates a taste for immediate gratification.

Unfortunately, it is harder to find convincing evidence of longer-term habit formation, and especially to find convincing evidence of *misprediction* of such longer-term changes. I discuss the limited evidence in the context of habit formation below.

Finally, before moving on to studying the implications of these errors, I emphasize something related to the dictum 'De gustibus non est disputandum': both of the errors discussed above are errors in implementing the preferences people have, and are not 'wrong preferences'. These models take as given preferences that people have, and predict behaviour and errors given those.

Implications of these errors for habit formation

Even fully rational people can form 'bad habits', and unless we want to moralistically embrace Mark Twain's observation, but miss the irony, our interest as a society ought to be focused in large part on under-standing *mistaken* bad habits. Yet there are several reasons to believe that many bad habits – and missing good habits – are due to the two errors discussed above, as well as other errors. First, at a casual empirical level, people have many bad habits that they vociferously say they don't want to have. This does not prove anything – people don't always say in words what they truly want, and they may not actually know.[8] But it would be policy folly and scientific silliness to ignore predictable expressions of people wishing things were different for them. The fact that parents and other loved ones wish people had better habits also means something.[9] And more direct measures of well-being, from quantitative evidence like Gruber and Mullainathan's (2005) arguments that people who are heavily taxed on tobacco are on average happier, to your own observations about the seeming happi-ness of people you know, indicate people may not have the levels of habits that make them happiest. Finally, the fact that even the most dedicatedly rational-choice research by economists studying habits falls so incredibly short of convincing that pure rationality rules the day, should be a strong signal that people are prone to decision-making errors.

What might the two types of errors discussed above say about habit formation? First, the direct implication of having a self-control prob-lem is a tendency to over-consume goods and activities with negative internalities, due to underweighting future health costs relative to current pleasures. People may eat too much, walk too little, etc. This simple and direct fact matters a lot, and is presumably what many people have in mind when they consider over-consumption to be a problem of societal and policy concern. This over-consumption inspires some of the policies I discuss below.

But it is not about the *habitual* nature of eating and exercise *per se*. This tendency to over-consume would be true even if these activities were not habit forming. Importantly, the case that *habit formation*

---

[8] And the fact that people say honestly that they wish they were thinner, or were in better physical shape, isn't *per se* the question we are interested in. Presumably, everybody wishes they were healthier. We need to know whether people wish they paid the cost to achieve these goals, not just that they wish the goals were achieved without cost.

[9] But it is likewise not proof; there are certainly wishes parents have for children that are themselves mistakes, or self-serving.

itself exacerbates the effects of self-control problems on over-consumption is not at all straightforward. If people are fully aware that some activity is habit forming, then short of complete (and unrealistic) unconcern about their future, it will change their behaviour. Even a person tempted by cake or by driving rather than walking who knows that current behaviour will influence her future behaviour and outcomes will take those effects into account. The observation that the misbehaviour of over-eating while young, say, is more costly if it leads to a taste for excessive eating while older, is correct as far as it goes. But that does not imply that the case for societal attention to correcting these self-control problems is any greater by dint of its habit formation. If young people (or their guardians) realize that the stakes are larger, they themselves will reduce the levels of an activity.

Consider a teenager who rightly or wrongly believes that a drug is harmful to her health and future, but *not* addictive. She then perceives the cost of using the drug as the direct costs, which she may count less than she should because of self-control problems. But if she believes that a drug is addictive, she'll now also recognize the cost of using the drug – that it will lead her to crave the drug in the future. This may in fact deter her without outside intervention. She will be *less* likely to engage in addictive activities than equally pleasurable non-addictive activities.

There is a similar – more subtle, but in fact more dramatic – reversal of common intuition regarding the effects of naivety about self-control. With any activity that is not habit forming, but involves trading off current pleasures against future health and other costs, then – in the absence of commitment devices – naivety has roughly no effect. Essentially, if eating dessert today has roughly no effect on either your taste for dessert in the future or on how bad future dessert will be for your health, then whether you are aware of your propensity to eat dessert tomorrow will not influence your tendency to eat dessert tonight. But if behaviour is habit forming, your theory of how you will respond in the future to habits you acquire today will influence your perceived cost of indulging today.

What effect will it have? Here, the common intuition that naivety about self-control is especially damning is not necessarily right. In fact, in the most basic settings, it is backwards. One might think that if you naively think you will avoid developing a bad habit in the future, then you will be insufficiently scared about acquiring the habit. But it is more painful to break yourself of a habit than to never acquire one; this is more or less what we mean by bad habits. If you naively believe that you will have the willpower to quit even if you develop a habit, then you perceive the cost of acquiring the habit as *more* costly than if you think you will continue to indulge anyhow. Likewise for good habits: letting yourself get out of shape is *more* tempting if you sophisticatedly realize you will just get out of shape in the future anyhow than if you naively think you'll make the difficult reinvestment in getting back in shape.

In many simple situations, then, naivety about future self-control may help you rather than hurt you to avoid bad habits. In other situations, sophistication may help you. If you have more complicated tastes – especially if you realize that your tastes will change with age and you will stop being tempted – then sophistication may help you avoid naively indulging in youth when it is attractive but then building an irreversible bad habit. And, related to this point, it turns out that sophistication may help tremendously in reforming a habit that you (for some reason) acquire. Intuitively, naivety can lead you to persistently, over-optimistically predict that you will 'quit tomorrow' – making you less motivated to quit today. The decision when to start withdrawing from a habit that you plan to withdraw from is psychologically and mathematically very similar to the type of 'procrastination' discussed in Akerlof (1991) and analysed in detail in O'Donoghue and Rabin (1999a). In situations where you must do something once involving an up-front cost with long-term benefits – precisely the case of changing a bad habit – naivety about your self-control problem almost always hurts you by making you repeatedly procrastinate under the false hypothesis that you will successfully complete the task tomorrow.

In sum, neither self-control problems *per se* nor naivety about future self-control problems necessarily lead to special mistakes in light of habit formation. People over-indulge in unhealthful behaviours because of self-control problems. But it is primarily the unhealthfulness *per se* – not the habit component – that causes the problem. Self-control problems predict that people over-consume unhealthy goods and activities, but by themselves there is no simple prediction that over-consumption is worse for habit forming goods than for non-habit forming goods.

The implications of projection bias, however, are less ambiguous: it does not lead to over-indulgence in non-habit forming vices, but *does* lead people to engage in too many bad habits. Although less sharply focused on by both researchers and policy-makers, I believe it is likely to be the larger error – although certainly there are cases where both in combination may do much more damage than either mistake alone would. Simply put: some evidence, and lots of intuition, suggests that people under-predict – or, if they intellectually predict, are too inattentive to it – the effects of habits. If you don't imagine at the time of choice how much your tastes will change if you change your lifestyle – if you don't believe that you'll ever come to enjoy veggies, or be satisfied with less to eat, or that exercise at the gym or walking up that flight of stairs will become easier over time – then you will under-invest in good habits and acquire many unplanned bad habits.

An interesting ancillary problem caused by projection bias for bad habits seems of clearest relevance to dieting: insofar as people under-appreciate variation in hunger levels – as hinted by the Read and van Leeuwen study cited earlier – then you may overeat *and* 'over diet' in an ineffective cycle of dieting and binge eating. When you just (over)ate for the day, and are very full, you may naively imagine that it is easy to refrain from eating. If you can't eat another bite right now, you may feel as if you can never eat another bite. You start the diet. And then you get hungry. Not only does the hunger lead you to eat (as it should), but you feel at such moments that it is unimaginable to go long without eating much – you may give up altogether on the diet. And so you eat until you can't eat another bite ...

Policy implications of these errors

I reiterate two points from earlier. First, unless we believe that it is likely that people are making mistakes, the fact that some activities are habit forming does not (in any way that I can understand) heighten the case for policy intervention, regulation or paternalism.

Second, if we decide we'd like to deter some activity, we should never forget the power of prices. The most practical policy we may employ if we reach the conclusion that people are doing too much of bad habits or too little of good habits is to tax the bad habits, and subsidize the good habits. If we want to get people to do less unhealthy eating, we should make it more costly; if we want people to do more exercise, we ought to make it cheaper. Of all those quoted above, Errol Flynn is classically considered the least wise, and his observation that

'My problem lies in reconciling my gross habits with my net income' does not satisfy our sense of depth in understanding habits. But he wisely noted that not having enough money to indulge his habits was a problem and surely recognized it is more of a problem for expensive habits than cheap ones. Flynn may have recognized something deep that the others did not: making something more costly is a pretty robust way to get people to do less of it.

Quite how to go about making bad habits more costly is of course harder, and certainly old-fashioned taxation and subsidies aren't the only instruments we ought to think about. But I worry that many concerned people might outsmart themselves while looking for more sophisticated determinants of behaviour and ignore the tried and true method of literally or metaphorically using prices to influence behaviour. Taxes and subsidies work to influence behaviour in virtually any domain and irrespective of whether and how people are irrational.

What does the nature of habit formation, and the potential errors exacerbated by habit formation, suggest about when and how to impose the prices? There is a simple logic of how to intervene that many of us have advocated that would work in principle for bad habits, but is much harder to see how to implement with either eating or exercise (or alcohol) than with more sharply addictive activities like smoking. We are likely to get more bang for the buck by targeting people when they are younger than when they are older. If we want to stop bad habits with as little effort and as little invasiveness as possible, we should stop them before they start. Indeed – and very importantly – for the various paternalistic and non-paternalistic goals, it is eminently plausible that, although we should want to stop bad habits and addictions before they start, we should not necessarily try to shut them down after they start. For good habits, the principle is that we should probably, when feasible, try to incentivize their creation but not necessarily subsidize their continuation.

The structure of habits and how to affect them with taxation and other regulations is an especially important issue for another important goal of public policy: progressive taxation and redistribution. If our ancillary goal is to change behaviour without too much undesirable redistributional effects, some argue (often sincerely, sometimes not so sincerely) that they do not want to tax vices because (as is empirically so) many of these vices are more prevalent among lower-income people. If we tax fatty food or tobacco, we are, in many more developed countries, disproportionately taxing the poor. As Gruber and Köszegi (2004) argue in the context of tobacco, however, there is an incompleteness to the intuition people have that the monetary tax incidence may be regressive, because poorer people are more likely to smoke or eat fatty food than wealthy people. The financial cost, in fact, may get things backwards. Simply put: a smoker pays a huge amount in taxes over the course of his or her lifetime. Raising taxes may get young people never to take up tobacco, and save them decades of extra taxes. The net tax burden from raising taxes on bad habits may be negative, and therefore be a means of redistributing money *towards* the groups engaging most in those bad habits.

Of course, there is a clear cost to taxing people, especially if many people are consuming goods at the right level. If we impose a heavy tax on crisps, then the many people who enjoy crisps will have to pay more. Economists have good reasons to argue that when people are 100 per cent rational, we should (depending on certain details of the structure of demand functions) tax different commodities at the same rate. If we would like to raise revenues corresponding to an average VAT rate of 10 per cent, we would often want to do so by having a uniform VAT. If people were 100 per cent rational, we would not, for instance, want to have a tax of 9 per cent on most items and 200 per cent on unhealthy food if that raised the same amount of taxes.

Here there is an issue with the way economists are and are not contributing to a mature and empirically grounded debate about the benefits and costs of 'sin taxes'. There are two interrelated doubts I have about economists' contribution to this debate, or at least something to watch out for as the debate over such taxes sharpens. First, related to both Gruber and Köszegi (2004) and O'Donoghue and Rabin (2006), adding even a bit of realistic self-control problems that are manifestly at least as consistent with observed demand as the 100 per cent rational model dramatically changes what economic theory says is the optimal tax. That is, economists have only to be a little bit wrong in our extreme rationality assumptions in order for our prescriptions for taxes to be pretty significantly wrong, and for the possibility that significant taxes on some unhealthy items are warranted. But this is closely related to a second problem with frequent framing by economists: even *assuming* that people are 100 per cent rational, all researchers ought to be forced to *quantify* the harm done by 'distortionary' taxes. That is, suppose that 100 per cent of those who ate junk food were 100 per cent rational in doing so. If we doubled the price of such food via taxes and lowered taxes on other items to keep revenue the same, how bad would that be, using the same types of measures (like 'consumer surplus') that economists already use? My sense is that the answer is often 'not bad at all'. Insisting that economists correctly identify what their own theories say is the *size* of the harm done from proposed policies, I believe, will change the nature of the debate, for both the societal and scientific good. Economists as a group have perhaps come up short of their usual scientific standards in their initial reactions to some of these debates. I think that is largely for the forgivable and inevitable reason that the potential benefits of many of the proposals are not something that economists have the familiarity and formal means to engage with. Hence, they simply report what their theory says is the best policy, rather than the costs of what they consider pointless departures from that best policy. Some of it may be for the (maybe marginally less forgivable, nor inevitable) reason that economists are so worried about supporting such policies for reasons that are unrelated to existing economic theories or evidence that they don't want to come clean about what those existing theories and evidence actually indicate. The two questions – the optimality of even fairly significant-seeming taxes for relatively small degrees of irrationality, and the fact that even maintaining 100 per cent rationality does not imply a huge cost – are related: theory tells us that the welfare costs of 'sin taxes' are small ('second order') to fully rational people and the welfare benefits are large ('first order') to those making the types of mistakes posited.

This, in turn, helps indicate a specific policy that will make sense in light of the errors discussed above, and to highlight a major theme in 'behavioural public policy' research. Under various names – cautious paternalism, conservative paternalism, benign paternalism, or libertarian paternalism and 'nudging' – research has proposed ideas of how to implement policies that do the least amount of harm to those who might be behaving fully rationally and those behaving badly. To illustrate, let us abstract away from the very real implementation problems (black markets, arbitrage, the costs of ID checks, etc.), and consider the following thought experiment that could be turned into a real policy experiment – or a real policy. Without taxing crisps or soda or cigarettes any more in total than we already do, consider merely changing the life cycle of the tax. Instead of (say) 10 per cent tax on unhealthy items for a person's entire life, consider heavy taxes for young people for these items, and no taxes when older, in a way calculated to leave the total tax burden the same overall if people do not change their behaviour. What would happen, according to different theories of motivation? If young people are acting according to fully rational models, fully realizing the habits they are forming and the costs they are incurring, then they will be made no worse off. Indeed, there is a behavioural prediction of the rational model: they will either keep consuming a lot in their youth and in their adulthood just like they did before, or they will stop in their youth and then start in their adulthood. But either way, economic theory based on full rationality says they will be just as well off as before. How might people who have self-control problems or projection bias behave? The prediction is that they are very likely to decrease consumption dramatically both in their youth *and* thereafter. This is because the prediction of these alternative models is that those who were forming these habits when young (at least the ones who were close to indifferent before) were not planning to do so. If people don't realize they will develop a lifelong habit as strong as they will, then they never thought they were going to pay taxes later in life just because of early consumption. We've now changed taxes so that they will pay the same *actual* total price of the habitual behaviour that they were in fact going to pay under the old taxes, but perhaps not the taxes they intended. If their old behaviour was based on not realizing they were starting a habit, this would tax them out of consumption. If their old behaviour was based on correct realization of their habit they were forming, it won't stop them consuming – and won't hurt them. More feasible and fine-tuned cousins of this hypothetical policy would improve the well-being of those over-consuming bad habits because of misprediction and would not hurt significantly (or at all) those doing so rationally.

This proposed policy, if feasible, would also of course provide empirical evidence on the role and rationality of habit formation in behaviour. But my focus on the case of young people leads to a second way I'd like to see economists more forcefully enter the policy debate on the role of habit formation in unhealthful behaviour. Here I want to remove my behavioural-economist, theoretical and welfare-analytic hats, to urge far greater focus on a simple, yet important, basic fact: a huge amount of our behaviour and welfare in the second half of our life is – in a coherent and important sense – determined by our choices in the first half of our life. Whether seen through William Wordsworth's famous line 'The child is the Father of the Man', or Dostoevsky's plain empirical statement 'The second half of a man's life is made up of nothing but the habits he has acquired during the first half', this is a simple empirical hypothesis that is of clear moral and policy relevance.

Is it true? I end this chapter not with exploring more policy implications, but with where I think some of the longer-term policy implications ought to begin: further empirical evidence. Just how important *is* the role of habit in eating, exercise and other healthful activities? Is it true that (say) changing children's eating habits will last them their whole life? How big is the effect? Again emphasizing my lack of familiarity with much of the empirical literature, I am still confident that very little convincing economic research exists trying to carefully observe the role of habit and prediction of habit in exercise, and almost none on long-run eating habits.

Empirical evidence on habit formation

There is one obvious approach we do *not* want to take to establish the role of habit in eating and exercise: compare the later behaviour of those who eat healthily early in life to those who do not eat healthily early in life. These will almost surely be positively correlated, and one often hears statistics of this sort presented as if it is laden with meaning. It is true that kids who eat more crisps tend to turn into the adults that eat more crisps. But we can be positive that much of this is not causal: children who like crisps better turn into adults who like crisps better, and so their intrinsic taste alone guarantees their consumption. What we want to know, to understand the benefits of policy trying to influence early-life healthfulness, is whether an 'exogenous' shift in eating crisps of the sort induced by a change in policy will change late-life crisp eating. Many of us are inclined to believe in both the likelihood that healthful behaviour is habitual, and that much unhealthful behaviour is mistaken and hence likely to benefit from policy oriented towards correcting it. However, unconvincing claims that correlation between behaviours early in life and late in life implies a causal role of habits undermines the scientific case for whether and how to pursue corrective policies. Nor is the heuristic that 'surely' some of the correlation is causal very convincing. In fact, we care a lot how much of it is. It is even possible that there is a positive correlation but a negative causal role. Children with a sweet tooth may grow into adults with a sweet tooth, even if eating sweets when young makes them less keen on sweets when old.

It is a tremendously hard empirical problem to tell whether early-life behaviour really turns into causal habits. In the domain of eating, it is especially difficult. One would want to know whether (say) two schools or similar school districts that had different school food policy *unrelated to the school populations* generated different habits later in life. This is a typical, and typically hard, empirical-economic problem. Another common technique is to try to look at natural experiments of some policy change that we know or suspect has an immediate affect on behaviour between two different close groups, and see the long-run effect. If some place banned soda machines from schools, for instance, then investigating whether years later there is a noticeable jump in habits of people at a certain age to those one year younger could indicate a habit forming change in behaviour at a formative age.

Another approach is to attempt to use the effect of past price changes on current behaviour, along the lines of the tobacco literature. Earlier economic identification of habits often *assumed* rational expectations. That means essentially looking for future price effects: something is habit forming (for a completely rational and informed consumer) in proportion to how much the person will react to perceived future prices in changing current behaviour. But the approach of looking at long-run effects of past prices does not assume rational expectations.[10] This is, empirically, a very hard thing to do. It is very difficult to separate out the effects of a lifetime of different prices, and it is very hard to find people who faced different prices for entirely 'exogenous' reasons.

The existing literature on the addictive nature of smoking attempts to make progress in that domain. While acknowledging the challenges to confident identification, Gruber (2001) probably gives the best guess. Using price variation across states and information on where people grew up, he estimates that something like 25–50 per cent of exogenous increases in youth smoking translates into adult smoking.

[10] See Pollak (1970).

That is, of every 100 young people priced out of smoking due to the range of tax changes he observes in the data, 25 (conservative estimate) or more likely 50 of them will never become smokers. Although I find Gruber's (2001) estimates more convincing, see Glied (2002, 2003), who argues that most of the effects of price-based tobacco reduction among the youth disappears by age 40. Although it relies on many more assumptions about the utility function and empirical estimation, Levy's (2009) estimates can be used to surmise that if we could stop people smoking at all before the age of 30, then two-thirds of them would never begin. Levy (2009) also provides evidence of the mistakes involved in smoking among the youth: inferring from the price responsiveness and other identification techniques, he suggests that beginning smokers suffer from projection bias, and are not predicting their future addiction much at all.

Cigarettes are, of course, both more habit forming and far easier to study concretely than 'eating habits'. It will be much harder to really learn about the long-run nature of eating or exercise habits. But to get a grip on shorter-run effects, some exciting new research by experimental economists has shed some light. Charness and Gneezy (2009) conducted a simple experiment at a gym that indicates that exercise is habit forming. During a treatment period, they randomly paid some non-gymgoers money to go to the gym, while others in their experiment were treated similarly but not incentivized to go to the gym. Unsurprisingly (prices again!), those who were paid to go the gym were more likely to go during the incentives period. Yet, surprisingly or not, this group was also more likely to go even after the incentives were removed. Although this effect wore off over time, there seemed to be a clear habituation to exercise. Acland and Levy (2010) replicated these results in a very similar design, also showing habituation that diminished over time. But they also had subjects in their study make incentivized predictions about their own future behaviour at various times and incentivized conditions, and were able to show that people were both naive about their self-control problem, and (importantly) that they under-appreciated the good habit formation associated with exercise. That is, before they were given incentives to go to they gym, they did not realize that this would make them more eager to go to the gym later. Although the timescales in these studies are necessarily not as long as we'd like, they provide evidence for habit formation and a guide to further research.

References

Acland, D. and Levy, M. R. (2010). Habit Formation, Naiveté, and Projection Bias in Gym Attendance. Mimeo.

Akerlof, G. (1991). Procrastination and Obedience. *American Economic Review* 81(2): 1–19.

Badger, G. J., Bickel, W. K., Giordano, L. A., Jacobs, E. A., Loewenstein, G. and Marsch, L. (2007). Altered States: The Impact of Craving on the Valuation of Current and Future Opioids. *Journal of Health Economics* 26(5): 865–76.

Baumeister, R. F., Heatherton, T. F. and Tice, D. M. (1994). *Losing Control: How and Why People Fail at Self-Regulation*. San Diego, CA: Academic Press.

Becker, G. S. and Murphy, K. M. (1988). A Theory of Rational Addiction. *Journal of Political Economy* 96(4): 675–700.

Becker, G. S., Grossman, M. and Murphy, K. M. (1991). Rational Addiction and the Effect of Price on Consumption. *American Economic Review* 81(2): 237–41.

(1994). An Empirical Analysis of Cigarette Addiction. *American Economic Review* 84(3): 396–418.

Bernheim, B. D. and Rangel, A. (2004). Addiction and Cue-Triggered Decision Processes. *American Economic Review* 94(5): 1558–90.

Charness, G. and Gneezy, U. (2009). Incentives to Exercise. *Econometrica* 77(3): 909–31.

Gilbert, D. T., Gill, M. J. and Wilson, T. D. (2002). The Future is Now: Temporal Correction in Affective Forecasting. *Organizational Behavior and Human Decision Processes* 88(1): 430–44.

Giordano, L., Bickel, W. K., Lowenstein, G., Jacobs, E. A., Marsch, L. and Badger, G. J. (2002). Mild Opioid Deprivation Increases the Degree that Opioid-Dependent Outpatients Discount Delayed Heroin and Money. *Psychopharmacology* 163: 174–82.

Glied, S. (2002). Youth Tobacco Control: Reconciling Theory and Empirical Evidence. *Journal of Health Economics* 21(1): 117–35.

(2003). Is Smoking Delayed Smoking Averted? *American Journal of Public Health* 93(3): 412–16.

Gruber, J. (2001). Youth Smoking in the 1990s: Why Did it Rise and What are the Long-Run Implications? *American Economic Review* 91(2): 85–90.

Gruber, J. and Köszegi, B. (2001). Is Addiction 'Rational'? Theory and Evidence. *Quarterly Journal of Economics* 116(4): 1261–303.

(2004). Tax Incidence When Individuals are Time-Consistent: The Case of Cigarette Excise Taxes. *Journal of Public Economics* 88(9–10): 1959–87.

Gruber, J. and Mullainathan, S. (2005). Do Cigarette Taxes Make Smokers Happier? *Advances in Economic Analysis and Policy* 5(1): article 4.

Herrnstein, R. J. and Prelec, D. (1992). A Theory of Addiction. In G. Loewenstein and J. Elster (eds.), *Choice Over Time*. New York: Russell Sage Foundation, pp. 331–60.

Laibson, D. (1997). Golden Eggs and Hyperbolic Discounting. *Quarterly Journal of Economics* 112(2): 443–77.

Levy, M. R. (2009). An Empirical Analysis of Biases in Cigarette Addiction. Mimeo.

Loewenstein, G., O'Donoghue, T. and Rabin, M. (2003). Projection Bias in Predicting Future Utility. *Quarterly Journal of Economics* 118(4): 1209–48.

Nisbett, R. E. and Kanouse, D. E. (1969). Obesity, Food Deprivation and Supermarket Shopping Behavior. *Journal of Personality and Social Psychology* 12(4): 281–94.

O'Donoghue, T. and Rabin, M. (1999a). Doing It Now or Later. *American Economic Review* 89(1): 103–24.

   (1999b). Addiction and Self Control. In J. Elster (ed.), *Addiction: Entries and Exits*. New York: Russell Sage Foundation.

   (2000a). The Economics of Immediate Gratification. *Journal of Behavioral Decision Making* 13(2): 233–50.

   (2000b). Addiction and Present-Biased Preferences. Mimeo.

   (2006). Optimal Sin Taxes. *Journal of Public Economics* 90(10–11): 1825–49.

Orphanides, A. and Zervos, D. (1995). Rational Addiction with Learning and Regret. *Journal of Political Economy* 103: 739–58.

Pollak, R. A. (1970). Habit Formation and Dynamic Demand Functions. *Journal of Political Economy* 78(4): 745–63.

Read, D. and van Leeuwen, B. (1998). Predicting Hunger: The Effects of Appetite and Delay on Choice. *Organizational Behavior and Human Decision Processes* 76(2): 189–205.

Wang, R. (2007). The Optimal Consumption and the Quitting of Harmful Addictive Goods. *The B.E. Journal of Economic Analysis and Policy* 7(1): article 15.

Wordsworth, William. (1807). "*My Heart Leaps Up When I Behold*," in *Poems, in Two Volumes*. London: Longman, Hurst, Rees, and Orme.

5.1 | *A response to Rabin*

ALEX VOORHOEVE

In his contribution to this book, Matthew Rabin offers an insightful analysis of three biases:

1. *projection bias*: the tendency to judge one's future wants by one's current desires;
2. *present bias*: the tendency to do what yields an attractive outcome in the moment in a way that is contrary to one's long-term interests; and
3. *naivety about present bias*: the failure to recognize one's susceptibility to present bias.

Rabin argues that these biases are irrational and details the self-harm they cause in the presence of habit forming choices. (This harm is understood in a liberal manner as a lesser degree of satisfaction of an individual's informed, long-term preferences.) He also argues that, to prevent this harm, governments should tax behaviour that leads to unhealthy habits.

Rabin's proposal invites the charge of paternalism. This charge is unwelcome to governments. To avoid it, they commonly appeal not to self-harm, but to the costs to *others* of unhealthy behaviour (e.g. in terms of higher state-funded health care provision) to justify intervention in choices regarding smoking, exercise and the consumption of fatty and sugary foods (De Marneffe, 2006).

I believe it is indeed important to avoid paternalistic interference when such interference limits informed, rational individuals' autonomy. However, with regards to unhealthy behaviour, the strategy of avoiding paternalism by appealing to harms to others has two weaknesses. First, it is unclear whether commonly targeted forms of unhealthy behaviour really do impose the net costs on others to which politicians appeal when justifying interventionist policies. For example,

I am grateful to Luc Bovens, Søren Flinch Midtgaard, Judy Jaffe, Joe Mazor, Harald Schmidt and audiences at the LSE and the Vejle Conference on Political Philosophy for helpful comments.

the British Prime Minister David Cameron has argued that 'obesity already costs our NHS a staggering £4 billion a year [and] within four years, that figure is expected to rise to £6.3 billion', and invoked these costs as part of the justification of the imposition of so-called 'fat taxes'.[1] But a careful recent study concludes that while obesity reduces the life expectancy of 20-year-olds by five years and increases health spending related to this behaviour, *total* lifetime health spending was greater for healthy-living people than for the obese (Van Baal et al., 2008, p. 249, emphasis added).

Second, the focus on third-party effects ignores the ways that interventions to prevent self-harm can be justified consistently with respect for autonomy. One way is to seek the consent of those who are interfered with. After all, an intervention to which an individual consents does not represent paternalistic interference (Feinberg, 1986, chapter 17). If Rabin is right about people's tendencies to choose outcomes that are contrary to their own considered preferences and about the ability of taxes to counteract these tendencies, then an enlightened majority might well consent to such taxes (the dissenting minority would then not be taxed *paternalistically*, but rather *for the sake of others*, who wish the taxes on themselves).

But even when such consent cannot be secured, one may appeal to so-called *soft paternalism*, which holds that the state has reason to constrain self-harming conduct without the consent of the people it constrains '*when but only when* that conduct is substantially non-voluntary' (Feinberg, 1986, p. 12, emphasis in original). Conduct is substantially non-voluntary, in the sense here intended, when it is insufficiently informed or performed by someone insufficiently capable of rational self-governance with respect to the conduct in question.

Soft paternalism attractively combines a concern with promoting individual well-being with respect for the rights of individuals to govern themselves when their decisions are substantially voluntary (Feinberg, 1986, pp. 12–16). In this response, I shall therefore ask whether there is a soft-paternalistic justification for the taxes that Rabin advocates. My answer will be nuanced. Rabin's description of these biases as 'irrational' suggests that the choices they prompt are substantially non-voluntary. However, I shall argue that Rabin's

---

[1] www.number10.gov.uk/news/speech-on-the-nhs/, and www.guardian.co.uk/politics/2011/oct/04/uk-obesity-tax-david-cameron, accessed November 2012.

description of these biases as 'irrational' is not always appropriate –
sometimes, for example, they are merely a form of preference change.
When they are due to the latter, the behaviour is fully voluntary, and
there exists no soft-paternalistic justification for coercive intervention.
I shall also argue that even when these biases *do* lead to substantially
non-voluntary choices, we should prefer policies that improve self-
knowledge and self-control to taxes. However, I shall note that Rabin's
analysis reveals circumstances under which these autonomy-enhancing
strategies will not be effective. In such cases, I shall conclude, Rabin's
taxes have a soft-paternalistic justification.

Habits

Rabin defines an activity as *habit forming* if and only if the marginal
expected[2] utility a person gets from consuming the good at that time
is higher when she has consumed more of it in the past. A habit is
bad if and only if past and current consumption has the additional
effect of lowering future expected utility levels. A habit is *good* if
and only if past and current consumption has the additional effect
of raising future expected utility levels. Here are two examples, also
represented in Table 5.1.1:

> Bad habit: smoking today increases the marginal utility (MU) of
> smoking tomorrow, while lowering the utility levels of smoking
> and not-smoking tomorrow.
> Good habit: running today increases the marginal utility of running
> tomorrow, while raising the utility level associated with running
> tomorrow and the utility level of not-running tomorrow.

Projection bias

Consider first a fully informed decision-maker who, at time t1, evalu-
ates an action by summing all present and future utilities generated by
that action. In our examples, such a decision-maker would avoid the
bad and choose the good habit.

---

[2] In this volume, Rabin does not extend his definitions to the risky context, but
this seems a natural extension. I make use of this extended definition when
discussing how naivety can be advantageous in the third section.

Table 5.1.1 *Utility levels and marginal utility in each period for two habits*

	A bad habit		
Time	t1	t2	t3
Action(s)			
Never smoke	6	6	6
	⟩ MU = 4		
Always smoke	10	7	0
		⟩ MU = 5	⟩ MU = 6
Smoke at t1, give up t2		2	
Smoke at t1 & t2, give up t3			−6

	A good habit		
Never run	6	6	6
	⟩ MU = −3		
Always run	3	7	9
		⟩ MU = 0	⟩ MU = 1
Run at t1, give up t2		7	
Run at t1 & t2, give up t3			8

Now introduce projection bias – a tendency to mispredict future utilities associated with an activity by adjusting them in the direction of the current utility of that activity. An example is provided in Table 5.1.2, which focuses on the choice between always abstaining from and always engaging in the habits described above. We can see that this would result in the decision-maker incorrectly judging that indulging in the bad habit is preferable to not indulging and that not cultivating the good habit is preferable to cultivating it.

Rabin describes projection bias as 'irrational' and believes we should counteract its effects by taxing bad habits (to reduce their perceived utility) and subsidizing good ones (to increase their attractiveness). Are these judgements justified?

One cause of projection bias may be mere lack of information. If a person lacks evidence for how something will affect her well-being, it may be sensible for her to extrapolate from her current experience of that thing. Moreover, in such cases, educating her about the consequences of her choices is better than taxing her, because the former does not limit her liberty.

Table 5.1.2 *Utility levels and marginal utility in each period as perceived by a decision-maker with projection bias at t1*

	A bad habit		
Time	t1	t2	t3
Action(s)			
Never smoke	6	6	6
Always smoke	10	8 (real utility = 7)	5 (real utility = 0)
	A good habit		
Never run	6	6	6
Always run	3	5 (real utility = 7)	6 (real utility = 9)

However, Rabin offers evidence that not all forms of projection bias are properly ascribed to a lack of information. He cites studies which show that people's current affective state influences their judgement of what would be best for them at a future time in which they will *not* be in this state, *even when these people possess abundant evidence of the shifts in their tastes.*

It is unclear what the cause is of this failure to take into account readily available information on one's future tastes. One hypothesis is that projection bias is the result of decision-making by the so-called 'intuitive system' (Kahneman, 2002). Such decisions are typically quick, automatic and require little mental effort; they are also strongly influenced by current stimuli. (In this, they contrast with decisions made by the reasoning system, which are slower, controlled, effortful and make use of different information.)

If this hypothesis is correct, then it might seem that the best policy response would be to encourage people to engage in deliberative decision-making. However, such encouragement may not be effective. Given our limited cognitive resources, it is sensible to make *some* decisions in a quick-fire way. Insofar as we do, we will be susceptible to projection bias.

In sum, although it seems unjustified to label projection bias 'irrational', it seems right to ascribe it to lack of information or imperfect processing of information. The behaviour to which it gives rise is therefore not wholly voluntary in the aforementioned sense, so that there may exist a soft-paternalistic justification for government action. Moreover, it may be that projection bias cannot be eliminated by providing individuals with information and encouraging them to engage in deliberative decision-making. Rabin may therefore be right that we have reason to counter its detrimental effects by taxing bad habits and subsidizing good ones.

Present bias and naivety

A person who displays *present bias* gives extra weight to well-being *now* over any future moment, but applies the same discount factor to all future moments. This gives rise to time inconsistency in the agent's preferences. By way of illustration, consider the smoking habit described in Table 5.1.1 as it would be evaluated by someone who assesses the utility of an action as two times the utility it yields in the current period plus the sum of utilities in all future time periods. At t1, this person will evaluate smoking as preferable to not-smoking.[3] However, at all preceding and all subsequent times, he will evaluate smoking as inferior to not-smoking.

Rabin regards such time-inconsistent preferences as irrational. Once again, this description is not always apt. Present bias could be displayed by a person who, at every point in time, deliberates well on the basis of all relevant information and is fully in control of himself. He merely undergoes preference change which always leads him to give extra weight to the pleasures of the moment. Such a person always does what he *then* most prefers. In this case, even though present bias leads to lesser satisfaction of the individual's long-term preferences, the behaviour to which it gives rise should not be regarded as irrational or non-voluntary (Parfit, 1986, part 2). Taxing it therefore lacks soft-paternalistic justification. This does not mean a government has no liberal policy instruments at its disposal, for it can empower citizens to stop their future selves from acting on present bias. An example is the Australian requirement on gambling providers to give customers the option to self-exclude from their venue or products.

Of course, present bias may instead be due to familiar faults in reasoning or self-control. For example, a person might prefer to gamble because his deliberation is clouded by excessive desire, which leads him to give less credence than he should to evidence that he will lose a lot of money. Or he may arrive at the right conclusion

---

[3] The utility of smoking is $(2 \times 10) + 7 + 0 = 27$; the utility of not smoking is $(2 \times 6) + 6 + 6 - 24$.

through deliberation (that he ought not to gamble) but fail to abide by it because of weakness of will. In such cases, it may indeed be appropriate to describe his present-biased choice as irrational and not fully voluntary. But even in such cases, a liberal government ought to prefer empowering citizens to control themselves (as the Australian policy does) to taxing them (as happens, for example, in Singapore, which heavily taxes gambling), at least where both are equally effective.

However, Rabin's analysis highlights a pitfall for policies that promote citizens' abilities to control their future selves. Such control depends on knowing that, in future, one will be biased towards the pleasures of the moment. Promoting such self-knowledge is therefore a component of an empowerment strategy. But, Rabin points out, such self-knowledge may be detrimental. Sophisticates, he writes, may be less likely than naifs to start an advantageous good habit, because they regard the chances that they will stick with the good habit as lower than the naifs. Self-knowledge may therefore be damaging.

To see why, imagine that present-biased Ahorita is considering embarking on an exercise regimen which would invariably do her good in the long run. Also suppose there is some uncertainty about the 'start-up costs' of this habit: it is certain to be unpleasant at t1, but at t2 there is an equal chance that it is either no longer unpleasant (because her body adapts quickly), or *very* unpleasant (because her muscles are sore). Finally, suppose that if it is *very* unpleasant, her present bias at t2 would lead her to quit the regimen at t2, but if it is no longer unpleasant, she will stick with it. How will Ahorita decide at t1?

If she is *sophisticated*, she will predict that if she were to start exercising at t1, there is a good chance that she will drop out at t2 and have suffered at t1 for nothing. Moreover, at t1, she will weight the unpleasantness of exercise in that period disproportionately heavily. Together, her present bias and sophisticated scepticism will make it less likely that she will start the healthy habit.

By contrast, if she is *naive* about her present bias, she will (falsely) predict that if she were to start exercising at t1, she would stick with it no matter what. Her naivety will therefore lead her to *overestimate* the expected benefits of starting the exercise regimen. Of course, her present bias at t1 will also lead her to *overweight* its expected cost. Her naivety therefore works against her present bias. Now, once she starts, she may drop out at t2. But there is also a good chance that she will stick with it, and this chance is sufficient (we can suppose) to make giving it a go worthwhile. Her naivety therefore makes it more likely that she will start and stick with an advantageous pattern of behaviour.

What are the lessons for policy? First, from a soft paternalist point of view, the best policy is one which informs citizens about their present bias while ensuring they have access to effective commitment devices to control their present bias. Second, in the absence of such devices, helping citizens to see the truth about themselves may not be good policy, because it may neither make them better off nor promote their pursuit of their long-term goals. Third, when present bias is irrational, effective commitment devices are not available and education alone will not help, governments have reason to turn to Rabin's proposed taxes and subsidies.

Conclusion

Projection bias, present bias and lack of self-knowledge make us less capable of fulfilling our long-term, considered desires. Rabin has argued in favour of using taxes to counteract these biases. By contrast, I have argued that respect for our rights of self-governance should lead us to prefer policies that help us to overcome these biases by education and by facilitating self-binding, where these will be effective. But I have also argued that a careful look at the way these biases work identifies circumstances in which (i) the biases lead to self-harming behaviour that is not fully voluntary and (ii) these autonomy-enhancing strategies will not be effective. In these circumstances, and only in these circumstances, governments have a soft-paternalistic justification for the use of taxes to counteract these biases.

References

De Marnette, P. (2006). Avoiding Paternalism. *Philosophy and Public Affairs* 68: 68–94.

Feinberg, J. (1986). *Harm to Self*. Oxford University Press.

Kahneman, D. (2002). *Maps of Bounded Rationality*. Nobel Prize Lectures (www.nobelprize.org/nobel_prizes/economics/laureates/2002/kahnemann-lecture.pdf).

Parfit, D. (1986). *Reasons and Persons*. Oxford University Press.

Van Baal, P., Polder, J., de Wit, A., Hoogenveen, R., Feenstra, T., Boshuizen, H., Engelfriet, P. and Brouwer, W. (2008). Lifetime Medical Costs of Obesity: Prevention No Cure for Increasing Health Expenditure. *PLoS Medicine* 5(2): 242–9.

6 | Confessing one's sins but still committing them: transparency and the failure of disclosure

SUNITA SAH, DAYLIAN M. CAIN
AND GEORGE LOEWENSTEIN

If financial advisers disclose the fact that they get a bonus if their clients invest in a particular product, how will clients use that information, and to what extent will the disclosure help them make a better decision? If at all, how might the disclosure alter the advice given by advisers, or how might it affect the relationship between advisers and their clients? In this chapter, we address these questions. Reviewing extensive evidence that casts doubt on the efficacy of disclosure, we conclude that disclosure is not a panacea; it often fails to serve its intended functions and may sometimes backfire, hurting the interests of those it was intended to protect.

Conflicts of interest, in which professionals have personal interests that conflict with their professional responsibilities, have been at the heart of many recent business fiascos. For example, the bubble in the American real estate market that burst in 2008 was partly supported by inflated ratings of collateralized mortgage bonds that were created by rating agencies that had financial ties to the issuers of those bonds. Many recent accounting scandals can be traced to conflicts of interest on the part of auditors, who received large consulting fees from the same firms they audited. Likewise, many health care professionals worry that similar problems have been created in medicine because of industry payments to physicians and fee-for-service compensation arrangements.

Conflicts of interest have received considerable attention from organizations such as the American Association of Medical Students, the Institute of Medicine and other policy-makers who have attempted to eliminate or manage these conflicts (for example, see www.amsascorecard.org for restrictions imposed on academic medical centres). However, even at academic medical centres, most of which have barred practices such as 'detailing' by pharmaceutical company representatives, many conflicts of interest remain untouched, including fee-for-service arrangements that encourage over-utilization. Moreover, most of the legislative measures that have been taken to mitigate problems associated with conflicts of interest in medicine, including the 2010 Patient Protection and Affordable Care Act, rely significantly on the perceived benefits of one particular solution: disclosure. Indeed, almost all attempts at rectifying the harmful effects of conflicts of interest in medicine, government, media, finance and academia include, or are limited to, disclosure.

At first glance, the logic for disclosure is compelling. In principle, disclosure should allow recipients of advice to take conflicted advice with a grain of salt, and advisers, knowing that their conflicts will be disclosed, should attempt to avoid conflicts or at least take credible steps to manage those conflicts, thus increasing the likelihood that their advice is trusted. However, disclosing conflicts of interest can also have surprising and unintended consequences, due to myriad psychological factors that affect both advisees receiving the disclosure and advisers who disclose their conflicts.

Perverse effects of disclosure (on advisees)

Given a choice, most advisees would opt for transparency. If their advisers have conflicts of interest, they would like to know about them. However, wanting such information is different from knowing what to do with it; in fact, psychological research suggests that advisees are unlikely to use the information very productively. First, advisees are often not particularly alarmed by the sort of disclosures used in everyday communications. For example, one study found that more than 90 per cent of patients expressed little or no worry about financial ties that researchers or institutions might have to drug companies (Hampson et al., 2006).

Second, even if advisees paid attention to the disclosure, their decision on what to do with it is likely to be suboptimal. In order to accurately discount for the biasing influences behind advice, the advisee must possess a psychological model of adviser behaviour that predicts both the impact of the conflict of interest on the advice and, as we discuss shortly, the impact of disclosure on that advice (Cain et al., 2011). Without an effective advice-discounting model, advisees have difficulty using disclosure effectively: they may ignore it, they may discount it but insufficiently so, or they may discount the advice too much. In some cases, disclosure might actually *increase* trust in the advice if the advisee interprets the disclosure as a sign of honesty or sees the adviser's payments as an indication of high professional status (Pearson et al., 2006).

Third, even if advisees attend to the disclosure and have a good mental model of how to react to it, they may be unable to react as they intend. Central to this idea is what psychologists call an 'anchoring' effect: advisees tend to fixate unconsciously on the advice initially given to them, even when they are aware that the advice should be discounted or totally ignored (Tversky and Kahneman, 1974). While many advocates of disclosure agree that disclosures should be clear and not buried in fine-print legalese, research on anchoring suggests that even clear disclosures (e.g. 'Warning: this advice was randomly generated; ignore it completely') fail to cause sufficient discounting of advice. The point is that even when advisees try to ignore advice, they have a surprisingly difficult time doing so.

Finally, a 'burden of disclosure' can be placed on advisees where they perversely feel increased pressure to adhere to the advice disclosed as conflicted, in spite of trusting that advice less. In a series of studies examining adviser–advisee interactions, Sah et al. (2012, 2013) showed that this burden of disclosure is the result of two psychological processes. The first mechanism at work is what we call *insinuation anxiety*: advisees fear that rejecting advice (once they learn about a conflict of interest) may give a negative signal to the adviser that they believe the advice is biased or the adviser corrupt. For instance, without disclosure, a customer may not want to invest in a new mutual fund due to risk aversion or satisfaction with his or her current fund. Advisees who receive disclosure may trust the advice less because of the disclosure (arguably the intended purpose of disclosure), or they may wish to reject the advice for the same reasons as without disclosure (risk aversion or satisfaction with their current fund). However, after disclosure, advice rejection is much more likely to signal distrust of the conflicted adviser – something the customer is understandably reluctant to communicate. The second mechanism for the burden of disclosure is the *panhandler effect*: congruent with literature on 'reluctant altruism' (Dana et al., 2006), advisees may feel pressure to help advisers obtain their personal interests once the advisers disclose those interests. For example, once an adviser discloses that he or she earns a large referral fee if the client enrols in a particular programme, the client may implicitly feel that he or she is being asked to 'help' the adviser get that fee.

Using experiments involving medical scenarios to test these mechanisms, we conducted a role-playing study to examine the impact of disclosure on advisees (Sah et al., 2012). Participants were asked to take the perspective of patients and received information about their medical history and current symptoms. Each participant heard a voice recording of his or her 'doctor', who informed them of two potential treatment options and then recommended one of those options. The recommended option was consistent in all conditions. The key manipulation was that, in one condition, the doctor disclosed that he would benefit if the patient took his recommendation, and, in the other condition, the patient was not informed about the doctor's conflict of interest. The doctor who disclosed was trusted significantly less than the doctor who did not disclose. However, relationship dynamics also created serious unintended effects. The patients who heard the disclosure reported that they felt much more uncomfortable about turning down the doctor's recommendation because they did not want to insinuate that the doctor was biased or corrupt. Therefore, disclosure created a significant burden on the patients and increased pressure to comply with the recommendation, even though they felt less trusting of the advice.

In a similar study, we showed that the burden of disclosure was not eliminated by the magnitude of the doctor's conflict of interest. Respondents (who role played as patients) experienced a similar pressure to comply (due to insinuation anxiety), whether or not the doctor had a small or large conflict of interest (Sah et al., 2012). Furthermore, stating that the disclosure was mandatory and required by law had no differential impact on participants' insinuation anxiety compared to those who may have attributed the information as voluntary disclosure. Whether the disclosure is mandatory or not, the patient still shows distrust by not complying with the doctor's recommendation.

Beyond these simulation studies, which could be construed as testing people's feelings about disclosure, we also conducted experiments with real payoffs, again focusing on the 'burden of disclosure' (Sah et al., 2013). In these experiments, 'advisers' instructed 'choosers' to select between two die-roll lotteries: 'roll A' or 'roll B'. These rolls resulted in different specific prize sets (for instance, a $5 Starbucks gift card if a '5' was rolled on die A). The prizes for the roll A lottery were superior in value to those of roll B; roll A had more than twice the expected value, and prior pilot studies revealed that more than 90 per cent of participants preferred roll A over roll B. Advisers gave advice about which die-roll lottery the chooser should pick, which was communicated in writing through a form that also contained full information on the prizes associated with each lottery. Since choosers had full information on the prizes, the advisers were not telling the choosers anything particularly informative about the lotteries other than how the advisers would make (or at least want the chooser to make) the choice. Some of the advisers were subject to a conflict of interest in that they would only receive compensation if the participant chose die-roll B, the inferior die roll. Half of these conflicted advisers were required to write out a word-for-word disclosure statement on the same communication form informing choosers of their self-interest, whereas the other conflicted advisers were told not to disclose their compensation. Other advisers were not subject to a conflict of interest and were compensated regardless of the chooser's choice.

Nearly all of the unconflicted advisers recommended the superior die-roll A (93 per cent), and all of the choosers who received this advice took it, reporting little pressure to accept the advice. In contrast, when advisers were subject to an undisclosed conflict of interest (they would benefit if the chooser selected the inferior die roll), many more (approximately 80 per cent) recommended the inferior die-roll B, and of choosers who received this biased advice, 52 per cent accepted the adviser's recommendation. This increased propensity to choose the inferior die roll was exacerbated when the adviser's conflict was disclosed. Of choosers who received biased advice and were informed of the conflict, 81 per cent picked the inferior die roll. These choosers picked die-roll B in spite of having full information on the prizes and on the adviser's conflict. Disclosure created increased compliance with advice that was clearly biased.

Choosers in the disclosure condition reported that they were less pleased with their choice and that they trusted the advice less than choosers who did not receive disclosure. Simultaneously, however, choosers with disclosure also indicated that they felt more pressure to help their advisers and also felt more uncomfortable about rejecting the adviser's recommendation. These feelings of social pressure medi-ated the relationship between receiving disclosure and complying with the adviser's advice. Disclosure significantly increased the pressure felt by choosers to comply with biased advice. The increased pressure was so great that, paradoxically, disclosure caused increased compliance – the opposite of the intended purpose of disclosure.

Perverse effect of disclosure (on advisers)

Disclosure can have a number of unintended effects on advisers as well (Cain et al., 2005, 2011). The first mechanism is *strategic exaggeration*: consciously exaggerating the bias in advice when disclosure is present. Strategic exaggeration is an attempt by conflicted advisers to counteract any potential discounting that disclosure may encourage in advisees. For instance, imagine that you are seeking advice on a financial investment. Your financial adviser receives compensation if you invest in a particular fund. It is easy to imagine that your financial adviser may exaggerate the benefits of the fund even more if he or she is *required* to disclose his or her conflict of interest.

Disclosure also creates an acceptable rationalization in the minds of advisers: the advisee has been informed of the risk of bias and the adviser can no longer be held responsible for the consequences, *caveat emptor* (Cain et al., 2011). Research suggests that displaying salient moral behaviour in one instance can cause people to believe that they are 'morally licensed' to behave less morally in subsequent situations (Monin and Miller, 2001). The suggestion here is that the adviser may treat disclosure (even mandated disclosure) as a sort of credit in a morality bank, and as long as the credits and subsequent debits balance out in the adviser's mind, his or her actions are justified (Zhong et al., 2009).

Cain et al. (2005, 2011) provide explicit support for the idea that disclosure leads conflicted advisers to give more conflicted advice. In one experiment (2005), 'advisers' were required to give 'estimators' a recommendation on the value of coins in several jars to which the advisers had closer viewing and about which they were given more information than estimators. Estimators were required to guess the total value of the coins in the jars after receiving advice and were rewarded for accuracy, i.e. estimators were paid according to how close their estimate was to the value of the jar. There were three main conditions appertaining to the advice given. In the no-conflict condition, advisers were paid according to their estimators' accuracy, so adviser and estimator objectives were aligned. In the two conflict conditions, advisers were rewarded more if the estimators *overestimated* the coin jar's value. One conflict condition required advisers to disclose this reward to their estimators, while the other had no such disclosure.

The results of this study provide support for the psychological mechanisms outlined above: conflicted advisers gave advice that was significantly more biased when their incentives were disclosed, and since estimators did not adjust properly for this exaggeration, they received lower payoffs than did estimators who received no disclosure. These findings were also replicated with experiments modelling a real-life situation of a homebuyer and a conflicted real estate agent, which also manipulated the presence/absence of disclosure when advisers' incentives were aligned with those of estimators (Cain et al., 2011). In these studies, without disclosure, the estimators seemed to assume that there was no conflict of interest, and with disclosure, advice worsened but was insufficiently discounted. Two other studies reported in the same paper provide explicit evidence of moral licensing and strategic exaggeration. For example, one of the studies features survey respondents who reported that it was more ethically acceptable to give blatantly misleading advice when a conflict had been disclosed than when it had not been disclosed.

Overcoming the limitations of disclosure

Making disclosure work: advisees

A series of follow-up experiments to the medical and die-roll studies (Sah et al., 2012, 2013) tested different remedies for the burden-of-disclosure effect. We found that those who could make their choices privately, or those who could change their minds afterwards, were less likely to follow biased advice than those who had to make their final choice in the presence of their advisers. Applied to financial decisions, the results suggest that people should not make significant commitments with their money until they have had time to think away from their advisers, or unless a cooling-off period is available where clients have the opportunity to cancel or change their minds without consequence. Applied to medicine, the research suggests that patients should think about their choice of treatment away from the pressures of the doctor's office.

Both the medical and die-roll studies also showed that disclosure provided by an external party, rather than directly from the adviser, significantly reduced the pressure to comply. In follow-up studies, however, we found that the burden was driven by *common knowledge* of the conflict between the adviser and advisee. In other words, when external disclosure was provided secretly (i.e. the adviser did not know that the advisee had this information), the burden was reduced, and when advisees were given this information from an external party and it was apparent that the adviser knew of the external disclosure, the burden reappeared. Common knowledge created the pressure both to avoid insinuating distrust to the adviser and to satisfy the adviser's self-interest. This is further evidence that the pressure to comply stems from what the advisee worries the adviser will think about non-compliance (e.g. 'Did the client think I was corrupt?' or 'Did the client knowingly refuse to help me?'). The physical presence of the adviser also increased the burden. When advisees had to make the decision in front of the adviser rather than in private, they were much more likely to comply.

With disclosure, advisees still need to know how much to discount the advice. Often, even *advisers* are unaware of how biased their advice is (Dana and Loewenstein, 2003); many of the problems of conflicts of interest stem from unintentional bias, rather than intentional corruption (Moore et al., 2005). How can one expect advisees to know how to accurately estimate and then counteract that bias if the advisers themselves cannot estimate it? Indeed, part of the problem with disclosure is that people often under-appreciate how dangerous conflicts of interest are to a well-meaning adviser. Disclosure is a warning of danger, but that danger is currently too often overlooked.

Cain et al. (2011, study 4) found that advisees who were able to contrast simultaneously advice from conflicted and unconflicted advisers gave far more weight to the unconflicted advice. Evidently, encouraging the presence and salience of unconflicted advice will be central to reducing the effects of biased advice (Robertson, 2010). In addition, research by Koch and Schmidt (2009) suggests that repeated feedback and multiple trials may educate and condition advisees on how to respond properly to disclosure. Although provocative, we worry that these conditions are typically very difficult to achieve in real-world settings. For example, in the situations in which they are most vulnerable, few decision-makers have the luxury of making multiple decisions and receiving explicit feedback about their consequences.

Making disclosure work: advisers

While the overwhelming experimental evidence demonstrates strategic exaggeration in advisers (Cain et al., 2011), a smaller (but still significant) group practised *strategic restraint*, decreasing bias in their advice for fear that disclosure would bring extra scrutiny to the advice. Indeed, research on disclosure of health and safety risks shows that, to the extent that disclosure is successful in reducing risks, its effects tend to work more by changing the behaviour of those creating the risks than by changing the behaviour of people facing the risks (Fung et al., 2007). Identifying the factors that bring on strategic restraint vs strategic exaggeration is key to determining the success of disclosure on advisers.

This research suggests that mandatory disclosure is most likely to have positive effects if, and to the extent that, it leads advisers to avoid conflicts of interest in the first instance. In another series of experiments, Sah and Loewenstein (2012) used a different paradigm – asking advisers to give estimators a recommendation of the number of filled dots in a large 30 × 30 grid of dots in which some dots were filled and some were clear. Estimators only viewed a small 3 × 3 subset of the grid and were paid for their accuracy in guessing the correct number of filled dots in the large grid. In the first experiment, all advisers were subject to a conflict of interest in that they were paid more if the estimators overestimated the number of filled dots. In the disclosure condition, advisers were required to inform the estimators of their conflict of interest. In the no-disclosure condition, estimators were unaware of their advisers' conflict. Consistent with the prior research, advisers gave more biased advice when they were required to disclose their conflict. However, in this experiment (and the prior experiments), advisers had no choice in experiencing the conflict of interest: it was inherent in their compensation system.

In the second experiment, Sah and Loewenstein (2012) allowed advisers to choose (1) to accept a conflict of interest and be paid well if the estimator overestimated, or (2) reject the conflict and be paid a smaller amount for the estimators' accuracy. Some advisers were subject to mandatory disclosure rules and knew they would have to disclose their conflict to the advisees, while others were not required to disclose their conflict. Sah and Loewenstein found that advisers under mandatory disclosure were more likely to reject the conflict of interest and give more accurate advice than those who did not have to disclose. The final study in this series added a condition with voluntary disclosure, which turned out to have similar effects as mandatory disclosure. Many advisers chose to reject the conflict and disclose that they had done so. This shows that disclosure can be beneficial when advisers have a choice to accept or reject the conflict.

The research of Church and Kuang (2009) also suggests that penalizing biased advisers may help improve the efficacy of disclosure. Unfortunately, bias is difficult to determine in real-world situations. For example, while many advisers labelled Enron a 'strong buy' even weeks before its collapse, it is not an easy task to determine who gave honest (albeit incorrect, perhaps unconsciously biased) advice versus those who intentionally misled their clients.

Conclusion

A thorough analysis of the research on disclosure indicates that conditions must be optimal for advisees to properly discount for biased advice and for advisers to behave as intended. Disclosure seems to work when advisers have a choice of whether or not to face a conflict of interest, and when advisees are immediately faced with unconflicted advisers. Using disclosure as a cure-all solution for conflicts of interest decreases these opportunities and professionals need to work harder to eliminate the presence of such conflicts.

Much of the research in other fields also concludes that having more information does not necessarily mean better decisions. Given the rules regarding disclosure during the discovery phase of a court case, law firms tend to overload opposing firms with documents in an attempt to inundate their opposition with information so that they cannot perform effective analysis (Brinkley, 2006).

People should have the right to receive accurate and complete information so as to make informed decisions, especially if regulators can learn how to enhance disclosure's effectiveness; disclosure, in the sense of providing as close to perfect information as possible, is desirable. However, if the person who receives the disclosure is overwhelmed by information with no way to discern what information is important, then disclosure will have little positive effect. In the words of David Weil, 'Transparency policies only work if they give users the information they need, when they need it, and in the form they need for making an effective decision' (2009, p. 22). Disclosure has many limitations, but there is also great opportunity for enhancing its beneficial effects.

If disclosure has pitfalls, however, perhaps the most significant is a kind of moral licensing effect we have not discussed to this point: the possibility that professions where disclosures of conflicts of interest are mandatory will feel morally licensed to not take more substantive measures in dealing with conflicts of interest. Disclosure alone is rarely sufficient to make much of a dent in the myriad problems caused by conflicts of interest. Disclosure will almost certainly have negative overall effects if it substitutes for more substantive interventions.

References

Brinkley, C. L. (2006). Stop Automaker Discovery Abuse. *Trial* 42: 20–8.

Cain, D. M., Loewenstein, G. and Moore, D. A. (2005). The Dirt on Coming Clean: Perverse Effects of Disclosing Conflicts of Interest. *The Journal of Legal Studies* 34: 1–25.

(2011). When Sunlight Fails to Disinfect: Understanding the Perverse Effects of Disclosing Conflicts of Interest. *Journal of Consumer Research* 37: 836–57.

Church, B. K. and Kuang, X. J. (2009). Conflicts of Interest, Disclosure, and (Costly) Sanctions: Experimental Evidence. *The Journal of Legal Studies* 38: 505–32.

Dana, J., Cain, D. M. and Dawes, R. (2006). What You Don't Know Won't Hurt Me: Costly (but Quiet) Exit in Dictator Games. *Organizational Behavior and Human Decision Processes* 100: 193–201.

Dana, J. D. and Loewenstein, G. (2003). A Social Science Perspective on Gifts to Physicians from Industry. *Journal of the American Medical Association* 290: 252–5.

Fung, A., Graham, M. and Weil, D. (2007). *Full Disclosure: The Perils and Promise of Transparency*. Cambridge University Press.

Hampson, L. A., Agrawal, M., Joffe, S., Gross, C. P., Verter, J. and Emanuel, E. J. (2006). Patients' Views on Financial Conflicts of Interest in Cancer Research Trials. *New England Journal of Medicine* 355: 2330–7.

Koch, C. and Schmidt, C. (2009). Disclosing Conflict of Interest: Do Experience and Reputation Matter? *Accounting, Organizations, and Society* 35: 95–107.

Monin, B. and Miller, D. T. (2001). Moral Credentials and the Expression of Prejudice. *Journal of Personality and Social Psychology* 81: 33–43.

Moore, D. A., Loewenstein, G. and Bazerman, M. (eds.) (2005). *Conflicts of Interest: Problems and Solutions from Law, Medicine, and Organizational Settings.* Cambridge University Press.

Pearson, S. D., Kleinman, K., Rusinak, D. and Levinson, W. (2006). A Trial of Disclosing Physicians' Financial Incentives to Patients. *Archives of Internal Medicine* 166: 623–8.

Robertson, C. (2010). Blind Expertise. *New York University Law Review* 85: 174–257.

Sah, S. and Loewenstein, G. (2012). Nothing to Declare: Disclosure Leads Advisors to Avoid Conflicts of Interest. Working paper.

Sah, S., Loewenstein, G. and Cain, D. M. (2012). Insinuation Anxiety: Increased Pressure to Follow Less Trusted Advice after Disclosure of a Conflict of Interest. Working paper.

  (2013). The Burden of Disclosure: Increased Compliance with Distrusted Advice. *Journal of Personality and Social Psychology* 104: 289–304.

Tversky, A. and Kahneman, D. (1974). Judgment under Uncertainty: Heuristics and Biases. *Science* 185: 1124–31.

Weil, D. (2009). Targeted Transparency. *Public Manager* 38: 22–4.

Zhong, C., Liljenquist, K. and Cain, D. M. (2009). Moral Self-Regulation: Licensing and Compensation. In D. D. Cremer (ed.), *Psychological Perspectives on Ethical Behavior and Decision Making.* Charlotte, NC: Information Age Publishing, pp. 75–89.

6.1 | *A response to Sah, Cain and Loewenstein*

ROBERT SUGDEN

When suppliers of products are better informed than consumers, consumers are vulnerable to exploitation. Perceptions of this problem have often been softened by common understandings of the role of the 'professional' – the doctor, the lawyer, the financial adviser, the car mechanic – as acting in good faith as an adviser to her client at the same time as selling services to him. But this traditional understanding seems to be decaying. There is an increasing public demand for transparency, and in particular for the mandatory disclosure of conflicts of interest. Sah, Cain and Loewenstein (SCL) discuss the limitations of this response.

SCL give a convincing account of the psychology of 'conflicted advice'. When there is common knowledge between the adviser and the advisee that the adviser has a conflict of interest, both parties are subject to influences that may undermine the benefit of disclosure.

Viewed through the lens of conventional game theory, the interaction between a conflicted adviser and an advisee is strategically complex. A self-interested adviser has an incentive to misrepresent her judgements; a self-interested advisee knows this and will discount for the bias; a self-interested adviser will anticipate this; and so on. One might construct a stylized game-theoretic model of this interaction, and assume that the rules of the game are common knowledge between rational players; but only a great leap of faith would justify one in treating the equilibria of such a model (there might well be more than one equilibrium) as informative about the real world. Reasonably enough, SCL give more attention to psychology than to rational choice.

As they explain, anchoring effects can make it difficult for advisees to discount advice, even when they have little confidence in its reliability. An advisee may perceive an adviser's disclosure of a conflict of interest as evidence of the adviser's honesty (even if disclosure is in fact a legal requirement), with the result that disclosure makes the advisee *more* susceptible to biased advice. After disclosure, an advisee may feel under pressure to accept conflicted advice, because it is now common knowledge that doing so would benefit the adviser, and because rejecting the advice might seem to signal suspicion about the adviser's good faith. On the other side of the transaction, an adviser may perceive disclosure as absolving her from the moral responsibility to act in the advisee's interests.

This analysis leads SCL to be sceptical of the value of compulsory disclosure. As their subtitle implies, the main thrust of their chapter is 'the failure of disclosure'. In more general terms, their analysis is presented as supporting the claim that (in implied contrast to the conclusions of rational-choice economics) 'having more information does not necessarily mean better decisions'. Significantly, however, SCL draw back from concluding that information about conflicts of interest should not be disclosed. Despite having presented evidence suggesting that disclosure may have adverse effects, they maintain that 'people should have the right to receive accurate and complete information so as to make informed decisions' and that 'disclosure, in the sense of providing as close to perfect information as possible, is desirable'. There seems to be some tension here.

The underlying problem is deeply embedded in behavioural welfare economics, as developed by, for example, Colin Camerer et al. (2003), Cass Sunstein and Richard Thaler (2003) and Douglas Bernheim and Antonio Rangel (2009). As a co-author and I have argued, the theoretical concepts and analytical techniques of neoclassical welfare economics can be given a range of alternative normative interpretations (McQuillin and Sugden, 2012). On one interpretation, welfare economics is fundamentally about individual well-being; the satisfaction of revealed preferences is used as a normative criterion, but only on the assumption that an individual's choices reveal her considered judgements about her well-being. On another interpretation, traditionally expressed in the concept of 'consumer sovereignty', the fundamental normative principle is one of opportunity or freedom of choice. The tension between these two interpretations was not felt until it began to become clear that individuals' choices often do not reveal stable and well-articulated preferences. Behavioural welfare economics responds to this problem by keeping well-being as the normative criterion but detaching the definition of well-being from individual choice. I have advocated the opposite approach, of using opportunity as the normative criterion without claiming that increases in opportunity necessarily increase well-being (Sugden, 2004). My sense is that SCL's general inclinations are towards behavioural welfare economics, but their appeal to the *right* to make one's own decisions on the basis of accurate information, whether or not that best promotes one's well-being, has some of the flavour of the opportunity-based approach.

SCL try to resolve this tension by arguing that the best solution to the problem of conflicts of interest is to eliminate those conflicts altogether. They conclude that mandatory disclosure, while morally necessary, is not enough. Professionals 'need to work harder to eliminate the presence of such conflicts'; professions need to 'take more substantive measures [than disclosure] in dealing with conflicts of interest'. SCL suggest that the most positive potential effect of mandatory disclosure is as an incentive to eliminate conflicts of interest. (The hypothesis that there is such an effect is supported by evidence that advisees are more ready to trust advice when it is not conflicted, and are conscious of and dislike the pressure to accept conflicted advice: see Cain et al., 2011 and Loewenstein et al., 2011.)

I can agree that there are some cases in which conflicts of interest on the part of professionals clearly work against the interests of their clients. But I think it is an over-simplification to treat conflict of interest *in general* as a pathology to be eliminated (or indeed as a sin to be confessed). Rather, it is a fact of economic life that has to be taken into account in understanding the evolution of market structures and in designing market regulations.

Consider a case that is currently important in the UK. The Financial Services Authority (FSA, the regulatory agency for the financial services industry) is introducing new regulations governing the retail sale of investment products such as pensions, annuities and unit trusts. Up to now, it has been common for the sale of those products to be intermediated by independent financial advisers, whose incomes are derived from commission payments from the providers of the products they recommend. The ensuing conflict of interest has been blamed for various highly publicized episodes of misselling. Under the new regulations, independent financial advisers will not be allowed to accept commission payments; instead, they must charge their customers directly for the advice they give. This policy (which seems sensible to me) is in the same spirit as SCL's recommendations. It eliminates a conflict of interest by enforcing a separation between the roles of adviser and provider.

However, the FSA regulations apply only to *independent* financial advisers, who are expected to make unbiased recommendations based on their knowledge of the whole range of financial products on the market. A retailer can declare that it sells only a limited range of products – typically because it is the retail arm of a particular provider – and in so doing can discharge itself from the obligation to give unbiased advice. Some commentators have predicted that the new regulations will lead to an increase in this form of vertical integration. Debarred from competing in terms of commission payments, providers may compete for sales by acquiring or setting up retail outlets; independent advisers may be squeezed out if consumers are resistant to more transparent charging. Such developments would be analogous to the growth of own-brand sales by supermarket chains and the corresponding decline of traditional grocers' shops.

Two generations ago, many customers perceived their grocers as sources of professional advice about what they should buy. If grocery is viewed in that old-fashioned way, the modern supermarket's promotion of its own brands reveals a gross conflict of interest, albeit one that is fully disclosed. In the same way, vertical integration in the financial services market might be seen as disclosure in a new guise, and thus as undermining what for SCL are the benefits of the new regulations. If one really wanted to eliminate conflicts of interest, the obvious regulatory solution would be to require the sale of all financial products to be intermediated by independent advisers, paid directly by their customers. But, as the FSA was presumably well aware, that would restrict competition and market innovation.

As markets evolve, people's understandings of market roles – and hence their understanding of conflicts of interest – can change. In the grocery case, I suggest, the modern shopper does not typically think of the supermarket as *advising* her to buy its own brands, and so the problem of how to deal with conflicted advice does not arise. When she considers buying a new type of own-brand product, she does not think of herself as assessing the truth or falsity of factual claims made by the supermarket. Instead, she treats the perceived price and quality characteristics of a supermarket's own brand as an *offer* that she can accept or reject. The supermarket's interest in the reputation of its brand comes to play a central role in sustaining the customer's trust in new products that carry that brand. Thus, market innovation has made redundant the role of the grocer as independent adviser. Innovation in the market for financial services may have similar consequences for the role of the independent financial adviser.

A well-ordered regulatory regime will facilitate the competitive process while allowing room for market structures to evolve in unpredicted directions. As Friedrich Hayek (1948) argued many years ago, markets work by integrating otherwise dispersed knowledge. Regulation may be able to help markets to work more effectively, but it cannot substitute for their role in solving the problem of division of knowledge. If that is right, the role of the regulator should not extend to deciding whether it is expedient to restrict flows of information. This way of thinking about markets may make it easier to reconcile the proposition that having more information does not necessarily mean better decisions with the intuition that conflicts of interest should be fully disclosed.

References

Bernheim, D. and Rangel, A. (2009). Beyond Revealed Preference: Choice-Theoretic Foundations for Behavioral Welfare Economics. *Quarterly Journal of Economics* 124: 51–104.

Cain, D., Loewenstein, G. and Moore, D. (2011). When Sunlight Fails to Disinfect: Understanding the Perverse Effects of Disclosing Conflicts of Interest. *Journal of Consumer Research* 37: 836–57.

Camerer, C., Issacharoff, S., Loewenstein, G., O'Donaghue, T. and Rabin, M. (2003). Regulation for Conservatives: Behavioral Economics and the Case for 'Asymmetric Paternalism'. *University of Pennsylvania Law Review* 151: 1211–54.

Hayek, F. (1948). *Individualism and Economic Order*. University of Chicago Press.

Loewenstein, G., Cain, D. and Sah, S. (2011). The Limits of Transparency: Pitfalls and Potential of Disclosing Conflicts of Interest. *American Economic Review, Papers and Proceedings* 101: 423–8.

McQuillin, B. and Sugden, R. (2012). Reconciling Normative and Behavioural Economics: The Problems to be Solved. *Social Choice and Welfare* 38(4): 553–67.

Sugden, R. (2004). The Opportunity Criterion: Consumer Sovereignty Without the Assumption of Coherent Preferences. *American Economic Review* 94: 1014–33.

Sunstein, C. and Thaler, R. (2003). Libertarian Paternalism is Not an Oxymoron. *University of Chicago Law Review* 70: 1159–202.

7 | *How should people be rewarded for their work?*

BRUNO FREY

The orthodox view

Recently, I met a couple. Joan has a management education and is employed as a human resource manager by a large international insurance firm with about 30,000 staff. George studied economics and now manages a well-respected family-run car dealing firm with fifteen employees in three locations.

When I talked to them about their professional activities, both emphatically stated: 'People should be paid according to their perform-ance.' Indeed, it was absolutely clear to both of them that performance pay induces people to work. Performance pay means that targets are fixed *ex ante*, and that those exceeding them get a bonus. Those not meeting the targets should be reprimanded or dismissed. In the case of George, each car sold should lead to a higher pay; in the case of Joan, those performing better than the target set should receive a higher salary. However, she did not tell me how 'performance' should or can be determined in the insurance business, except in relation to the direct selling of insurance contracts.

The couple knew that I am an academic economist and they were glad to tell me that their view corresponds exactly to what they learnt in their respective university courses.

Some questions

I first probed George, the car dealer, concerning some problems with performance pay. I asked him whether he really pays a bonus directly linked to the number of cars sold by an employee. I suggested that this would lead his employees to sell cars 'at all costs'. They would disregard the interests of the customers, as well as of his firm.

George immediately agreed and stated that this would certainly be bad for his well-established firm because he is interested in keeping his customers happy so that they come back to the firm in the future. He even mentioned several other drawbacks of a performance pay linked to the number of cars sold, such as that employees would then tend to 'steal' potential customers from each other, and between locations.

It turned out that in reality, George does not use performance pay in his firm. Rather, he links his employees' salary to the *total* number of cars sold and the revenue generated in *all* three locations. Moreover, he became concerned about the cost of running his firm, and therefore decided to link the salaries to the overall profit, rather than to the revenue, of his firm.

While George is convinced that pay for performance is the right, and academically approved, way to compensate people, in reality he does not act accordingly. The salary he pays does not directly relate to the incentives to work hard. A particular employee is able to shirk profits from the work of all other employees. The harder they work, the higher is his salary. He has no incentive to work hard because he is able to free ride on the public good produced by his colleagues.

George's situation is typical. He would ruin his business if he paid his employees strictly according to performance. Instead, he is letting his experience of life guide him. He refrains from producing a public good situation by putting trust in individual employees and by letting them share *ex post* in the profit they helped to generate.

Joan's job situation is different. While she is equally convinced that 'pay for performance' is the right and only reasonable way to reward employees, she is not in a position to change the firm's compensation policy. The firm is large, and hierarchy dominates.

On being asked, it turned out that she is well aware of the high direct cost of running the compensation system. Her unit counts about 30 well-paid people. She even agrees that to identify and measure 'performance' in a large insurance firm is extremely difficult. Her knowledge is corroborated by a huge literature in management telling us that it is impossible to measure strictly performance when the activity is multi-dimensional (e.g. Argote et al., 2003; Latham et al., 2005; Neely and Neely, 2002).[1] Joan also realizes from her experience that 'you get what you pay for'. In economics, this principle is known

---

[1] This is an old topic in the social sciences, visible, for example, in the impossibility of aggregating individual preferences; see Arrow (1951), Sen (1970) and many other scholars.

as 'multiple tasking' (Holmstrom and Milgrom, 1991). Rational employees put all their effort into the activities on which their pay depends and disregard the rest. Clearly, if it is not possible to specify *in detail* all the activities expected by an employee, this may lead to inefficiencies and huge costs to the firm.

But there is one aspect that neither Joan nor the literature consider. There is a fundamental, but often neglected, principle in the social sciences: 'Whenever an index is important, it will be manipulated.' This 'manipulation principle' lies behind Goodhart's Law (see Chrystal et al., 2003) in monetary policy: as soon as the quantity of money has become a policy target, it will be manipulated. As a consequence, the systematic relationship between money and economic magnitudes such as national income no longer holds. Sociologist Donald Campbell has gained the same insight in a more general context (see Campbell, 1976).

For the case of performance wages the 'manipulation principle' means that the employees invest effort to influence the performance index in their favour. Indeed, often it is more advantageous to them to manipulate the performance measure than to put effort into working well according to the relevant performance index.

Various motivations to work

Joan and George have quite typical views about why people work, namely because they are paid for doing so. If not compensated by money, they would not work. This seems so obvious that it is not called into question. This view is supported by standard economic theory as can be seen from any textbook on microeconomics. The classical supply curve of labour (as shown in Figure 7.1) is based on the relative price effect which translates this view into a marginal effect: the higher the monetary compensation offered, the more work in terms of time and intensity will be offered (see Becker, 1976, 1993).

Recently, economic theorists have taken into account that people are not only extrinsically motivated but that they may to some extent also be intrinsically motivated. This means that the supply curve of labour indicates that people are willing to put in work even if they are not paid (see Figure 7.2).

The extent of intrinsically supplied work is subject to a psychological anomaly. Most people state that they have a considerable amount of intrinsic motivation. This is reflected by the large amount of voluntary

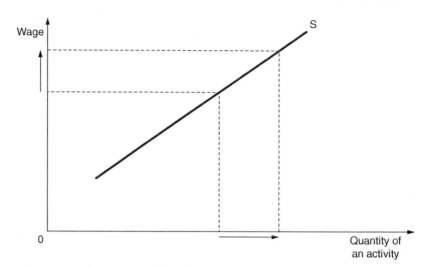

Figure 7.1 Relative price effect of supply curve

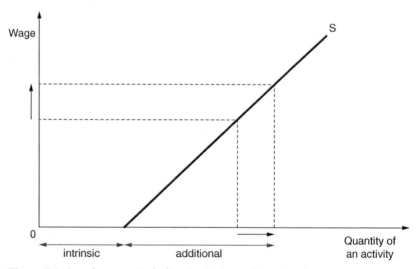

Figure 7.2 Supply curve including intrinsic work motivation

work offered in most countries of the world. Not all voluntary work is done because people are willing to undertake work they find gratifying as such. Some part is motivated by an effort to get experience in work or to establish connections useful for future employment. Nevertheless, the literature (see e.g. Deci et al., 1999; Lindenberg, 2001) clearly suggests that intrinsic motivation plays a large role that is consistent with what people state about their own motivation. Interestingly enough, the same people *assume* that *other* persons are less, or not at all, intrinsically motivated than they themselves. Others 'must' therefore be induced by money to work. This explains well the undisputed support for 'pay for performance'.

People educated in economics or management at a university that takes psychological economics or behavioural economics into account are by now aware of what has been termed 'motivational crowding theory' (Bénabou and Tirole, 2003; Frey, 1992, 1997; Frey and Jegen, 2001; Le Grand, 2003). It postulates a systematic effect of extrinsic on intrinsic motivation.

The 'crowding out effect' states that intrinsic motivation is undermined when people are paid to fulfil a task. Obviously, this effect can only take place if employees are to some extent intrinsically motivated when they perform a task. This is the first condition. For many types of work this condition does not hold, especially for menial, simple and repetitive work. Somewhat surprisingly to academic observers, empirical evidence suggests that even in these cases people are (to some extent) proud of performing their work well. The picture of human beings performing *only* if they are forced to do so by money or by command is wrong. The converse statement, of course, does not hold. Except wealthy persons, or those receiving income from some other source (e.g. from government) people could not survive without receiving monetary compensation. A realistic view of the labour market considers simultaneously extrinsic and intrinsic incentives.

There is a second condition for the crowding out effect. External intervention via monetary compensation must be considered by the employees in question as 'controlling'. This means that they feel that the wage offered for work makes it unnecessary, or even ridiculous, to maintain their intrinsic motivation for the task that they perform. Interest in the task as such has become unnecessary and is therefore crowded out. The extent to which individuals feel controlled by working for money differs widely. There are people who are rather resistant, especially those who are self-confident and refuse to have their inner feelings dictated by their employers. In that case, the crowding out effect is small or does not exist at all. Paying people to fulfil particular tasks then has no negative consequences for labour supply. In contrast, there are professions, in which individuals self-select or are selected into, where work is solely undertaken for

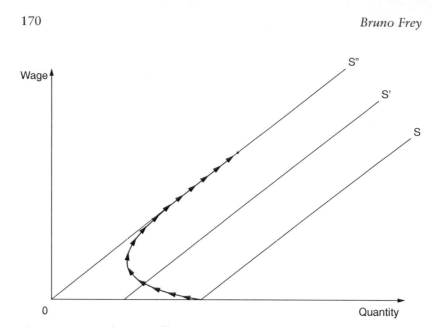

Figure 7.3 Crowding out effect on labour supply

monetary benefit. This may apply to the many materialistically ingrained employees in the financial sector. Even if they initially entered these sectors partly because of an interest in the work as such, they will quickly lose this intrinsic motivation. As soon as it is fully crowded out, a pay-for-performance scheme functions, and the more effort they put in their work, the more highly they are paid. It must immediately be added that this does not hold for all, or even a majority, of managers even in the financial sector, let alone in other sectors of the economy. When you ask a highly paid manager whether he or she would work more for more money, he or she invariably responds that they already work at full capacity. It follows that the monetary compensation has no direct incentive effect on work but serves as an indicator of one's worth compared to other managers.

Provided the two conditions hold, a pay increase may lead to a reduction in effort, as shown in Figure 7.3. The figure is drawn such that the relative price effect of higher pay for more work (a movement along the supply curve) is over-compensated by the reduction in intrinsic work motivation (a leftward shift of the supply curve). It must be noted that this crowding out effect does not necessarily obtain. It may well be that this effect is so weak that the relative price effect dominates. Motivation crowding theory does not postulate a mechanical relationship. Rather, it emphasizes that the interaction between extrinsic and intrinsic motivation depends on identifiable conditions.

Motivation crowding theory also considers a 'crowding in effect'. There are conditions under which external interventions via money lead to a strengthening of intrinsic work motivation. This is in particular the case when the compensation received indicates that the superiors therewith acknowledge the good work performed. Performance pay then serves to bolster the intrinsic interest in the work. As a result, a pay increase raises work time and effort by the relative price effect as well as by strengthening the underlying interest in the work itself.

Relevance for economic theory

Motivation crowding theory makes a relevant contribution to economics in several regards. It suffices to mention two aspects.

First, intrinsic motivation is closely linked to *creativity* (see the experimental evidence by Amabile, 1996, 1998), thereby establishing the basis for innovation and growth. It would be difficult to argue that people can be induced to be creative by offering them money. Rather, the search for new ideas is an intrinsic characteristic of extraordinary people. Creative people often do make money but this is more a consequence of seeking innovations, and not the underlying incentive. To build a dynamic theory of the economy merely based on extrinsic motives misses a crucial feature.

Second, the crowding out effect *reverses* the conventional relative price effect. A pay increase reduces, rather than increases work input, and therefore introduces a completely new element into theory. For quite some time, behavioural economics has taken into account 'anomalies' to received economic theory (see e.g. Dawes, 1988; Frey and Eichenberger, 1994; Kahneman et al., 1982; Thaler, 1992). Examples are:

- the endowment effect
- the reference point effect
- the opportunity cost effect
- certainty and small probability effects
- anchoring effects
- availability and representative biases
- over-confidence effects
- framing effects

These anomalies have greatly contributed to a better understanding of human behaviour than that offered by assuming the *homo economicus* position (e.g. Frey and Eichenberger, 1994; Simon, 1982). However, these anomalies only modify the strength of the relative price effect, and do not reverse it. In this sense, the crowding out effect is more fundamental as it postulates that the price system leads to behavioural reactions so far not considered in conventional economic theory.

How can people be induced to work?

Many scholars have learnt to accept Motivation crowding theory (see e.g. Bénabou and Tirole, 2003), but they rarely see any alternative to inducing people to work by offering them a corresponding monetary compensation. In the following, four alternatives are discussed (see also Frey and Osterloh, 2002, 2006; Osterloh and Frey, 2000, 2006). However, this does not mean that they can substitute for monetary pay, at least if the crowding out effect does not dominate. Rather, the alternatives discussed can serve as complements, if carefully applied.

Careful selection and job matching

When hiring, a firm's representatives can make a great effort to find persons who are interested in the task and do not only seek the job because of the monetary compensation attached. A close matching of the job requirements with the applicant's interests and capacities helps to have staff that feel part of the firm. When care is taken to have intrinsically motivated employees in appropriate jobs, the management can 'let them work'. The need for monitoring and controlling is strongly reduced, which makes the firm more efficient.

Conserving intrinsic motivation

The least a successful employment policy by a firm can do is to conserve the intrinsic motivation its workers originally have. This sounds trivial but is often neglected. The joy of work is in many cases undermined not only by trying to steer employees' behaviour solely by money, but also by supervising and monitoring them too closely. Many people intrinsically interested in the work they do have been de-motivated by bureaucratic interferences – and not only in the public sector.

Fixed wage and ex post *overall evaluation*

As mentioned above, money may be used as a signal of appreciation if the recipient perceives that his or her work has been well done. Bonuses may serve this purpose but there is always the danger that the intrinsic motivation will be crowded out. A wage independent of reaching pre-determined targets does not run this danger. The superiors make clear that they pay an adequate (market) salary but that the employees' task is to work – rather than to try to game the pay-for-performance system. The adjustment of the fixed wage over time is based on an overall *ex post* evaluation of the employee. If such evaluation is considered to be fair by the employees, they are even ready to accept a lower wage increase, or no increase at all; the employees trade off any potential wage increase against the procedural utility gained by the fair process (on procedural utility and the respective empirical evidence, see Frey et al., 2004).

Building up intrinsic motivation

A more effective way to raise intrinsic motivation is to emphasize the good performance of the worker by handing out an *award*. This possibility is discussed in more depth in the next section.

Awards as incentives

Ubiquity of awards

There is an enormous number of awards in the form of orders, medals, decorations, prizes, titles and other honours. There are few, if any, areas of society in which awards are not used. Awards are equally ubiquitous in monarchies as in staunch republics. In the French Republic, for instance, the Légion d'honneur plays an important role, and the United Kingdom has an extensive system of awards and titles (House of Commons, 2004). In the United States, the President and Congress bestow medals, and the armed forces give purple hearts, bronze and silver stars (Cowen, 2000, p. 93). It is well known that a flood of orders, medals and titles (such as 'Hero of the Soviet Union' or 'Hero of Socialist Labour') was handed out in communist countries, as well as in right- and left-wing dictatorships.

Awards are also hugely popular in the arts, culture and the media. Prominent examples are the Academy Awards (Oscars), the prizes handed out by the film festivals at Cannes, Venice and Berlin, the Booker Prize and the Prix Goncourt in literature, and the Pulitzer Prizes. In sports, athletes receive the honour of being chosen 'Sports Personality of the Year', and of being admitted into one of the many halls of fame. The International Football Association bestowed on Pelé and Franz Beckenbauer the 'FIFA Centennial Order of Merit'. Awards are also used extensively in religious organizations. The Vatican, for instance, confers many different awards, such as the Order of Christ and the Order of the Holy Sepulchre of Jerusalem.

Academia also has an elaborate and extensive system of awards. Consider the universities handing out the titles of honorary doctor, professor or senator, or professional associations awarding an enormous number of medals, the most important one probably being the Fields Medal in mathematics. There are prestigious fellowships in the many academies of science (e.g. Fellow of the Royal Society). And then, of course, there are the Nobel Prizes.

There is a widespread use of awards in the corporate sectors of market economies. Many firms honour their employees as 'Employee of the Year', 'the Month' or 'the Week'. There seems no limit to the ingenuity of inventing new awards. The media support this by creating their own awards such as 'Best Managers' (*BusinessWeek*), 'CEOs of the Year' (*Financial World*) or 'Person of the Year' (*Time*). In Britain, the leaders of many large corporations are decorated with orders and titles.

Literature

The science of *phaleristics* (the Greek and Roman word for award) has produced a large literature on *specific* awards, in particular on orders, decorations and medals. It is mainly devoted to presenting the historical facts about individual orders as well as the rules according to which an order is handed out. Useful discussions on the present state of orders, focusing on Britain, are provided in Phillips (2004) and a report by the House of Commons (2004). Awards and related issues have been discussed in a considerable literature in sociology.[2]

---

[2] For example, Bourdieu (1979); Braudy (1986); De Botton (2004); Elster (1983); and Marmot (2004).

With few exceptions, these works address social recognition and distinctions in general, but do not analyse particular types of awards. The psychological literature (a survey is given in Stajkovic and Luthans, 2003) provides important insights into the mechanisms through which awards work on the individual level. Personnel psychology systematically compares the impact of different human resource practices on performance (see Combs et al., 2006 for a recent meta-analysis).

Despite the importance of awards in society, economists have largely disregarded them. Some literature in economics provides insights into isolated aspects of awards such as the signal emitted (see Spence, 1974), the competition induced (e.g. Lazear and Rosen, 1981), and in terms of incentives in a principal–agent relationship in a firm (surveys are provided by Gibbons, 1998 and Prendergast, 1999). In behavioural economics, aspects such as esteem, identity, status and reputation have been analysed.[3]

There may be various reasons why economists have so far neglected awards. First, as they are not fungible, awards may be considered inferior instruments for inducing effort compared to monetary compensation. Second, awards may just be one result of high motivation and success and not a contributing cause. Third, awards may not be perceived as different from monetary incentives. It could be assumed that they are only valued by the recipients due to the ancillary bonus or to the extent to which they induce increases in future income. However, it has been demonstrated in experiments that people value status independently of any monetary consequence; they are even willing to incur material costs to obtain it (Huberman et al., 2004).

Differences between awards and pay

Awards and monetary compensation have various characteristics differentiating them (see Besley, 2005; Frey, 2007; Frey and Neckermann, 2006; Neckermann and Frey, 2007):

---

[3] Examples of recent economic works addressing aspects related to awards are: analyses of status incentives (e.g. Auriol and Renault, 2001; Besley and Ghatak, 2008; Dubey and Geanakoplos, 2005; Ederer and Patacconi, 2004; Fershtman et al., 2001; Loch et al., 2001), rewards as feedback (Sururov and van de Ven, 2006), social recognition (Brennan and Pettit, 2004; English, 2005), reciprocity (e.g. Fehr and Gächter, 2000; Fehr and Schmidt, 2004), identity (Akerlof and Kranton, 2005), conventions (e.g. Young, 1993), superstars and positional goods (Frank, 1985; Hirsch, 1976; Rosen, 1981).

- The material costs of awards may be very low, or even nil, for the donor, but the value to the recipient may be very high. In contrast to monetary compensation, award givers need to take into account that the value of an award decreases with the number of awards in circulation since the prestige associated with winning an award depends on its scarcity.
- Awards are always given in public, normally at a specially arranged ceremony. In contrast, the size of monetary compensations, i.e. salaries, tends to be hidden.
- Accepting an award establishes a special relationship, in which the recipient owes (some measure of) loyalty to the donor. The respective contract is, however, tacit, incomplete and difficult, or even impossible, to enforce by the donor. Monetary compensation in contrast typically does not induce loyalty. Quite the opposite is true: payments can easily be used as justification for working for a principal/an organization that one publicly denounces.
- Awards are better incentive instruments than monetary payments when the recipients' performance can be determined only vaguely. Criteria for awards are typically a broad and not clearly specified set. Therefore, performance can be globally evaluated *ex post*. Monetary compensation, on the other hand, almost always needs to be clearly specified contractually *ex ante*.
- Awards are less likely than monetary compensation to crowd out the intrinsic motivation of the recipients. Typically, awards are perceived as supportive rather than controlling. This lies in the social nature of awards and the fact that the associated *ex post* performance measurement is less intrusive and allows the consideration of input factors such as motivation and work ethic as well as a broad assessment of performance dimensions that are hard to measure. Further, unlike pure monetary payments, awards are less likely to destroy the signal value of actions requiring special commitment or of actions beyond what is typically expected. When payments are involved it is not clear for observers whether the behaviour was driven by dedication and commitment or solely by the money. In principle the same holds for awards because they are also extrinsic incentives. However, awards are less powerful extrinsic incentives, so that the signal value of special behaviours is raised.

- Awards are not taxed, while monetary income is. In countries with high marginal tax rates it is therefore relatively more attractive to receive an untaxed award than to receive a highly taxed monetary compensation.

These considerations make it clear that there are indeed many major differences between awards and monetary compensation that are well worth analysing.

Channels of influence

Awards work as incentives via a number of channels that have been shown to influence human behaviour. Among others, awards motivate because:

- winning an award makes the recipient feel good about himself irrespective of monetary or status consequences, hence even without others knowing about the award;
- they are typically conferred by a principal whose opinion the agent values, and because of the social prestige they generate and recognition they bring from the peer group;
- they are typically set up as tournaments and many agents enjoy competing, i.e. working towards an award generates procedural utility, and hence pleasure irrespective of the outcome;
- awards create and establish role models: they distribute information about successful and desirable behaviour and create loyalty.

While the general term 'award' implies that the different existing honours and prizes pertain to the same group of incentives, specific awards differ vastly from one another in terms of what component is most salient. Some awards are clearly competition prizes, while others more closely resemble feedback or praise. Some awards are valuable in monetary terms, while others come with neither monetary nor other material benefits. Among state orders awards can be identified that convey legislative power, such as the title of a Lord among the British orders, while other orders are purely honorific, such as the title Knight. Awards differ greatly with respect to the social recognition and prestige they will bring to the recipient. In general, awards bestowed within private institutions including those in for-profit firms differ from other awards mainly in that the money coming with them is of greater importance. Nevertheless, managers clearly indicate that they use awards to give special recognition that goes above and beyond pure material compensation to chosen employees.

The realm of awards is quite vague. The semantics are unclear and the various types of awards are not well defined. These unclear distinctions are no accident, but an important feature of awards.

Criteria

All awards share certain essential features that warrant the analysis of awards as one phenomenon. Awards are handed out according to a *broad set* of criteria. Typically, the various performance dimensions and how these are weighed to determine the winner are not clearly specified. Consider, for example, an award for exceptional customer service. It is not normally made explicit which specific behaviours count and how important these are. Rather, the criteria are left vague. This way, donors, for instance, avoid the risk that employees will only focus on the activities specified rather than on whatever would be best in the situation at hand. This leads to another feature of awards, namely the *subjective element* in determining the winner. Also, awards are *not enforceable*. While awards are typically handed out in a manner that makes the reasons for choosing the particular recipient transparent, non-recipients cannot claim an award by trying to establish that their performance was better. In Germany as well as in many other countries state orders are, for instance, the only governmental acts besides presidential pardons that are not subject to administrative law. A further characteristic of awards is their *tournament character* and the fact that all awards serve as incentives, be it direct or indirect. Awards are direct incentives when they are announced *ex ante* to be granted for certain kinds of performance within a given period of time, such as the customer service award granted for the best customer service in the current year. Awards are indirect incentives when they stimulate other individuals to engage in similar tasks by establishing that this kind of behaviour is deemed desirable. Examples of awards with indirect incentive effects are state orders handed out for exceptional moral courage, such as saving lives.

Conclusion

Most people take it for granted that 'people work because they are paid accordingly'. It follows that 'pay for performance' must be the correct system to compensate employees. Those who perform better than the target set should receive a higher pay, those who perform less well than the target should get a lower wage, or should be dismissed.

A look at how employees are paid in reality suggests that pay for performance is rarely strictly applied. Practitioners are aware of the negative consequences of applying this system. Some of the negative consequences have been extensively discussed in the literature (e.g. Bebchuk and Fried, 2004). The most important are that:

- 'performance' is rarely identifiable and measurable to any degree of precision – except perhaps for very simple tasks;
- the 'multiple tasking effect' leads to possibly important, but unpredictable, tasks being neglected;
- the performance targets are systematically manipulated by the employees subjected to them.

This chapter goes beyond these well-known problems of performance pay and focuses on the effect of various incentives for employees to work. To consider only extrinsic motivation is too narrow; when intrinsic motivation is taken into account possible negative effects of pay for performance become visible, in particular the 'crowding out effect'.

There are viable alternatives to pay for performance:

- carefully selecting and socializing new employees;
- maintaining the intrinsic work motivation people have;
- using fixed wages and *ex post* overall evaluations;
- offering people awards to cater for human beings' fundamental desire for recognition.

Awards have several important advantages over pay for performance. One is that they allow the use of vague, broad and subjective criteria that are crucial when it comes to unexpected, or impossible to expect, events. Awards enable superiors to reward employees who act in their interest under extraordinary circumstances. While awards have been rarely analysed in economics, they are widely used in the public sector, in the arts, sports and media, in academia, as well as in the for-profit corporate sector. The fact that awards are used in so many areas of human life should serve as a signal that they might fulfil an important role.

It is high time to give up the idea that money is the only thing that matters for performance. Rather, there are a variety of incentives to be considered: in addition to the extrinsic incentives provided by monetary pay or other material compensation, the symbolic value of awards and intrinsic motivation are crucial.

References

Akerlof, G. A. and Kranton, R. E. (2005). Identity and the Economics of Organization. *Journal of Economic Perspectives* 19: 9–32.

Amabile, T. (1996). *Creativity in Context: Update to the Social Psychology of Creativity*. Boulder: Westview Press.

(1998). How to Kill Creativity. *Harvard Business Review* 76(5): 76–87.

Argote, L., McEvily, B. and Reagans, R. (2003). Managing Knowledge in Organizations: An Integrative Framework and Review of Emerging Themes. *Management Science* 49(4): 571–82.

Arrow, K. J. (1951). *Individual Values and Social Choice*. New York: Wiley.

Auriol, E. and Renault, R. (2001). Incentive Hierarchies. *Annales d'Économie et de Statistique* 63: 261–82.

Bebchuk, L. A. and Fried, J. (2004). *Pay Without Performance: The Unfulfilled Promise of Executive Compensation*. Cambridge, MA: Harvard University Press.

Becker, G. S. (1976). *The Economic Approach to Human Behavior*. University of Chicago Press.

(1993). Nobel Lecture: The Economic Way of Looking at Behavior. *Journal of Political Economy* 101: 385–409.

Bénabou, R. and Tirole, J. (2003). Intrinsic and Extrinsic Motivation. *Review of Economic Studies* 70: 489–520.

Besley, T. (2005). *Notes on Honours*. Mimeo. London School of Economics.

Besley, T. and Ghatak, M. (2008). Status Incentives. *American Economic Review* 98: 206–11.

Bourdieu, P. (1979). *La Distinction: Critique Sociale du Jugement*. Paris: Les Éditions de Minuit.

Braudy, L. (1986). *The Frenzy of Renown: Fame and Its History*. New York: Oxford University Press.

Brennan, G. and Pettit, P. (2004). *The Economy of Esteem: An Essay on Civil and Political Society*. Oxford University Press.

Campbell, D. T. (1976). *Assessing the Impact of Planned Social Change*. Occasional Paper Series 8. The Public Affairs Center, Dartmouth College.

Chrystal, K., Mizen, A. and Mizen, P. D. (2003). Goodhart's Law: Its Origins, Meaning and Implications for Monetary Policy. In P. D. Mizen (ed.), *Central Banking, Monetary Theory and Practice: Essays in Honour of Charles Goodhart*. vol. 1. Cheltenham: Edward Elgar, pp. 221–43.

Combs, J., Hall, A. and Ketchen, D. (2006). How Much Do High-Performance Work Practices Matter? A Meta-Analysis of their Effects on Organizational Performance. *Personnel Psychology* 59: 501–28.

Cowen, T. (2000). *What Price Fame?* Cambridge, MA: Harvard University Press.

Dawes, R. M. (1988). *Rational Choice in an Uncertain World*. San Diego and New York: Harcourt Brace Jovanovich.

De Botton, A. (2004). *Status Anxiety*. New York: Pantheon Books.

Deci, E. L., Koestner, R. and Ryan, R. M. (1999). A Meta-Analytic Review of Experiments Examining the Effects of Extrinsic Rewards on Intrinsic Motivation. *Psychological Bulletin* 125(6): 627–68.

Dubey, P. and Geanakoplos, J. (2005). *Grading in Games of Status: Marking Exams and Setting Wages*. Mimeo. Cowles Foundation, Yale University.

Ederer, F. and Patacconi, A. (2004). *Interpersonal Comparisons, Status and Ambition in Organisations*. Mimeo. Department of Economics, University of Oxford.

Elster, J. (1983). *Sour Grapes: Studies in the Subversion of Rationality*. Cambridge University Press.

English, J. F. (2005). *The Economy of Prestige: Prizes, Awards, and the Circulation of Cultural Value*. Cambridge, MA: Harvard University Press.

Fehr, E. and Gächter, S. (2000). Fairness and Retaliation: The Economics of Reciprocity. *Journal of Economic Perspectives* 14: 159–81.

Fehr, E. and Schmidt, K. (2004). Fairness and Incentives in a Multi-Task Principal–Agent Model. *Scandinavian Journal of Economics* 106: 453–74.

Fershtman, C., Weiss, Y. and Hvide, H. (2001). *Status Concerns and the Organization of Work*. Mimeo. Eitan Berglas School of Economics, Tel Aviv University.

Frank, R. H. (1985). *Choosing the Right Pond: Human Behavior and the Quest for Status*. New York: Oxford University Press.

Frey, B. S. (1992). Tertium Datur: Pricing, Regulating and Intrinsic Motivation. *Kyklos* 45: 161–84.

(1997). *Not Just for the Money: An Economic Theory of Personal Motivation*. Cheltenham: Edward Elgar.

(2007). Awards as Compensation. *European Management Review* 4: 6–14.

Frey, B. S. and Eichenberger, R. (1994). Economic Incentives Transform Psychological Anomalies. *Journal of Economic Behavior and Organization* 23(2): 215–34.

Frey, B. S. and Jegen, R. (2001). Motivation Crowding Theory. *Journal of Economic Surveys* 15(5): 589–611.

Frey, B. S. and Neckermann, S. (2006). Auszeichnungen: Ein vernachlässigter Anreiz. *Perspektiven der Wirtschaftspolitik* 7: 271–84.

Frey, B. S., Benz, M. and Stutzer, A. (2004). Introducing Procedural Utility: Not Only What, but Also How Matters. *Journal of Institutional and Theoretical Economics* 160(3): 377–401.

Frey, B. S. and Osterloh, M. (eds.) (2002). *Successful Management by Motivation: Balancing Intrinsic and Extrinsic Incentives*. Berlin: Springer Verlag.

Frey, B. S. and Osterloh, M. (2006). *Evaluations: Hidden Costs, Questionable Benefits, and Superior Alternatives*. IEW Working Paper No. 302. University of Zurich.

Gibbons, R. (1998). Incentives in Organizations. *Journal of Economic Perspectives* 12: 115–32.

Hirsch, F. (1976). *Social Limits to Growth*. Cambridge, MA: Harvard University Press.

Holmstrom, B. and Milgrom, P. (1991). Multitask Principal-Agent Analyses: Incentive Contracts, Asset Ownership, and Job Design. *Journal of Law, Economics, and Organization* 7(2): 24–52.

House of Commons, Select Committee on Public Administration (2004). *A Matter of Honour: Reforming the Honours System. Fifth Report of Session 2003–04*. London: Stationery Office.

Huberman, B., Loch, C. and Öncüler, A. (2004). Status as a Valued Resource. *Social Psychology Quarterly* 67: 103–14.

Kahneman, D., Slovic, P. and Tversky, A. (eds.) (1982). *Judgement under Uncertainty: Heuristics and Biases*. Cambridge University Press.

Latham, G. P., Almost, J., Mann, S. and Moore, C. (2005). New Developments in Performance Management. *Organizational Dynamics* 34: 77–87.

Lazear, E. and Rosen, S. (1981). Rank-Order Tournaments as Optimum Labor Contracts. *Journal of Political Economy* 89: 841–64.

Le Grand, J. (2003). *Motivation, Agency, and Public Policy*. Oxford University Press.

Lindenberg, S. (2001). Intrinsic Motivation in a New Light. *Kyklos* 54: 317–43.

Loch, C., Yaziji, M. and Langen, C. (2001). The Fight for the Alpha Position: Channeling Status Competition in Organizations. *European Management Journal* 19: 16–25.

Marmot, M. G. (2004). *The Status Syndrome: How Social Standing Affects our Health and Longevity*. New York: Times Books/Henry Holt.

Neckermann, S. and Frey, B. S. (2007). *Awards as Incentives*. IEW Working Paper No. 334. University of Zurich.

Neely, A. D. and Neely, A. (eds.) (2002). *Business Performance Measurement: Theory and Practice*. Cambridge University Press.

Osterloh, M. and Frey, B. S. (2000). Motivation, Knowledge Transfer, and Organizational Forms. *Organization Science* 11: 538–50.

(2006). Shareholders Should Welcome Knowledge Workers as Directors. *Journal of Management and Governance* 10(3): 325–45.

Phillips, Sir H. (2004). *Review of the Honours System*. London: Cabinet Office.

Prendergast, C. (1999). The Provision of Incentives in Firms. *Journal of Economic Literature* 37: 7–63.

Rosen, S. (1981). The Economics of Superstars. *American Economic Review* 71: 845–58.

Sen, A. (1970). *Collective Choice and Social Welfare*. San Francisco: Holden-Day; republished 1979, Amsterdam: North Holland.

Simon, H. A. (1982). *Models of Bounded Rationality*. Cambridge, MA: MIT Press.

Spence, A. (1974). *Market Signaling*. Cambridge, MA: Harvard University Press.

Stajkovic, A. and Luthans, F. (2003). Behavioral Management and Task Performance in Organizations: Conceptual Background, Meta-Analysis, and Test of Alternative Models. *Personnel Psychology* 56: 155–94.

Sururov, A. and van de Ven, J. (2006). *Discretionary Rewards as a Feedback Mechanism*. Working Paper 2006-16. Amsterdam Centre for Law & Economics.

Thaler, R. H. (1992). *The Winner's Curse: Paradoxes and Anomalies of Economic Life*. New York: Free Press.

Young, H. P. (1993). The Evolution of Conventions. *Econometrica* 61: 57–84.

7.1 | *A response to Frey*

MATTEO M. GALIZZI

In his chapter, Bruno Frey takes an original look at 'pay for performance', arguably one of the most quoted lessons from economic science. The belief that people work because they are paid accordingly is one of the conceptual cornerstones commonly taken for granted by economists, and implies that those who perform better than predefined targets should receive higher pay, while those who fail to do should be paid less, or even dismissed.

Yet, Frey notices, a look at reality suggests that pay for performance is rarely applied in strict terms. Frey argues that this is because practitioners are rightly aware of the negative consequences of implementing a 'pure' pay-for-performance system, and reviews the main negative consequences discussed in the literature (interestingly mostly from management studies): (i) performance is rarely identifiable and measurable to any degree of precision, except for very simple tasks; (ii) the 'multiple tasking effect' implies that possibly important, but not included, tasks are completely neglected as employees, rationally, put all their efforts in the activities on which their pay depends; (iii) the performance targets are systematically manipulated by the employees, who can invest much effort in influencing the performance index in their favour.

Frey goes beyond these problems in pay for performance and more generally addresses whether it is sensible to stick to the concept of extrinsic motivation as a channel through which to incentivize higher levels of effort and output. He refers to motivational crowding theory, to which he has been the principal contributor, and argues that pay for performance can crowd out workers' intrinsic motivation.

Frey then discusses four alternatives to pay for performance that can induce people to work, namely (i) carefully selecting and hiring the job candidates genuinely interested in the task, and closely matching the job requirements with applicants' interests and capabilities; (ii) continuously maintaining intrinsic motivation, for instance by not

184

undermining the joy of work with excessive pressure for measuring outputs, too close supervision and monitoring, or too many bureaucratic interferences; (iii) using fixed wages, adjusted over time based on an overall *ex post* evaluation of the employee, according to evaluation procedures that are considered fair by the employee; (iv) recognizing good performance by handing out awards, rather than monetary payments.

Frey concludes by discussing the role and nature of awards. Interestingly, awards and prizes have been rarely studied in economics, despite the fact they are widely used in the real world (and perhaps arguably even more than narrowly defined pay-for-performance schemes), which signals that they play an important role in a broad variety of contexts: from academia and research to corporate business, from politics, institutions and regimes to sport, from arts to journalism.

Frey notes that awards have some important advantages over pay for performance. First, they allow the use of vague and broad subjective criteria that better serve the purpose of compensating overall *ex post* performance, and not just narrowly defined tasks. Second, thanks to their high symbolic value, they cater to the human need for recognition and thus foster, rather than crowd out, intrinsic motivation.

Frey's chapter is highly inspiring and enjoyable, and convincingly constructed. It contains a novel perspective on the economics of awards and prizes that will motivate further work in this direction, and also offers other fascinating insights; for instance, when Frey argues that intrinsic motivation is ultimately linked to creativity.

Eight minor thoughts came to my mind on corresponding specific aspects where perhaps stronger supportive arguments are needed if future work is planned in this area. Finally, I offer a few thoughts on some experimental design issues in testing the role of awards compared to financial incentives.

First, the discussion of the negative consequences of pay for performance perhaps deserves stronger support. Direct empirical evidence may be brought forward to show that pay for performance has serious limitations. Some interesting insights, for instance, come from recent experiments directly testing the relationship between pay for performance and effort (Ariely et al., 2009). Although rather recent in economics, this line of work refers back to psychological research documenting the 'choking under pressure' phenomenon; that is, situations where increased effort can result in a *decrement* in performance (Baumeister, 1984).

Ariely et al. (2009) explicitly discuss four channels through which choking under pressure can occur in the presence of pay-for-performance schemes: (i) effort above an optimal level can produce supra-optimal levels of arousal, which in turn can decrease performance; (ii) consciously thinking about the task shifts control of behaviour from automatic to controlled mental processes, for tasks which are highly practised and automated; (iii) large incentives can occupy the mind and attention of the worker with thoughts about the reward itself, distracting her from the task; and, perhaps most importantly, (iv) specific pay-for-performance incentives can narrow individuals' focus to some dimensions of the work, which can be detrimental for jobs that 'involve insight or creativity' (Ariely et al., 2009, p. 453), a situation which closely evokes the link between creativity and intrinsic motivation mentioned by Frey.

Second, the argument that intrinsic motivation coincides with creativity is indeed fascinating. Intrinsic motivation and creativity are both associated with a high sense of fulfilment with a task or a job, and this is more likely to be the case when the task is a direct expression of individual creativity, that is, when creativity shapes the final outcomes and the reflection of individual input is evidently and universally recognized. From this perspective, the tasks where one should observe higher levels of creativity and intrinsic motivation are the ones which are the opposite of the 'alienating' works in the Marxian sense: the ones where the worker cannot see the final outcome of her effort. Although some evidence exists on the links between creativity and subjective well-being (e.g. Dolan and Metcalfe, 2012), more experimental and empirical evidence is needed on the exact relationship between intrinsic motivation and creativity.

Third, an aspect which perhaps deserves stronger support is the argument that pay for performance is rarely applied in a strict sense in the real world. While I agree that it is rarely applied in its 'pure' form, virtually all job contracts are *partly* based on pay for performance, and this practice is rapidly spreading across many working contexts to which this scheme was not traditionally applied, from medical doctors to researchers, from judges to school teachers. Frey is absolutely right in pointing out that, despite its increasing diffusion, there is not yet conclusive scientific evidence on whether pay for performance (i) works in any context; (ii) works better than other compensation schemes; and (iii) has no unintended consequences spilling over into other aspects of the job relationship, for instance by crowding out intrinsic motivation. One can claim that the widespread use of pay-for-performance schemes implies that crowding out of intrinsic motivation is rarely a serious concern in real-world contexts, perhaps because it is believed that many jobs do not imply any intrinsic motivation at all. As argued by Frey, this may be because much work is tedious and menial, or because workers self-select into jobs which are coherent with their (lack of) intrinsic motivation, or because the original motivation quickly disappears, absorbed by more materialistic considerations, as for some jobs in the financial sector, for instance. Yet, the abnormal compensation schemes and performance-based bonuses in the financial sector have been blamed as facilitating factors for some of the distorted practices that led to the boom and bust of the financial markets and the onset of the 2008 financial crisis. The observation that many highly paid traders and financial managers, if asked whether they would work for more money, invariably respond that they are already at full capacity, is a good argument to agree with Frey that in those cases extra monetary compensation cannot possibly push further effort, and only serves as an indicator of one's worth compared to colleagues. One may thus provocatively argue why, if it is only for signalling the worth of good employees compared to colleagues, banks and financial companies should not opt for handing out 'pure awards' with no money attached to them, rather than costly bonuses.

Fourth, there seems to be room for more direct experimental evidence also on a couple of claims related to the overall perception of intrinsic motivation, namely to test (a) whether people indeed assume that others are less, or not at all, intrinsically motivated than they are; and (b) whether more intrinsically motivated individuals are also more keen on thinking so than not-so-intrinsically motivated subjects. Similarly, one may wonder whether it is possible to provide details of some direct evidence in support of the claim that even in menial, simple and repetitive work, employees are proud of performing their work well.

Fifth, the dichotomy between financial incentives, on the one hand, and 'symbolic' awards on the other, seems more appropriate as a benchmark than a fully fledged description of the ways people get paid for their work. There may actually be an entire spectrum of possible options to reward people for their work and performance, starting from 'pure' awards with no monetary component at all, to bundles of both awards and monetary prizes which still entail a high symbolic and signalling value (e.g. Nobel Prizes), to in-kind compensatory awards (e.g. books for best MSc student, health-related goods, gym fees, health insurance schemes) to earmarked monetary compensation (school fees for the children, health insurance for the spouse, research funds for conferences, travel expenses and so on). A taxonomy of different effects attached to different rewards may be useful.

Sixth, and related, on the links between awards and intrinsic motivation, in principle, it can indeed be argued that the fact that they are typically handed out in public ceremonies makes awards also evident signs of status and public recognition, which also appeal to *extrinsic* motivation. Actually, in some circumstances, awards and prizes may appeal to extrinsic motivation even more than financial incentives. The fact that awards are handed out based on broad, rather than specific, criteria is a good point, but still disregards that many awards can be very specifically defined as well (e.g. the most-quoted paper in 2012 in a scientific journal, the best teaching scores, etc.).

Seventh, the argument that payments can be easily used as justification for working for a principal/employer that one publicly denounces, as opposed to the loyalty aspect inherently related to awards, is another excellent point, and relates to the typical argument used by an employee to break up, with very little sense of guilt, a working relationship to which the employer may expect some degree of loyalty: 'Well, they pay me more, what should I do?' Related to that, however, one may also notice that, in general, awards inherently require that the entity at the top of the hierarchy which assigns the award/prize is surrounded by a well-accepted and universally recognized authority. This is generally the case with awards from monarchies, and presidents of the republic, as well as prizes to best employees within private companies, awarded by the CEO, or to professionals assigned by the top governing board (Nobel Prize Selecting Committees, the Royal Society, etc.). In some other situations, however, such a universally well-accepted authority may not exist, or there is some ambiguity or 'noise' about the true authority, for instance because of two competing 'schools', 'views' or 'camps' in the field, organization or practice. If so, direct monetary compensation may be preferred by the recipient, since money has a more universally accepted and 'neutral' signalling power of recognition of the quality of the work, and the recipient may feel less exposed to an alleged involvement and engagement with a controversial awarding authority (e.g. a regime, a business club, a party-leaning magazine).

Finally, awards may cater to the human need for recognition by boosting self-esteem and confidence. This is not incompatible with crowding in intrinsic motivation, and may be the main behavioural driver to maintain and enhance intrinsic motivation. In order to disentangle this 'pure effect' of awards from potentially different behavioural explanations, a neat experimental test of the different crowding out/in effects of awards versus monetary payments would need to focus on a very specific type of award. In particular, (i) awards should not entail any type of economic consequences in terms of inherent monetary values attached to them (e.g. sums of money handed out together with the prize/award), or in terms of higher future monetary rewards, compensations or salaries as indirect consequences of the award itself (e.g. pay increases for being best employee, financial bonuses to the best banker/trader); and (ii) the existence, nature and type of the award, and the criteria on which it is based, should be publicly known in advance of the effort. Condition (i) is necessary (but not sufficient) to ensure that awards may be perceived, at least to some extent, as different from monetary incentives. Condition (ii) is necessary to partly deal with the concerns related to the causality direction between awards and effort discussed by Frey. In fact, if awards are not publicly known, or are handed out following completely obscure criteria, it is unlikely that corresponding effort will be exerted by individuals in advance.

Moreover, by their 'symbolic' nature, awards present peculiar aspects compared to money, which necessarily introduce some degree of confounding explanatory factors. For instance, in order to estimate the 'pure effect' of awards as a booster of personal self-esteem and motivation, one should also be able to control for the award's value to the recipient as a factor satisfying human vanity and need of being in the spotlight. As awards are often quintessentially assigned in public ceremonies or announcements, disentangling the two effects may be difficult in practice. Similarly, due to the fact that awards are typically handed out by a donor whom the recipient respects, the symbolic value of an award also incorporates a sense of gratification from having a special relationship with a 'personal idol'. All in all, it seems that more direct experimental evidence is needed to compare head-to-head monetary incentives and awards across a range of contexts.

References

Ariely, D., Gneezy, U., Loewenstein, G. and Mazar, A. (2009). Large Stakes and Big Mistakes. *Review of Economic Studies* 76: 451–69.

Baumeister, E. (1984). Choking Under Pressure: Self-Consciousness, and Paradoxical Effects of Incentives on Skilful Performance. *Journal of Personality and Social Psychology* 46(3): 610–20.

Dolan, P. and Metcalfe, P. (2012). The Relationship Between Innovation and Subjective Wellbeing. *Research Policy* 41(8): 1489–98.

8 | Influencing the financial behaviour of individuals: the mindspace way

PAUL DOLAN

Introduction

The question of how to improve population-wide financial capability is of increasing concern to policy-makers.[1] This chapter is focused on how recent advances in behavioural economics can help us better understand financial decision-making and, ultimately, to design interventions that make it easier for us to behave in ways that improve our financial capability. Behavioural economics seeks to combine the lessons from psychology with the laws of economics (Kahneman, 2003). The basic insight of behavioural economics is that human behaviour is guided not by the dictates of rationality embodied in a super-computer that can analyse the costs and benefits of every action. Instead, it is led by our very human, sociable, emotional and sometimes fallible brain. Psychologists have been studying these characteristics for more than a century, and writers and thinkers for much longer (Triplett, 1898). In a nutshell, the mental shortcuts that serve us so well in much of life can also get us into trouble, both as individuals and as societies.

Consistent with these observations, two very general paradigms have emerged in recent years – models that aim to change cognitions (such as beliefs and attitudes), and models that change the context (environment or situation) within which the person acts. Most traditional interventions prompt changes in cognitions to bring about behaviour change (Webb and Sheeran, 2006). This may involve providing new information or changing the incentives. The presumption is that people will analyse the relevant pieces of information, the numerous incentives offered to them, and act in ways that reflect their best interests. In contrast, the second route relies mostly on contextual changes to bring about behaviour change, where the focus is on the more automatic processes of judgement and influence.

---

[1] This chapter is a shorter version of Dolan et al. (2012).

The context model recognizes that people are sometimes seemingly irrational and inconsistent in their choices. As a result, it focuses more on changing behaviour without 'changing minds'.

We recognize that the most effective and sustainable changes in behaviour will come from the successful integration of interventions designed to change cognitions and contexts but, until recently, the second route has received relatively less attention from researchers on behaviour change than the first. We also recognize that there may be significant public concern over attempts at influencing citizen behaviour and there are many ethical and normative issues associated with the use of influence techniques that may depend on the automatic mind. We leave these issues to one side here, focusing on the evidence in relation to behaviour change which can then be fed into the normative debate.

The next section of the chapter reviews the evidence relating to the more traditional interventions that seek to improve financial capability through information and education designed to 'change minds'. These interventions are generally designed to improve financial literacy, making it easier for people to 'read' financial markets and improve financial decision-making. Such interventions can lead to changes in behaviour but, somewhat unsurprisingly, tend to work best on those who are most open to being informed and educated (who tend to be the better educated in the first place). Traditional interventions may therefore serve to widen the gap between those with high and low levels of financial capability and, insofar as policy-makers are interested in improving the financial capability of those at the lowest levels, there will be interest in looking for interventions to augment the standard approaches.

Recent developments in behavioural theory show that 'changing contexts' can have a powerful effect on behaviour: we can change behaviour by sometimes quite subtle changes to the environment or choice architecture. The following section therefore focuses on what we consider to be the nine most robust contextual effects on behaviour. It builds on a framework under the mnemonic 'mindspace' to represent nine effects on behaviour operating largely on the 'automatic' system: messenger, incentives, norms, defaults, salience, priming, affect, commitments and ego (Dolan et al., 2010). A review of the academic literature shows that all the effects have the potential to bring about changes in behaviour that increase financial capability. We are not yet at the stage, however, where we can say very much about the marginal impact of each effect, or about the impact of different combinations of effects.

The final section provides some concluding remarks. It is clear that changes in the 'choice architecture' (Thaler and Sunstein, 2008) can change behaviour, and banks and other financial institutions are increasingly alert to the opportunities that this brings. We therefore need to conduct further research – ideally using field experiments – into the robustness of the various environmental effects on different finance-related behaviours. Alongside this research, we should seek to establish the degree to which there is political will and public permission to change the choice architecture in particular ways. We have seen the power of defaults (changing from 'opt-in' to 'opt-out') in pension plans, for example, and there is certainly scope to go much further. It would help if there were better empirical evidence and normative debate before we go too far.

Changing minds

Traditional population-wide behaviour change interventions rely on using information, to provoke reflective mental processing, and as a result to change certain cognitions (beliefs) which can have a direct effect on behavioural responses. Such 'traditional' interventions attempt to educate agents to make better informed decisions. Thus, information leads to explicit appraisals of costs/risks and benefits related to different behaviours, and ultimately changes beliefs about such behaviours.

Giving out information has become a prominent part of the policy-maker's toolkit, and its importance is recognized through the impact of feedback (Thaler and Sunstein, 2008), which, as we shall see below, must be salient to recipients. Almost five decades of research on whether changes in cognitions engender population-wide behaviour change have been embodied in dozens of psychological theories and documented in hundreds of publications. The domains of application cover most maladaptive and problematic behaviours, which have been the focus of public policy concern. The richest cluster of models and data comprises numerous theories in social and health psychology, which assume that providing information that changes various beliefs produces intentions to change one's behaviour and these in turn affect behaviour (Vlaev and Dolan, 2009).

The impact of education and information on behaviour is consistent with the standard economic model, so the greater amount of information we have, the more likely we are to calculate accurately the payoffs for each decision. Financial literacy is low, however, and those who benefit from education and information are usually the better educated and informed to start with. Lusardi (2007; Lusardi et al., 2010) finds that financial illiteracy in the US is widespread. This is especially true for young adults, those with a low education, women, African-Americans and Hispanics. Interestingly, close to half of older workers do not know which type of pensions they have and the large majority of workers know little about the rules governing social security benefits. Notwithstanding the low levels of literacy that many individuals display, however, very few rely on the help of experts or financial advisers to make savings and investment decisions (Lusardi et al., 2010).

The evidence from Meier and Sprenger (2008) argues that a main limit to financial literacy is people's time preferences. They analyse a field experiment, where a short, free credit counselling and information programme was offered to more than 870 individuals. About 55 per cent chose to participate. Independently, they elicited time preferences using incentivized choice experiments both for individuals who selected into the programme and those who did not. They show that the two groups differ in their measured discount factors, in that individuals who choose to acquire personal financial information through the credit counselling programme discount the future less than individuals who choose not to participate, i.e. impatient people do not select the help and financial education.

Although it is difficult to draw conclusions about when individuals seek advice, the research literature strongly suggests that individuals who do solicit advice are more likely to follow that advice than individuals who receive unsolicited advice. Indeed, a robust finding is that individuals who receive advice by default tend to significantly discount it (Bonaccio and Dalal, 2006; Yaniv, 2004a, 2004b; Yaniv and Kleinberger, 2000). While explicitly solicited advice is perceived as helpful, unsolicited advice or imposed support is perceived as intrusive, which might even lead to the wrong behaviours (Deelstra et al., 2003; Goldsmith, 2000; Goldsmith and Fitch, 1997). In a related vein, Gino (2008) shows that individuals are significantly more receptive to advice that they pay for, rather than advice they get for free. This also resonates with a study by Waber et al. (2008), where patients recover faster with a placebo if they know that the placebo was expensive.

Since some individuals actively choose to seek out advice, any correlations between actual behaviour and advice may be the result of self-selection: individuals who are particularly prone to certain types of investing behaviour may also be more likely to seek out advisers. Hackethal et al. (2009) find that self-selection largely explains their finding of better outcomes for advisees in the context of German internet brokerage accounts. Hung and Yoong (2010) try to unpick causality by providing advice to those who ask for it and those who do not ask, and compare to a standard control group. They find that unsolicited advice has no effect on investment behaviour but when advice is optional, individuals with low financial literacy are more likely to seek it out. In spite of this negative selection on ability, individuals who actively solicit advice indeed perform better. Solicited advice does indeed appear to have more of an effect than unsolicited advice, although the magnitude of self-selection effects can over-shadow actual treatment effects.

In one of the largest studies on the impacts of financial education, Bernheim and Garrett (2003) found that savings rates increase significantly with the provision of employer-based education. Employees who are offered retirement education are far more likely to participate in 401(k) programmes, and to make larger contributions to their plans. The effects of education are particularly pronounced among those least inclined to save; however, there is some indication that education stimulates 401(k) contributions among high savers. Using data from Merrill Lynch, and a telephone survey of 3,500, the authors employ a difference-in-difference approach and assume that timing of the introduction of state-mandated financial education is exogenous. They conclude that the mandates led to a 1.5 per cent higher savings rate.

There is, however, evidence against Bernheim and Garrett's result. Using similar census data, Cole and Shastry (2008) allow for the inclusion of state fixed effects to control for unobserved, time-invariant heterogeneity in savings behaviour across states, as well as non-parametric identification of the treatment effect itself (rather than a linear measure of years-since-mandate-began employed by Bernheim and Garrett). Once these three enhancements are implemented, all treatment effects fall to precisely zero. Therefore, these results cast doubt on whether financial literacy as implemented under this programme had any effect at all.

Education and information may not be so successful because of the nature of people's beliefs about their future financial behaviour. Standard theories in economics and psychology assume that beliefs precede behaviour but an accumulation of evidence suggests that the causality may in fact go in the opposite direction. Goetzmann and Peles (1997) show that investors' choice of mutual funds tends to induce selective perception of information about the efficacy of their choice – they find that even well-informed investors tend to bias their perceptions about past performance.

Financial information and education designed to 'change minds' can change behaviour but, somewhat unsurprisingly, tend to work best on those who are most open to being informed and educated (who tend to be the better educated in the first place). Recent developments in behavioural theory show that 'changing contexts' can have a powerful effect on behaviour: we can change behaviour by sometimes quite subtle changes to the choice architecture.

Changing contexts: mindspace

The elements summarized in Table 8.1 and described in this section are those effects that, from laboratory and field research in social psychology, cognitive psychology and behavioural economics, I consider to be the most robust effects for changing behaviour that operate largely, but not exclusively, on the automatic system (see Dolan et al., 2010 for further details).

Messenger

We are heavily influenced by who communicates information, and this effect is mediated by the reactions we have to the source of that information (Durantini et al., 2006). In an experiment on enrolment in the Tax Deferred Account (TDA) in the US by Duflo and Saez (2003), a random sample of employees in a subset of departments were encouraged to attend a benefits information fair organized by a university. Enrolment in the TDA eleven months after the fair was significantly higher in departments where some individuals were treated (i.e. encouraged to attend) than in departments where nobody was treated. This finding may be the consequence of messenger effects and social norm effects. The messenger effects are that friends and

Table 8.1 *Mindspace categories*

Messenger	We are heavily influenced by who communicates information.
Incentives	Our responses to incentives are shaped by predictable mental shortcuts such as strongly avoiding losses.
Norms	We are strongly influenced by what others do.
Defaults	We 'go with the flow' of pre-set options.
Salience	Our attention is drawn to what is novel and seems relevant to us.
Priming	Our acts are often influenced by subconscious cues.
Affect	Our emotional associations can powerfully shape our actions.
Commitments	We seek to be consistent with our public promises, and reciprocate acts.
Ego	We act in ways that make us feel better about ourselves.

colleagues in the same department are telling their colleagues about the benefits of enrolment, and social norm effects operate by creating the norm of enrolment within a department.

Incentives

One of the basic laws of economics is that we respond to incentives. It is undoubtedly true that lowering interest rates makes people save less, spend more, and people are more likely to get into debt – these are rational responses. Gross and Souleles (2002) analyse how people respond to the supply of credit using a unique credit card dataset, and they find that increases in the limit to credit generates an immediate and significant rise in debt. Yet minor barriers to saving, such as application costs or waiting times, can also discourage participation out of proportion to the magnitude of the costs they impose (Bertrand et al., 2006). Our focus here is on predictable mental shortcuts to incentives that can be categorized in three broad ways: loss aversion, hyperbolic discounting and mental accounting.

First, losses loom larger than gains because we dislike losses more than we like gains of an equivalent amount (Kahneman and Tversky, 1979). Benartzi and Thaler (1995) showed that the equity premium is consistent with what loss-averse investors require to invest in stocks, provided that they evaluate their portfolio performance annually.

At horizons as short as a year, the likelihood that stocks under-perform relative to bonds requires a substantial compensation in terms of returns, given loss aversion. At a longer horizon, the likelihood of under-performance decreases, and the implied equity premium decreases. Their model assumes that investors, when evaluating the holdings, make no distinctions between realized gains/losses and 'paper' gains/losses. Investors, however, may treat the two utility carriers asymmetrically and derive utility (or disutility) only from realized gains and losses. Investors may even go as far as distancing themselves from the paper losses. For instance, Karlsson et al. (2005) show that, when the stock market is doing poorly, investors are substantially less likely to look at their holdings on the internet.

Second, we prefer to live for today at the expense of tomorrow. We usually prefer smaller, more immediate payoffs to larger, more distant ones. £10 today may be preferred to £12 tomorrow. This is consistent with standard economic theory. But when we, as many of us will, prefer £12 in eight days to £10 in a week's time, we are exhibiting dynamic inconsistency. This set of preferences implies that we have a very high discount rate for now compared to later, but a lower discount rate for later compared to later still. This is referred to as hyperbolic discounting. Ausubel (1999) provides tentative evidence of this impatience with credit card offers. Pre-introductory and post-introductory interest rates were randomized across the sample. Ausubel found that consumers are at least three times as responsive to changes in the introductory interest rate as compared to dollar-equivalent changes in the post-introductory interest rate. The extent to which this is explained by hyperbolic discounting, as opposed to simple impatience, requires further investigation.

Third, we mentally allocate money to discrete bundles. We think of money as sitting in different 'mental accounts' – salary, savings, expenses, etc. Spending is constrained by the amount sitting in different accounts and we are reluctant to move money between such accounts (Thaler, 1999). This means that accounts may encourage people to save or spend money by explicitly 'labelling' accounts for them, but still leaving freedom to choose how the money is used. Mental accounting means that identical incentives vary in their impact according to the context: people are willing to take a trip to save £5 off a £15 radio, but not to save £5 off a refrigerator costing £210 (Thaler, 1985). One recent policy innovation to encourage this behaviour has been the advent of federal tax split refunds in the US. Since 2007, individuals have been able to split their refunds across multiple accounts, including savings accounts and IRAs (Karlan and Morduch, 2010). Evidence suggests that this policy might work to encourage saving (Beverly et al., 2006).

Norms

We tend to do what those around us are already doing. Social and cultural norms are the behavioural expectations, or rules, within a society or group (Bicchieri, 2006). People often take their understanding of social norms from the behaviour of others. Some social norms have a powerful automatic effect on behaviour (e.g. buying on credit, being quiet in a library) and can influence actions in positive and negative ways. As mentioned earlier, Duflo and Saez (2003) show how norms operate in the context of enrolment into the TDA: the financial behaviour of work colleagues affects the decision about whether to enrol or not. In a novel study of the effect of norms and peer groups, Karlan (2007) tested whether better-connected groups perform better in terms of loan repayments and savings in Peru, where banks lend to groups rather than individuals. He finds that stronger social connections of the group lead to higher repayments and savings.

Defaults

Defaults are the options that are pre-selected if an individual does not make an active choice. The best examples of defaults have come from financial behaviour. Madrian and Shea (2001) consider the effect of a change in a default on the contribution rates in retirement savings in the US. Before the change, the default is non-participation in retirement savings; after the change, the default is participation at 3 per cent in a money market fund. Madrian and Shea (2001) find that the change in default has a very large impact: one year after joining the company, the participation rate in 401(k)s is 86 per cent for the treatment group and 49 per cent for the control group. Choi et al. (2004) extend the Madrian and Shea findings to show that they are generalizable to six companies in different industries with remarkably similar effect sizes. In a further study, Cronqvist and Thaler (2004) examine the choice of retirement funds in Sweden after the privatization of social security. They find that 43 per cent of new participants chose the default plan, despite the fact that the government encouraged individual choice, and despite the availability of 456 plans. Three years later, after the end of the advertisement campaign encouraging individual choice, the proportion choosing the default plan increased to 92 per cent.

Salience

Our behaviour is greatly influenced by what our attention is drawn to (Ariely et al., 2003; Kahneman and Thaler, 2006). In our everyday lives, we are engaged with a range of stimuli, but we tend to filter out unconsciously much irrelevant, redundant and familiar information. Simplifying the information in choice environments, for example by making the most relevant information salient, is therefore necessary. As an example of where attention is directed, Hossain and Morgan (2006) provide evidence from an online auction that people respond too much to the sales price and too little to the postage and packing price. Brown et al. (2008b) hypothesize that when consumers think in terms of consumption, annuities are viewed as valuable insurance, whereas when consumers think in terms of investment risk and return, the annuity becomes a risky asset because the payoffs depend on an uncertain date of death. To test this, they randomized frames to a group of over 50s, and found that the vast majority of individuals prefer an annuity over alternative products when the question is framed in terms of consumption, while the majority of individuals prefer non-annuitized products when the questions are presented in terms of risk and return. Brown et al. (2008a) demonstrate that this result is not dependent on the initial purchase price.

Priming

Priming explains that people's subsequent behaviour may be altered if they are first exposed to (primed by) certain stimuli such as words, sights or sensations (and these effects are real and robust). Priming has the potential to change financial behaviour in the field, but we do not know enough about the sustainability for priming to change long-term behaviour. One small-scale experiment is that of Stewart (2009) who uses the same anchoring approach that was made famous by Ariely et al. (2003) and Tversky and Kahneman (1974). Stewart uses the anchoring approach to minimum repayments on hypothetical credit card debt. He finds that the minimum-repayment information anchors the size of hypothetical repayments. Interestingly, Feinberg (1986) found that being primed with a credit card makes you more likely to spend more on a good, and spend quicker. Prelec and Simester (2001) auctioned sports tickets off to MBA students, where one condition was payment by credit card and the other condition was paying by cash. They found that when payment was by credit card, the average bid was 60–110 per cent higher than the cash bid.

Affect

Affect (the experiencing of emotion) is a powerful force in decision-making. Emotional responses to words, images and events can be rapid and automatic, so that people can experience a behavioural reaction before they realize what they are reacting to (Zajonc, 1980). Some studies have examined the link between emotions and financial decision-making directly. In Landry et al. (2006), in a door-to-door marketing of a fundraising appeal, the authors found that the physical attractiveness of the door-to-door salespeople was far more important to some than the lottery that was being offered. They found that a one-standard deviation increase in physical attractiveness among women solicitors increases the average contributions by 50–135 per cent. Similarly, in a developing country setting, Bertrand et al. (2010) find that adding a photo of a woman to a direct mail solicitation increases the likelihood of borrowing by just as much as dropping the interest rate by 30 per cent – for both men and women.

Commitments

Individuals tend to procrastinate and delay taking decisions that could be in their long-term interests (O'Donoghue and Rabin, 1999). Many people are aware of their weakness of will and use commitment devices to achieve long-term goals. Thaler and Benartzi's (2004) Save More Tomorrow (SMT) scheme enabled each employee to commit a portion of their future salary increases towards retirement savings. They found that 78% joined from those who were offered SMT;

80% of that 78% remained in the programme through the fourth raise; and importantly, the average savings rate increased from 3.5% to 13.6% over 40 months. Ashraf et al. (2006) offered an account with a commitment device to 842 randomly determined households in the Philippines with a pre-existent bank account. Access to funds in these accounts was constrained to reaching a self-specified savings goal or a self-specified time period. The commitment savings product was taken up by 202 households. A control group of 466 households was offered a verbal encouragement to save but no commitment. Savings in the full treatment group was 80 per cent higher than in the control group.

A question remains, however: to what extent are such commitments about binding one's behaviour, or are they in fact merely about creating structure (Karlan and Morduch, 2010)? Karlan and Zinman (2009) test the effects of simply making savings more salient by sending clients simple reminders to make deposits. They find that even with no commitment, the reminders can be successful in increasing savings rates (by 6 per cent) and helping clients meet savings goals (a 3 per cent increase in the likelihood of reaching one's goal).

Ego

Evidence shows that we behave in a way that supports the impression of a positive and consistent self-image. When we are doing well, we attribute it to ourselves; when we do badly, we blame other people or the situation we are in – the 'fundamental attribution error' (Miller and Ross, 1975). Benartzi (2001) provides field evidence of over-inference and/or self-image protection, where the likelihood of employees investing in employer stock depends strongly on the past performance of the stock. In companies in the bottom quintile of performance in the past ten years, 10 per cent of employee savings are allocated to employer stock, compared to 40 per cent for companies in the top quintile. This difference does not reflect information about future returns. Companies with a higher fraction of employees investing in employer stock under-perform over the next year relative to companies with a lower fraction. Adkins and Ozanne (2005) discuss the impact of a low literacy identity on consumers' behaviour, and argue that when low literacy consumers accept the low literacy stigma, they perceive market interactions as more risky, engage in less extended problem solving, limit their social exposure and experience greater stress.

Discussion

We identify two reasons why new models of behaviour change are needed in general, and in consumer finance in particular. First, existing theories and methods leave a substantial proportion of the variance in behaviour, beyond the effect of rational (conscious) intentions, to be explained (Sheeran, 2002; Webb and Sheeran, 2006). Second, there has been a recent accumulation of evidence, particularly in behavioural economics but also in social and cognitive psychology, that human decisions are very susceptible to various subtle changes in the environment (Ariely, 2008; Thaler and Sunstein, 2008). Traditional approaches to behaviour change in finance have not yet fully integrated this evidence, even though it potentially improves population-wide financial capability. Failing to take this evidence into account also threatens the success of policies that aim to encourage individuals to take personal responsibility for their financial affairs.

It is reasonable to conclude from the review of the literature presented here that there is scope to alter the environment in ways that encourage greater levels of financial capability. This process is at a relatively early stage, but there is significant opportunity for well-structured research leading to interventions being implemented and evaluated to ensure that financial capability does indeed improve. In contrast to education and basic information, the mindspace framework offers the potential to influence financial behaviour in ways that may not widen existing inequalities (which most education and information programmes tend to do). Interventions based on our automatic system are more likely to have a universal effect across people with different socio-demographic backgrounds.

There are a few caveats here that offer future research opportunities. First, some of the evidence on financial decisions is derived from the laboratory as opposed to the field. Second, a great deal of the evidence comes from the developing world, mainly because field experiments have become very popular in development economics (Duflo and Kremer, 2005). So, further research would be welcome in the developed world, especially with respect to field evidence in the US and the UK. With respect to particular areas, there needs to be further work on the impact of messenger, priming, norms and ego in financial decision-making.

We are not yet at the stage where we know the marginal effects of different elements of mindspace, in isolation or in combination with other elements. So we need to field test different combinations of effects. A greater focus on the automatic system suggests that it may be more effective to identify a potentially effective intervention and conduct an experiment with a broad population group. This approach contrasts with traditional segmentation analysis based on studying small population groups in depth before determining an appropriate intervention. It also contrasts with traditional market research, which as a guide to behaviour is almost hopeless – not because we are liars but because we do not really know what drives behaviour. We are driven by unconscious triggers and as soon as we tap the conscious mind, we have removed large parts of the reasons for our behaviour.

We recognize that the most effective and sustainable changes in behaviour will come from the successful integration of cultural, regulatory and individual change – drink-driving demonstrates how stiff penalties, good advertising and shifting social norms all combined to change behaviour quite significantly over a couple of decades (Yanovitsky and Bennett, 1999). We certainly need to better integrate changing cognitions and improving financial literacy with changing contexts that may directly lead to improved financial capability. The choice environment is rarely neutral and 'choice architects' will always be shaping our decisions whether we like it or not. This chapter suggests that further experimentation could lead to significant improvements in the 'choice architecture' of the financial services industry.

References

Adkins, N. and Ozanne, J. (2005). The Low Literate Consumer. *Journal of Consumer Research* 32: 93–105.

Ariely, D. (2008). *Predictably Irrational: The Hidden Forces that Shape our Decisions*. London: HarperCollins.

Ariely, D., Loewenstein, G., and Prelec, D. (2003). Coherent Arbitrariness: Stable Demand Curves Without Stable Preferences. *Quarterly Journal of Economics* 118: 73–105.

Ashraf, N., Karlan, D. and Yin, W. (2006). Tying Odysseus to the Mast: Evidence from a Commitment Savings Product in the Philippines. *Quarterly Journal of Economics* 121: 635–72.

Ausubel, L. M. (1999). Adverse Selection in the Credit Card Market. Unpublished manuscript.

Benartzi, S. (2001). Excessive Extrapolation and the Allocation of 401(k) Accounts to Company Stock. *Journal of Finance* 56: 1747–64.

Benartzi, S. and Thaler, R. H. (1995). Myopic Loss Aversion and the Equity Premium Puzzle. *Quarterly Journal of Economics* 110: 73–92.

Bernheim, B. D. and Garrett, D. M. (2003). The Effects of Financial Education in the Workplace: Evidence from a Survey of Households. *Journal of Public Economics* 87: 1487–519.

Bertrand, M., Karlan, D., Mullainathan, S., Shafir, E. and Zinman, J. (2010). What's Advertising Content Worth? Evidence from a Consumer Credit Marketing Field Experiment. *Quarterly Journal of Economics* 125(1): 263–306.

Bertrand, M., Mullainathan, S. and Shafir, E. (2006). Behavioral Economics and Marketing in Aid of Decision Making among the Poor. *Journal of Public Policy and Marketing* 25: 8–23.

Beverly, S., Scheider, D. and Tufano, P. (2006). Splitting Tax Refunds and Building Savings: An Empirical Test. In J. M. Poterba (ed.), *Tax Policy and the Economy*, vol. 20. Cambridge, MA: National Bureau of Economic Research, pp. 111–61.

Bicchieri, C. (2006). *The Grammar of Society: The Nature and Dynamics of Social Norms*. New York: Cambridge University Press.

Bonaccio, S. and Dalal, R. S. (2006). Advice Taking and Decision-Making: An Integrative Literature Review, and Implications for the Organizational Sciences. *Organizational Behavior and Human Decision Processes* 101: 127–51.

Brown, J. B., Kling, J. R., Mullainathan, S., Wiens, G. R. and Wrobel, M. V. (2008a). *Framing, Reference Points, and Preferences for Life Annuities*. The Retirement Security Project, October.

Brown, J. B., Kling, J. R., Mullainathan, S. and Wrobel, M. V. (2008b). Why Don't People Insure Late-Life Consumption? A Framing Explanation of the Under-Annuitization Puzzle. *American Economic Review* 98: 304–9.

Choi, J. J., Laibson, D., Madrian, B. and Metrick, A. (2004). For Better or Worse: Default Effects and 401(K) Savings Behavior. In D. A. Wise (ed.), *Perspectives on the Economics of Aging*. University of Chicago Press, pp. 81–121.

Cole, S. and Shastry, G. K. (2008). If You Are so Smart, Why Aren't You Rich? The Effects of Education, Financial Literacy, and Cognitive Ability on Financial Market Participation. Working paper.

Cronqvist, H. and Thaler, R. H. (2004). Design Choices in Privatized Social-Security Systems: Learning from the Swedish Experience. *American Economic Review* 94: 424–8.

Deelstra, J. T., Peeters, M. C. W., Schaufeli, W. B., Stroebe, W., Zijlstra, F. R. H. and van Doornen, L. P. (2003). Receiving Instrumental Support at Work: When Help is Not Welcome. *Journal of Applied Psychology* 88: 324–31.

Dolan, P., Elliott, A., Metcalfe, R. and Vlaev, I. (2012). Influencing Financial Behavior: From Changing Minds to Changing Contexts. *Journal of Behavioral Finance* 13(2): 126–42.

Dolan, P., Hallsworth, M., Halpern, D., King, D. and Vlaev, I. (2010). Mindspace: Influencing Behaviour Through Public Policy. London: Cabinet Office and Institute for Government.

Duflo, E. and Kremer, M. (2005). Use of Randomization in the Evaluation of Development Effectiveness. In O. Feinstein, G. K. Ingram and G. K. Pitman (eds.), *Evaluating Development Effectiveness*, vol. 7. New Brunswick, NJ: Transaction Publishers, pp. 205–32.

Duflo, E. and Saez, E. (2003). The Role of Information and Social Interactions in Retirement Plan Decisions: Evidence from a Randomized Experiment. *Quarterly Journal of Economics* 118: 815–42.

Durantini, M. R., Albarracin, D., Earl, A. and Mitchell, A. L. (2006). Conceptualizing the Influence of Social Agents of Behavior Change: A Meta-Analysis of the Effectiveness of HIV-Prevention Interventionists for Different Groups. *Psychological Bulletin* 132: 212–48.

Feinberg, R. A. (1986). Credit Cards as Spending Facilitating Stimuli. *Journal of Consumer Research* 13: 348–56.

Gino, F. (2008). Do We Listen to Advice Just Because We Paid for It? The Impact of Advice Cost on Its Use. *Organizational Behavior and Human Decision Processes* 107: 234–45.

Goetzmann, W. N. and Peles, N. (1997). Cognitive Dissonance and Mutual Fund Investors. *Journal of Financial Research* 20: 145–58.

Goldsmith, D. J. (2000). Soliciting Advice: The Role of Sequential Placement in Mitigating Face Threat. *Communications Monographs* 67: 1–19.

Goldsmith, D. J. and Fitch, K. (1997). The Normative Context of Advice as Social Support. *Human Communication Research* 23: 454–76.

Gross, D. B. and Souleles, N. S. (2002). Do Liquidity Constraints and Interest Rates Matter for Consumer Behavior? Evidence from Credit Card Data. *Quarterly Journal of Economics* 117: 149–85.

Hackethal, A., Haliassos, M. and Jappelli, T. (2009). *Financial Advisors: A Case of Babysitters?* CEPR Discussion Papers 7235.

Hossain, T. and Morgan, J. (2006). Plus Shipping and Handling: Revenue (Non) Equivalence in Field Experiments on eBay. *Advances in Economic Analysis and Policy* 6(2): article 3.

Hung, A. and Yoong, J. (2010). *Asking for Help: Survey and Experimental Evidence on Financial Advice and Behavior Change.* RAND Working Paper WR-714-1.

Kahneman, D. (2003). A Perspective on Judgment and Choice: Mapping Bounded Rationality. *American Psychologist* 58: 697–720.

Kahneman, D. and Thaler, R. (2006). Anomalies: Utility Maximisation and Experienced Utility. *Journal of Economic Perspectives* 20: 221–34.

Kahneman, D. and Tversky, A. (1979). Prospect Theory: An Analysis of Decision under Risk. *Econometrica* 47: 263–91.

Karlan, D. (2007). Social Connections and Group Banking. *Economic Journal* 117: F52–F84.

Karlan, D. and Morduch, J. (2010). Access to Finance. In D. Rodrik and M. Rosenzweig (eds.), *Handbook of Development Economics*, vol. 5. Amsterdam: North-Holland, pp. 4703–84.

Karlan, D. and Zinman, J. (2009). *Expanding Microenterprise Credit Access: Using Randomized Supply Decisions to Estimate the Impacts in Manila*. Yale University, Dartmouth College, and Innovations in Poverty Action Working Paper.

Karlsson, N., Loewenstein, G. and Seppi, D. J. (2005). The 'Ostrich Effect': Selective Attention to Information about Investments. Unpublished manuscript.

Landry, C. E., Lange, A., List, J. A., Price, M. K. and Rupp, N. G. (2006). Toward an Understanding of the Economics of Charity: Evidence from a Field Experiment. *Quarterly Journal of Economics* 121: 747–82.

Lusardi, A. (2007). *Household Saving Behavior: The Role of Literacy, Information and Financial Education Programs*. NBER Working Paper 13824.

Lusardi, A., Mitchell, O. S. and Curto, V. (2010) *Financial Literacy among the Young: Evidence and Implications for Consumer Policy*. Dartmouth College Working Paper.

Madrian, B. and Shea, D. F. (2001). The Power of Suggestion: Inertia in 401(k) Participation and Savings Behavior. *Quarterly Journal of Economics* 116: 1149–87.

Meier, S. and Sprenger, C. (2008). *Discounting Financial Literacy: Time Preferences and Participation in Financial Education Programs*. Federal Reserve Bank of Boston, Public Policy Discussion Paper No. 07-5.

Miller, D. T. and Ross, M. (1975). Self-Serving Biases in the Attribution of Causality: Fact or Fiction? *Psychological Bulletin* 82: 213–25.

O'Donoghue, T. and Rabin, M. (1999). Doing It Now or Doing It Later. *American Economic Review* 89: 103–24.

Prelec, D. and Simester, D. (2001). Credit-Card Effect on Willingness to Pay. *Marketing Letters* 12: 5–12.

Sheeran, P. (2002). Intention-Behavior Relations: A Conceptual and Empirical Review. In W. Strobe and M. Hewstone (eds.), *European Review of Social Psychology*, vol. 12. Chichester: Wiley, pp. 1–30.

Stewart, N. (2009). The Cost of Anchoring on Credit Card Minimum Repayments. *Psychological Science* 20: 39–41.

Thaler, R. H. (1985). Mental Accounting and Consumer Choice. *Marketing Science* 4: 199–214.

(1999). Mental Accounting Matters. *Journal of Behavioral Decision Making* 12: 183–206.

Thaler, R. H. and Benartzi, S. (2004). Save More Tomorrow: Using Behavioral Economics to Increase Employee Saving. *Journal of Political Economy* 112: S164–S187.

Thaler, R. H. and Sunstein, C. R. (2008). *Nudge: Improving Decisions about Health, Wealth and Happiness*. New Haven: Yale University Press.

Triplett, N. (1898). The Dynamogenic Factors in Pacemaking and Competition. *American Journal of Psychology* 9: 507–33.

Tversky, A. and Kahneman, D. (1974). Judgment under Uncertainty: Heuristics and Biases. *Science* 185: 1124–30.

Vlaev, I. and Dolan, P. (2009). *From Changing Cognitions to Changing the Context: A Dual-Route Model of Behaviour Change*. London: Imperial College Business School.

Waber, R. L., Shiv, B., Carmon, Z. and Ariely, D. (2008). Commercial Features of Placebo and Therapeutic Efficacy. *Journal of the American Medical Association* 299: 1016–17.

Webb, T. L. and Sheeran, P. (2006) Does Changing Behavioral Intentions Engender Behavior Change? A Meta-Analysis of the Experimental Evidence. *Psychological Bulletin* 132: 249–68.

Yaniv, I. (2004a). The Benefit of Additional Opinions. *Current Directions in Psychological Science* 13: 75–8.

(2004b). Receiving Other People's Advice: Influence and Benefit. *Organizational Behavior and Human Decision Processes* 93: 1–13.

Yaniv, I. and Kleinberger, E. (2000). Advice Taking in Decision Making: Egocentric Discounting and Reputation Formation. *Organizational Behavior and Human Decision Processes* 83(2): 260–81.

Yanovitsky, I. and Bennett, C. (1999). Media Attention, Institutional Response and Health Behaviour Change: The Case of Drunk Driving 1978–1996. *Communication Research* 26: 429–53.

Zajonc, R. B. (1980). Feelings and Thinking: Preferences Need No Inferences. *American Psychologist* 35: 151–75.

8.1 | *A response to Dolan*

SANDER VAN DER LINDEN

Introduction

Paul Dolan argues that there are two broad approaches to behavioural change: changing *minds* and changing *contexts*. He argues that while the former approach relies more heavily on conscious and reasoned processes, the latter predominantly deals with the subconscious, automated system of the human brain and attempts to facilitate change by altering the 'environmental context' in which people make decisions. In particular, he notes that the latter approach (i.e. changing contexts) has received relatively little attention in the past and that, by focusing on altering people's choice environment, 'mindspace' represents a promising framework for improving the public's financial capabilities. In explaining the rationale behind the development and application of the mindspace framework, he states: 'new models of behaviour change are needed in general, and in consumer finance in particular[, as] existing theories and methods leave a substantial proportion of the variance in behaviour, beyond the effect of rational (conscious) intentions, to be explained'.

It is important to understand that the first part of Dolan's argument does not (or should not) flow from the latter. While new models of behavioural change are undoubtedly needed, the existing theories and methods that Dolan seems to be referring to are (unlike mindspace) not meant to prescribe behavioural change; rather, they are concerned with explaining proportional variance in behaviour. The fact that existing models are not able to account for a larger range of variance in the public's financial behaviour undoubtedly calls for new models and methods that potentially can, but this is not what mindspace brings to the table: *explaining* and *changing* behaviour are two related, but categorically different things. Second, there is a good amount of research that looks beyond the effect of 'conscious intentions' that Dolan did not explicitly cover. In this response, I would like to take a step back and shed some light on not only the difference but also (perhaps more importantly) the interrelation between *models of behaviour* and *theories of change* and how this distinction helps to illuminate the potential and role of mindspace in changing the public's financial behaviour.

Getting the distinctions right

In behavioural science, a distinction is made between *models of behaviour* and *theories of change*. While models of behaviour aid in understanding specific behaviours by identifying the underlying factors that determine and influence them, theories of change show how behaviours can be changed and/or change over time (Darnton, 2008). While *theories of change* more commonly depict generic processes, for the most part, models of behaviour are diagnostic, designed to explain the determinant psychological factors and the relative importance of those factors in predicting and explaining a given behaviour. In addition, change theory is more pragmatic and aims to support interventions in either changing existing or encouraging the adoption of new behaviours.

Yet, while there is no doubt that models of behaviour and theories of change have distinct purposes, they are also highly complementary. In fact, successfully trying to change any given behaviour involves a thorough understanding of all of the factors that determine and influence the behaviour under investigation. Hence, it is important for evaluators to not only look at behavioural outcomes, because it is from studying the psychological determinants of behaviour that we gain understanding of why certain interventions were successful or not (GCN, 2009; Steg and Vlek, 2009) and where and how to try out future strategies for changing behaviour (Hamid and Cheng, 1995). Indeed, in an overview of how applied *behavioural* models can assist consumer finance, Xiao (2008) mentions that in order to help change undesirable financial behaviours, it is pivotal to first gain a better understanding of how such financial behaviours are formed in the first place.

Moving beyond false dichotomies

As Dolan highlights, the traditional focus of public policy has been on using (persuasive) information to change people's *cognitions*. This preoccupation with 'conscious change' undoubtedly grew out of early knowledge–attitude–behaviour models, followed by expectancy-value frameworks such as the 'theory of reasoned action' (Fishbein and Ajzen, 1975) and its successor the 'theory of planned behaviour' (Ajzen, 1991). While some of these traditional behavioural models, at their core, do assume that human behaviour is goal-directed (i.e. 'conscious'), the application of existing – and the quantity, scope and orientation of new – models has shifted to include a wide range of behavioural determinants, including emotions, habits, norms and even environmental/contextual factors (e.g. see Schwartz, 1977; Stern et al., 1999; Triandis, 1977; van der Linden, 2011), investigating virtually all types of behaviour (including consumer finance). For example, recent research points to the increasing role of moral norms in explaining individual investment behaviour (e.g. Hofmann et al. 2008). A recent model presented by Shim et al. (2010) explains how environmental factors such as parental guiding, work and high school education influence the financial habits, attitudes and behaviours adopted by young adults. Research also shows that women tend to worry more about financial risks and accordingly, Sethi-Iyengar et al. (2004) show that women enrol in voluntary pension plans in greater numbers and make larger contributions than men.

The general idea is that the discussion should not revolve around changing minds (i.e. conscious change) or changing contexts (i.e. sub-conscious change). In fact, the practical value of making distinctions between 'reflective, conscious' and 'automated, subconscious' parts of the brain is fairly limited, as most real-life behaviour is the result of careful integration of both processes (e.g. Camerer et al., 2005). As neuroscientist Damasio (1994, 1999) has pointed out in a series of clinical cases, these two processes operate in parallel and continuously interact with each other. For example, people are unable to make rational decisions without the presence of subtle, instinctive emotional cues. Similarly, the analytical processing of scientific information can elicit strong emotions. In other words, the traditional notion of two separate functional systems (emotion versus cognition) is no longer scientifically defensible (Ochsner and Phelps, 2007).

The role of mindspace

'There has been a recent accumulation of evidence, particularly in behavioural economics but also in social and cognitive psychology, that human decisions are very susceptible to various subtle changes in the environment' (Dolan, this volume).

Dolan points out a crucial and valid point here: human decisions are strongly influenced by environmental conditions and mindspace goes a long way towards providing a framework that taps into these 'contextual factors'. However, behavioural change frameworks such as *'nudge'* and *'mindspace'* essentially assume that the government should act as a 'teacher' and steer citizens down the path that is most beneficial to them and society as a whole. By slightly altering people's choice environment, the cost of behavioural change is essentially minimized. Yet, not all researchers agree with this approach to behavioural change. For example, a concept known as *'think'* strategies relies on the notion that individuals can step away from day-to-day life and reflect on a wide range of public policy choices. It assumes that people are *'knowledge hungry'*, *'learn to process new information'* and reach *'new heights of reflection'* (John et al., 2011). Thus, 'think' requires active deliberation and assumes that individuals would want to engage in (public) debates about important (financial) issues.

While both approaches have their merits, it is not unreasonable to assume that on their own, both 'think' and 'mindspace' are perhaps on equally unrealistic ends of the behaviour spectrum as human behaviour is neither fully deliberative, nor fully automatic; people are neither completely autonomous nor entirely social (Jackson, 2005) and so attempting to focus solely on changing one aspect of behaviour, at best, under-appreciates many other important determinants. Hence, a combination of various types of interventions is likely to be preferable, a standpoint that Dolan also seems to agree with.

While different in their specific focus, *nudge* (Thaler and Sunstein, 2008), *think* (John et al., 2011) and *mindspace* (Dolan et al., 2012) can all be considered *'theories of change'* and that is exactly where their contribution lies. Models of behaviour do not just focus on cognitions or attitudes; in fact, regardless of whether they focus on norms, emotions, habits or conscious intentions, they add to the empirical evidence base from which change interventions can draw. For example, an increasing body of research is pointing out that a substantial amount of variance in individual financial risk-taking behaviour actually has a genetic basis (Kuhnen and Chiao, 2009). Applied models that deal with the behavioural determinants of consumer finance provide policy-makers and researchers with more information on what factors drive the behaviour under investigation. Yet the fact that some individuals have a genetic predisposition towards more financial risk taking does not mean that these individuals will also take more risk, as the effect of genetic predispositions on behaviour is mediated (or mitigated) by environmental influences. To illustrate, individuals with the so-called '*warrior*' gene (i.e. a predisposition for violent behaviour) will generally not become violent unless the individual is exposed to an environment that would be conducive to eliciting such behaviour (Caspi et al., 2002). In the same way, individuals who are prone to financial risk taking might in fact not do so when the environment stimulates them to do the opposite (i.e. save money). Hence, here is where *theories of change*, such as *mindspace*, can prove potentially useful, for example, by designing a choice environment that discourages people from taking financial risks.

Conclusions

The mindspace framework presented by Dolan et al. (2012) fills an important gap in terms of much-needed behavioural change strategies that look at how to provide an environment that is more conducive to our physical, mental as well as financial well-being. Yet, while the adopted mindspace framework builds on relatively broad and dispersed research on human behaviour, future research could focus more on strengthening the connection between findings put forth by specific behavioural models and how theories of change (e.g. mindspace) can utilize this information to try and create an environment that is more conducive to altering or improving the public's financial capabilities.

For example, many types of financial behaviours can be delineated, ranging from relatively simple behaviours such as applying for and using a credit card to more complex decisions about investments and pension plans. It is very likely that these behaviours differ systematically in their determinants (i.e. applying for a credit card is not the same as figuring out a 401(k) plan). Of course it is possible to test out different behavioural change strategies in a 'hit or miss' type manner, finding out 'what works' through an iterative (experimental) process of trial and error. Yet, is it not presumptuous to think that sustainable behavioural change can be achieved without understanding the factors that underlie, drive and differentiate the behaviours under investigation? In conclusion, determining tradeoffs between the extent of environmental adjustments (e.g. default enrolment in employer pension funds) and more cognitive-based strategies (e.g. improving financial literacy) is (or should be) contingent on a thorough understanding of all the (conscious and subconscious) determinants of the target behaviour.

References

Ajzen, I. (1991). The Theory of Planned Behaviour. *Organizational Behaviour and Human Decision Processes* 50: 179–211.

Camerer, C., Loewenstein, G., and Prelec, D. (2005). Neuroeconomics: How Neuroscience Can Inform Economics. *Journal of Economic Literature* 43: 9–64.

Caspi, A., McClay, J., Moffitt, T. E., Mill, J., Martin, J., Craig, I. W., Taylor, A. and Poulton, R. (2002). Role of Genotype in the Cycle of Violence in Maltreated Children. *Science* 297: 851–4.

Damasio, A. R. (1994). *Descartes' Error: Emotion, Reason, and the Human Brain*. New York: Grosset and Putnam.

(1999). *The Feeling of What Happens*. New York: Harcourt-Brace.

Darnton, A. (2008). *Reference Report: An Overview of Behavioural Change Models and their Uses*. Government Social Research (GSR) Behaviour Change Knowledge Review.

Dolan, P., Hallsworth, M., Halpern, D., King, D., Metcalfe, R. and Vlaev, I. (2012). Influencing Behaviour: The Mindspace Way. *Journal of Economic Psychology* 33: 264–77.

Fishbein, M. and Ajzen, I. (1975). *Belief, Attitude, Intention, and Behaviour: An Introduction to Theory and Research*. Reading, MA: Addison-Wesley.

Government Communication Network (GCN) (2009). *Communications and Behaviour Change* (www.behaviourworksaustralia.org/wp-content/uploads/2012/09/commongood-behaviourchange.pdf).

Hamid, P. N. and Cheng, S. T. (1995). Predicting Anti-Pollution Behaviour: The Role of Molar Behavioural Intentions, Past Behaviour and Loss of Control. *Environment and Behaviour* 27: 679–98.

Hofmann, E., Hoelzl, E. and Kirchler, E. (2008). A Comparison of Models Describing the Impact of Moral Decision Making on Investment Decisions. *Journal of Business Ethics* 82: 171–87.

Jackson, T. (2005). *Motivating Sustainable Consumption: A Review of Evidence on Consumer Behaviour and Behavioural Change*. A report to the Sustainable Development Research Network. London: SDRN.

John, P., Cotterill, S., Moseley, A., Richardson, L., Smith, G., Stoker, G. and Wales, C. (2011). *Nudge, Nudge, Think, Think: Experimenting with Ways to Change Civic Behaviour*. London: Bloomsbury Academic Publishing.

Kuhnen, C. M. and Chiao, J. Y. (2009). Genetic Determinants of Financial Risk Taking. *PLoS One* 4: e 4362.

Ochsner, K. N. and Phelps, E. (2007). Emerging Perspectives on Emotion–Cognition Interactions. *Trends in Cognitive Sciences* 11: 317–18.

Schwartz, S. (1977). Normative Influences on Altruism. In L. Berkowitz (ed.), *Advances in Experimental Social Psychology*, vol. 10. New York: Academic Press, pp. 221–79.

Sethi-Iyengar, S., Huberman, G. and Jiang, W. (2004). How Much Choice is Too Much? Contributions to 401(k) Retirement Plans. In O. S. Mitchell and S. P. Utkus (eds.), *Pension Design and Structure: New Lessons from Behavioral Finance. Part I. Research on Decision-Making Under Uncertainty*. Oxford University Press, pp. 83–96.

Shim, S., Barber, B., Card, N. A., Xiao, J. J. and Serido, J. (2010). Financial Socialization of First-Year College Students: The Roles of Parents, Work and Education. *Journal of Youth Adolescence* 39: 1457–70.

Steg, L. and Vlek, C. (2009). Encouraging Pro-Environmental Behaviour: An Integrative Review and Research Agenda. *Journal of Environmental Psychology* 29: 309–17.

Stern, P. C., Dietz, T., Abel, T., Guagnano, G. A. and Kalog, L. (1999). A Value-Belief-Norm Theory of Support for Social Movements: The Case of Environmentalism. *Human Ecology Review* 6: 81–97.

Thaler, R. H. and Sunstein, C. R. (2008). *Nudge: Improving Decisions about Health, Wealth and Happiness*. New Haven: Yale University Press.

Triandis, H. (1977). *Interpersonal Behaviour*. Monterey, CA: Brooks and Cole.

van der Linden, S. (2011). Charitable Intent: A Moral or Social Construct? A Revised Theory of Planned Behaviour Model. *Current Psychology* 30: 355–74.

Xiao, J. J. (2008). Applying Behaviour Theories to Financial Behaviour. In J. Jing Xiao (ed.), *Handbook of Consumer Finance Research*. New York: Springer, pp. 69–81.

9 | *Decision analysis from a neo-Calvinist point of view*

D R A Z E N   P R E L E C

By neo-Calvinist point of view, I refer to analysis focused on assessing the diagnostic significance of policy decisions, rather than establishing the direct consequences of decisions. Diagnostic significance refers to information revealed by an irrevocable act, information about some underlying collective value or belief. Decisions, especially those that break with precedent, can expose the tradeoffs between competing values, tradeoffs that society tacitly endorses. In these situations, the role of analysis might be not so much to recommend a course of action, but to clarify what is at stake, the 'diagnostic risk' as it were, created by the choice.

Here I outline a simple framework for how this analysis might proceed. The core ideas are taken from an earlier self-signalling model of choice (Bodner and Prelec, 2003; Prelec and Bodner, 2003). That model postulated a distinction between two types of utility: utility that flows directly from the causal consequences of choice, and diagnostic utility, which is the pleasure or pain derived from learning something positive or negative about one's own internal state, disposition, ability or future prospects. People are presumed to be chronically uncertain about where they stand with respect to these broad attributes, which in turn makes their choices diagnostic. Anticipation of diagnostic reward, or fear of diagnostic pain, promotes self-control and inhibits self-indulgence.

The new aspect considered in this chapter is that the self-signalling agent is taken to represent a unified collective, such as a nation, society or corporation. With self-signalling agents, individual or collective, standard decision analysis methods are no longer appropriate. The question then becomes how these methods might be usefully modified or adapted.

I start by looking at the motivational paradox inherent in the Calvinist doctrine of predestination, and argue that Calvinism brings into sharp relief an otherwise universal mechanism for self-control and self-management. We treat this mechanism – the mechanism that

216

sustains motivation even in the absence of any causal link between actions and outcomes – as a purely naturalistic, psychological phenomenon. I then review the self-signalling model, and conclude with a speculative discussion of how decision analysis might be adapted to this new setting.

The Calvinist solution to the problem of self-control

As is well known, a distinctive aspect of the Calvinist religious system is the doctrine of predestination, which asserts that God has divided mankind into two categories, the elect, who will enjoy eternal life, and the rest, who will not:

> By an eternal and immutable counsel, God has once and for all determined, both whom he would admit to salvation and whom he would condemn to destruction ... This counsel, as far as concerns the elect, is founded on his gratuitous mercy, totally irrespective of human merit. (Calvin, *Institutes* III, 21, 7)

The die has been cast before birth and nothing a person does during his lifetime can change the outcome. Effort, good deeds, fulfilling duties and so on will not help. One might ask how this fatalistic doctrine could compel such stringent uniformity of conduct and observance. If one were designing doctrines from scratch, and wanted to create a set of beliefs to encourage virtue, it is not likely one would incorporate a belief in predestination, which takes all power over the final outcome away from the individual. On the face of it, the message seems to be: relax, it's all been decided anyway. But relaxation is the last thing associated with Calvin and the system erected in Geneva, a 'most perfect theocracy' where even details of dress and haircut were regulated.

From the standpoint of rational behaviour, the motivational power of the doctrine is mysterious. What are the incentives for virtue, if virtue cannot accomplish the one goal that a believer values above all others? Max Weber proposed a solution to this puzzle over a hundred years ago, in his classic work *On the Protestant Ethic and the Spirit of Capitalism*:

> however useless good works might be as a means of attaining salvation, nevertheless they are indispensable as a sign of election. They are the technical means, not of purchasing salvation, but of getting rid of the fear of damnation.

In practice this means that God helps those who help themselves. Thus the Calvinist, as it is sometimes put, himself creates his own salvation, or, as would be more correct, the conviction of it. But this creation cannot, as in Catholicism, consist in a gradual accumulation of individual good works to one's credit, but rather in a systematic self-control which at every chosen moment stands before the inexorable alternative, chosen or damned.

Weber not only identified the source of motivation, but also of its tendency to impose order, regularity and pattern on a series of actions:

[The Calvinist] could not hope to atone for hours of weakness or of thought-lessness by increased good will at other times. The God of Calvinism demanded of his believers not single good works, but a life of good works combined into a unified system ...

The moral conduct of the average man was thus deprived of its planless and unsystematic character and subjected to a consistent method for conduct as a whole. It is no accident that the name of Methodists stuck to the participants in the last great revival of Puritan ideas in the eighteenth century, just as the term Precisians, which has the same meaning, was applied to their spiritual ancestors in the seventeenth century.

On Weber's account, predestination, the very aspect of doctrine that should have eroded self-control, paradoxically served to enhance it. Radical uncertainty about underlying conditions endowed even minor actions with great significance. As actions became more systematic and regimented (precision, method, purity), deviations become easier to spot. Thus, order and planning gave rise to even more order and planning, in a self-reinforcing cycle.

A parallel line of thought appears in George Ainslie's discussion of rule-governed behaviour and compulsion (Ainslie, 1992). Theoretical approaches to self-control within economics have emphasized the temporal aspect of the problem, the conflict between the near and the far. This conflict, however, does not capture a key – perhaps *the* key – aspect of the self-control decision, which is the problem of scale. Let us take a standard example – smoking. Monterosso and Ainslie state the problem concisely:

Consider a smoker who is trying to quit, but who craves a cigarette. Suppose that an angel whispers to her that, regardless of whether or not she smokes the desired cigarette, she is destined to smoke a pack a day from tomorrow on. Given this certainty, she would have no incentive to turn down the cigarette – the effort would seem pointless. What if the angel whispers instead that she is destined never to smoke again after today, regardless of her current choice? Here, too, there seems to be little incentive to turn down the cigarette – it would be harmless.

Only if future smoking is in doubt does a current abstention seem worth the effort. But the importance of her current choice cannot come from any physical consequences for future choices; hence the conclusion that it matters as precedent. (Monterosso and Ainslie, 1999)

Again, we have a pre-existing condition (one is either destined to smoke, or destined not to smoke), which is not caused but only revealed by the current action. What keeps the smoker from smoking is the immediate loss in expectations about long run health that would be triggered by a single cigarette; the physical consequences of smoking one cigarette are of course negligible.[1]

We may use the term 'self-signalling' to refer to actions taken in order to provide good news about some personal characteristic or state, even when such actions do not cause that state. The basic assumption is that certain deep characteristics – which could be values, abilities or beliefs – cannot be deduced through introspection, but can only be revealed through actual choice. Such characteristics are 'cognitively inaccessible' (Bodner and Prelec, 2003). In this setting the choice becomes potentially diagnostic, which in turn creates a motive to self-signal the desired characteristics through a virtuous choice.[2]

Self-signalling by unified collectives

Societies and other corporate collectives also live in conditions of uncertainty about their deep characteristics. Are they generous, are they just, are they destined to survive or to perish? Political rhetoric tends to strike characteristic Calvinist notes when there is a conflict between expediency and broader values or self-esteem. For example, scanning a few recent headlines: 'How we care for orphans as a society

[1] However, being forced to smoke the cigarette at gunpoint, or doing so in order to achieve some worthwhile purpose (e.g. to please your host), would not lead to the same loss in expectations. Only free actions are informative, on this account.

[2] See Ginossar and Trope (1987), Mijovic-Prelec and Prelec (2010), Quattrone and Tversky (1984) and Sanitioso et al. (1990) for laboratory psychological evidence supporting self signalling.

shows what kind of society we are',[3] 'Are We a Nation Doomed to be Violent?',[4] 'Is Canada a Country That Hates Its Young?'[5] By bringing pre-existing conditions into the picture, the rhetoric amplifies the stakes on what may be a minor or narrow issue. Granted, orphans are important, but the decision is not just about them. Rather, lack of care for orphans is symptomatic of a deeper disorder. The rhetoric invokes Calvinist intuitions about pre-existing conditions, which are revealed rather than caused by the current decision.

It is plausible that the deep values that define a society are not fully accessible by collective introspection, whether informal or formalized through social science research. Political liberties, guarantees of due process, protection against threats and catastrophes, beliefs in national mission, uniqueness and destiny are examples of such characteristics. No matter how much research is done, there remains a margin of uncertainty that is only resolved through an actual test. Indeed, one might suppose that a greater range of characteristics is inaccessible at the social level than at the individual one. Preferences and beliefs that are individually inaccessible surely remain so in the aggregate, and collective preferences and beliefs are distributed among the crowd. It is hard to tell how a collective would react in a new situation, faced with unexpected challenges and tests. Protections afforded by constitutional guarantees against imprisonment without trial or against torture exist on paper, but will they hold up in exceptional times? Even if one could elicit information about deep characteristics, there is a matter of credibility. Official representatives, who are in a position to see how decisions are made, have strong incentives to disguise the real picture. Hence, any direct expressions of core preferences or beliefs may be treated as indicators of the official ideology, not fact.

Analysis for a self-signalling decision-maker

What might be the role of decision analysis in this setting, when underlying values and beliefs are inaccessible? Or, to put it differently, is there any way to exploit the objectivity and analytical rigour of

---

[3] http://conhomeusa.typepad.com/platform/2011/04/conservative-solutions-orphans.html.

[4] http://indiancountrytodaymedianetwork.com/ict_sbc/are-we-a-nation-doomed-to-be-violent/.

[5] http://montrealsimon.blogspot.com/2011/05/is-canada-country-that-hates-its-young.html.

decision analysis in situations where decisions have diagnostic rather than causal significance?

It will be helpful to begin with a stylized account of decision analysis in the traditional mode, with a single decision-maker representing a unified collective confronted with a choice between actions x, y, z, etc. Prior to analysis, she is unclear about her values (preferences) and her beliefs (subjective probabilities over relevant events). Formally, one would say that the decision-maker does not know her *type*, θ, which is a catch-all variable representing values, or beliefs, or both.[6] Uncertainty about θ translates into uncertainty about the actual utility function over actions, $u(x,\theta)$, which the decision-maker presumably wishes to maximize. If choosing without benefit of analysis, by gut feel, the decision-maker would go with the action x that maximizes $\sum_{\theta} p(\theta)u(x,\theta)$, where $p(\theta)$ represents uncertainty about one's type.

In the ideal scenario governing the traditional mode, the end result of decision analysis will be to clarify the decision-maker's actual type, $\theta°$, which is to say, her beliefs, desires and abilities. This process may involve a combination of discussion and formal elicitation exercises, where the decision-maker is presented with hypothetical choices, and reveals preferences and probabilities through these choices. Enlightened by the results of analysis, the decision-maker will then choose to maximize the exact utility criterion $u(x,\theta°)$, instead of the imprecise criterion, $\sum_{\theta} p(\theta)u(x,\theta)$.

Traditional decision analysis does, therefore, acknowledge that the discovery of true values and beliefs is a complex process, and, indeed, that is the very reason why professional assistance is brought into play. But the difficulty in extracting underlying characteristics is purely cognitive, not motivational, and can be solved by entertaining hypothetical scenarios and choices.

For a self-signalling decision-maker the underlying characteristics – preferences and beliefs – are radically inaccessible: they cannot be mapped out by any purely intellectual exercise. However, these characteristics may be revealed through actions. Exactly how they are revealed will depend on the underlying decision rule, mapping characteristics to actions. To move forward with analysis within the broad framework of utility maximization, one would need to specify the

---

[6] In the case of belief, θ would be probability vector $\theta = (\theta_1,..,\theta_n)$ over events $S_1,..,S_n$.

general form of the utility function that the self-signalling agent is trying to optimize.

We follow here the specification given in Bodner and Prelec (2003), which is arguably the simplest model of this phenomenon.[7] As before, $u(x, \theta^\circ)$ will denote the utility associated with action x. This is the 'deep desire' for x, cognitively inaccessible but nevertheless registering an impact on choice. As before, explicit beliefs about θ are defined by a self-image distribution, $p(\theta)$. The value of this self-image is, in turn, determined by a separate utility function, $V(\theta)$, which indicates how much utility would be gained by discovering the true θ. This function represents the only new element in the theoretical setup.

By intentionally choosing one outcome over others, the decision-maker potentially learns something about the inaccessible θ. Hence, a deliberate action leads to an updating of the self-image, from $p(\theta)$ to $p(\theta|x)$. The updated self-image generates a second form of utility, called diagnostic utility: $\sum_\theta p(\theta \mid x) V(\theta)$, which is computed by replacing the prior self-image $p(\theta)$ with the posterior $p(\theta|x)$. Diagnostic utility captures the extent to which choices provide good or bad news about θ: Total utility = Outcome utility + Diagnostic utility:[8]

$$U(x, \theta^\circ) = u(x, \theta^\circ) + \sum_\theta p(\theta \mid x) V(\theta)$$

Whether an action provides information about θ will depend on the inferential process that specifies how the updated self-image $p(\theta|x)$ is computed from the choice and from prior beliefs $p(\theta)$. There are two endogenous approaches to such inferences, i.e. approaches requiring no new parameters beyond the ones already given, viz. $u(x,\theta)$, $V(\theta)$ and $p(\theta)$ (Prelec and Bodner, 2003). A rational inference rule assumes full awareness about the self-signalling criterion. This means that $p(\theta|x)$ must properly discount the signalling value of an ostensibly virtuous action for the fact that the action is partly motivated by anticipated favourable inferences. This carries to a logical conclusion the basic idea in self-perception theory (Bem, 1972), namely, that the process of inferring hidden beliefs and desires from overt behaviour is the same

---

[7] For related models of signalling between temporally differentiated multiple-selves, see Benabou and Tirole (2004) and Bernheim and Thomadsen (2005).

[8] It would be more correct to write: $u(x, \theta^\circ) + \sum_\theta (p(\theta \mid x) - p(\theta)) V(\theta)$, but to simplify, we omit the constant term $\sum_\theta p(\theta) V(\theta)$ representing expected utility of the prior self-image.

irrespective of whether the inferences pertain to someone else or to ourselves. Just as we might discount someone else's good behaviour as being due only to a desire to impress, so too we could discount our own behaviour for ulterior motives. The second, and perhaps more plausible, inferential rule assumes no awareness of diagnostic motivation, and hence all actions are treated as the result of simple maximization of outcome utility. There is no discounting for diagnostic motivation. In that case, a good action is taken at face value, resulting in an overly optimistic self-image. Descriptively, this may be the more realistic model of self-signalling. However, a normative analysis, as pursued here, would require the rational inference rule.

To complete the model in either variant one imposes a consistency requirement between choice of x as a function of θ, and inference about θ as a function of observed x. This means that the updated self-image $p(\theta|x)$ places positive probability only on those characteristics θ that maximize utility in light of $p(\theta|x)$ (total utility for the rational variant, or outcome utility for the face-value variant). The formal requirements for equilibrium are that if action x is taken with positive probability for some $\theta°$, then for all y, $U(x, \theta°) \geq U(y, \theta°)$. Conversely, $p(\theta°|x) > 0$ implies: for all y, $U(x, \theta°) \geq U(y, \theta°)$.[9]

Here is how the model might interpret the smoker's dilemma, as presented by Monterosso and Ainslie. The deep characteristics in play are the smoker's beliefs about future smoking: is he destined to smoke always or never? Let us suppose that the angel did indeed whisper something, but the whisper is cognitively inaccessible. The hand that might or might not reach for the cigarette has heard the message but the conscious mind has not. Furthermore, no amount of assisted armchair analysis will reveal the contents of the message. What decision analysis might do, however, is to establish how the utility parameters depend on the message. To be concrete, let us suppose that these parameters indicate that the diagnostic utility of finding out that one will never smoke is +2 units irrespective of beliefs about future smoking. This is the value of good news. Let us also suppose that the desire to smoke this single cigarette increases as a function of deep

---

[9] There remains the case of out-of-equilibrium beliefs. One possibility is to adapt the following criterion: if x fails to maximize $U(x,\theta)$ for any θ, then $p(\theta|x) > 0$ only for characteristics θ for which the loss associated with x relative to any other action y (hence measured by $\text{Max}_y\{U(y,\theta) - U(x,\theta)\}$) is minimized (see Cho and Sobel, 1990).

belief about future smoking: the desire is $+1$ if the angel whispered: 'you will never again smoke' and $+3$ if: 'you will smoke forever'. A positive interaction between deep beliefs and current desire for a cigarette is psychologically plausible: resignation that one will smoke forever is a likely incentive cue, triggering a craving to smoke now; alternatively, deep belief in future smoking and momentary desire might both be linked to a chronic appetite for smoking, and so on.

We have then a situation where the desire for the cigarette will fall short of diagnostic utility if the smoker deep down truly believes that he will never again smoke, and will exceed diagnostic utility if he deep down truly believes that he will smoke forever. Thus, the decision analyst can state with confidence that the smoker will smoke this cigarette if and only if deep down he believes that he will smoke a pack a day from tomorrow on. The cigarette taken now exposes an underlying lack of conviction about the long run.[10] Moreover, conviction, or lack thereof, is fully warranted: the smoker will smoke this cigarette if and only if he is destined to smoke forever. This last statement is all that the analyst would convey to the smoker, leaving the final decision up to him.

This is a hugely stylized example, but it conveys the essence of an analysis conducted in a neo-Calvinist spirit. The starting position is a radical scepticism about our ability to introspect desires and beliefs, either as individuals or as organized collectives. Verbal affirmations, for example of intentions to stop smoking, cannot be trusted. The standard procedures of decision analysis are likewise of no help, because they also rest on purely hypothetical scenarios and choices. Since access to deep characteristics is barred, the main function of traditional policy analysis – to rationally arrive at an optimal course of action – cannot be carried out. Instead, the goal of analysis should be to clarify the diagnostic significance of each possible action and present that information to the decision-maker.

The first step in this process would be to define the deep characteristics (θ) that are at diagnostic risk. Such characteristics would have to be (a) pre-existing, that is, not created by the decision, (b) uncertain, (c) inaccessible by armchair analysis and (d) potentially relevant, that

---

[10] The story could be fleshed out in other ways of course. One could hypothesize that the unknown type parameter refers to how much one cares about future health (rather than belief about future smoking); in that case, the decision to smoke the current cigarette would expose an underlying lack of concern about future health.

is, exerting influence on the action taken. In the policy domain, prominent categories of characteristics would include collective values (expressed as tradeoffs between competing objectives), collective abilities (knowledge, competence, determination) and collective beliefs about future prospects (destiny, survival, national prestige).

To link these characteristics to the self-signalling model, one would express them in terms of outcome utilities, $u(x,\theta)$. From the standpoint of the model, a characteristic is nothing more than the associated outcome utility function. The tools for assessing $u(x,\theta)$ could be taken from the standard decision analytic arsenal – choices between lotteries and tradeoff analysis – except that the questions would be thoroughly depersonalized. The decision-maker would be asked to consider a hypothetical scenario in which society deep down holds values or beliefs θ, and then, acting as an agent on behalf of that society, express preferences between different x, y that would be most consistent with the specified values and beliefs. This would require separate elicitation exercises for each possible θ, a process that could be simplified by assuming parametric forms for $u(x,\theta)$.

The second step would be to assess the diagnosticity of different possible actions, that is, to pin down the updated self-image distribution $p(\theta|x)$ for each possible x. One might think that this could be done by direct elicitation of $p(\theta|x)$, as a straightforward probability inference conditional on action x. The direct approach has two drawbacks, however. First, the probabilities may not be credible, because if the decision-maker is inclined to choose some particular $x°$, that may lead him to rationalize the choice by providing an excessively favourable assessment of $p(\theta|x°)$. Second, the distribution $p(\theta|x)$ should in principle be derived from the equilibrium condition, and it is unreasonable to expect a respondent to be able to compute an equilibrium.

The better approach, instead, would be to formally derive $p(\theta|x)$ from $V(\theta)$, $p(\theta)$ and the already extracted $u(x,\theta)$. One could attempt to elicit $V(\theta)$ and $p(\theta)$ by treating θ as 'certain knowledge that $\theta = \theta°$', and presenting the decision-maker with choices between lotteries on θ, and between lotteries and modifications to the status quo. The exercise would challenge the decision-maker to make tradeoffs between levels of deep characteristics, and to judge whether certain levels are superior to the current state of affairs. These tradeoff choices would reveal the official, public values, and official current self-image, but, of course, not the actual underlying values and beliefs. The exercise would map out the official ideology of the unified collective.

The final step of the analysis is purely deductive, namely, to compute equilibria consistent with the extracted parameters, $u(x,\theta)$, $V(\theta)$ and $p(\theta)$. The result would be both an action rule that specifies x as a function of θ, and a diagnostic inference rule that specifies how the updated self-image $p(\theta|x)$ depends on x. These two rules would comprise the bulk of the report conveyed back to the decision-maker.

Previously I have said that the goal of analysis should only be to clarify the diagnostic significance of each possible action, and not to select one particular action as best. An apparent exception to this arises whenever analysis yields a unique pooling action as the only equilibrium consistent with the extracted parameters. The exception is only apparent, because even a slight deviation from the pooling action would trigger a strong negative inference on the usual refinement criteria (Cho and Sobel, 1990). The pooling equilibrium is essentially a rule, stating that something must be done or not done irrespective of deep desires and beliefs. Pooling would be expected in situations where diagnostic utility looms much larger than any outcome utilities at stake, for any type. In that case, the message sent to the decision-maker would be simple indeed: whatever temptations are in play, you should cut deliberations short and do the right thing; the diagnostic risk to self-image is just too high.

In a pooling equilibrium, the diagnostic value of actions is highly asymmetrical. Doing wrong, which is to say, deviating from the pooling action, leads to a severe loss in self-image; however, doing right, which is to say, sticking with the pooling action, leaves the self-image exactly where it was before. This fits well with the traditional interpretation of Calvinist inference: a life of virtue does not guarantee salvation, but a dissolute life is proof of damnation.

Summary

I have outlined here one way in which diagnostic utility could be introduced into policy analysis. Diagnostic considerations are a staple of political argument, as shown by rhetorical phrases such as 'Are we a society that allows, tolerates, cares about X?' It is as if the underlying levels of commitment by society to stated values – the true collective preferences – are unknown. In these circumstances, a decision with even minor consequences, concerning due process, say, may be tremendously informative about a larger issue, such as whether the liberties guaranteed by the US Constitution would survive under stress. A full cost–benefit for policy analysis should then take into account these diagnostic implications. None of this is intended to minimize the formidable difficulties in carrying out this project in an actual policy dilemma. Even if it is true, as I have implied, that everyone, including policy-makers, is to some degree a genetic Calvinist, it is far from evident that people in authority would accept the diagnostic interpretations as served up by a technical, outside agency.

References

Ainslie, G. (1992). *Picoeconomics: The Strategic Interaction of Successive Motivational States Within the Person*. New York: Cambridge University Press.

Bem, D. (1972). Self-Perception Theory. In L. Berkowitz (ed.), *Advances in Experimental Social Psychology*. New York: Academic Press, pp. 1–62.

Benabou, R. and Tirole, J. (2004). Willpower and Personal Rules. *Journal of Political Economy* 112: 848–87.

Bernheim, B. and Thomadsen, R. (2005). Memory and Anticipation. *Economic Journal* 115: 271–304.

Bodner, R. and Prelec, D. (2003). Self-Signalling and Diagnostic Utility in Everyday Decision-Making. In I. Brocas and J. Carillo (eds.), *Psychology of Economic Decisions*, vol. 1. Oxford University Press, pp. 105–24.

Cho, I. and Sobel, J. (1990). Strategic Stability and Uniqueness in Signaling Games. *Journal of Economic Theory* 50: 381–413.

Ginossar, Z. and Trope, Y. (1987). Problem Solving in Judgment under Uncertainty. *Journal of Personality and Social Psychology* 52: 464–74.

Mijovic-Prelec, D. and Prelec, D. (2010). Self-Deception as Self-Signaling: A Model and Experimental Evidence. *Philosophical Transactions of the Royal Society B: Biology* 365: 227–40.

Monterosso, J. R. and Ainslie, G. (1999). Beyond Discounting: Possible Experimental Models of Impulse Control. *Psychopharmacology (Berl)*. 146: 339–47.

Prelec, D. and Bodner, R. (2003). Self-Signaling and Self-Control. In G. Loewenstein, D. Read and R. F. Baumeister (eds.), *Time and Decision*. New York: Russell Sage, pp. 277–98.

Quattrone, G. and Tversky, A. (1984). Causal versus Diagnostic Contingencies: On Self-Deception and on the Voter's Illusion. *Journal of Personality and Social Psychology* 46: 237–48.

Sanitioso, R., Kunda, Z. and Fong, G. T. (1990). Motivated Recruitment of Autobiographical Memory. *Journal of Personality and Social Psychology* 59: 229–41.

Weber, M. (2002). *The Protestant Ethic and the Spirit of Capitalism*. Trans. P. Baehr and G. C. Wells. Penguin Books.

9.1 | *A response to Prelec*

LUC BOVENS

Outcome and diagnostic utility

At the heart of Drazen Prelec's chapter is the distinction between outcome utility and diagnostic utility. This distinction becomes interesting when a strict regard for outcome utility prompts us to do one thing, whereas taking into account diagnostic utility prompts us to do something else. Let us look at Prelec's paradigm cases.

(i) A Calvinist is considering whether to engage in a single sinful (and pleasurable) action.
(ii) A person who has quit smoking is considering whether to smoke just one single cigarette.
(iii) Rather than investing in a scheme that benefits orphans, a nation is considering whether to make a different investment that has greater public benefits (say roadworks).

The outcome utility of the single sinful action, smoking the single cigarette and making a different investment is positive, but the diagnostic utility is negative. The diagnostic utility of the single sinful action is the utility that is associated with not being among God's chosen; the diagnostic utility of smoking the single cigarette is the utility associated with being a weak-willed person who won't be able to stick to her resolution of quitting smoking; and the diagnostic utility of choosing the different investment is the utility associated with being the kind of society that is heartless and does not care about the needy. A neo-Calvinist decision-maker will refrain from the actions in (i), (ii) and (iii) on the grounds of their negative diagnostic utility, although their outcome utility is positive.

Observing and intervening in causal networks

There is a particular distinction in the literature on causal networks, namely the distinction between *observing* and *intervening*, that maps

228

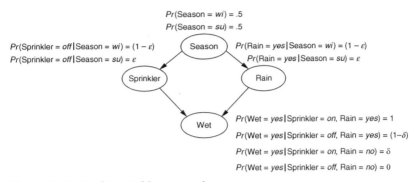

Figure 9.1.1 Pearl's sprinkler network

onto Prelec's distinction between diagnostic and outcome utility. I will explore the connection between both frameworks.

Here is a slightly simplified version of Pearl's paradigm example (Pearl, 2000, p. 15). Let there be the binary variables season (*winter* or *summer*), rain (*yes* or *no*), sprinkler (*off* or *on*) and wet (*yes* or *no*). The chance of rain (in California) is greater in winter than in summer. People tend to turn their sprinklers on more often in summer than in winter. Rain and sprinklers tend to make the pavement wet, though rain's effect is substantial while the sprinkler's effect is marginal. Figure 9.1.1 represents this causal structure and if we insert low values for δ and ε, then the probabilities in the figure match our description of weather patterns and sprinkler settings in Californian seasons and the effect of rain and sprinklers on pavements.

Let us slightly change the example to bring in utilities. Suppose that the water does not drip onto the pavement but onto a bush and that the utility of a wet bush (i.e. a bush that is sufficiently wet to flower) is 1 and of a dry bush (a bush that is insufficiently wet to flower) is 0. Hence the expected utility equals the probability of Wet = *yes*.

What is the change in expected utility of *observing* that someone has (rather than has not) turned on the sprinkler? Let us set ε as approaching 0 and δ at 1/6 in the graph. Winter makes it very likely that there is rain and that the sprinkler is off, whereas summer makes it very likely that there is no rain and that the sprinkler is on. Rain and sprinkler action provide certainty that the bush will flower, rain by itself a 5/6 chance, sprinkler action by itself 1/6 chance and no rain or sprinkler action provide certainty that the bush won't flower. Now suppose that we observe that someone has turned on the sprinkler. Then we can infer that it is very likely to be summer. Hence it is very likely that there is no rain and so the expected utility is (roughly) $\delta = 1/6$. Suppose that we observe that nobody has turned on the sprinkler. Then we can infer that it is very likely to be winter. Hence there is likely to be rain and the expected utility is (roughly) $(1 - \delta) = 5/6$. So observing that the sprinkler is on rather than off entails a *drop* in expected utility of $(1 - \delta) - \delta = (5/6 - 1/6) = 2/3$.

What is the change in expected utility of *intervening* by turning on the sprinkler (rather than not turning it on)? If it's summer, then the expected utility of turning on the sprinkler is 1/6 and of not turning on the sprinkler is 0. If it's winter, then the expected utility of turning on the sprinkler is 1 and of not turning on the sprinkler is 5/6. So either way, intervening by turning on the sprinkler (rather than leaving it turned off) entails a *rise* of expected utility of $\delta = 1/6$.

In Prelec's terms, the diagnostic utility of the sprinkler being on rather than off is negative: observing that the sprinkler is on rather than off is bad news since it entails a drop in expected utility. However, the outcome utility of the sprinkler being on rather than off is positive: intervening to turn the sprinkler on is a good thing to do since it entails a rise in expected utility.

I will show now how Prelec's cases of neo-Calvinism have the same structure as Pearl's paradigm example.

Let us start with the case of the Calvinist. Committing a single sinful action is like the sprinkler being turned on. Being destined to heaven is like rain. Being among God's chosen is like wintertime in California. We can simply substitute these new variables into Figure 9.1.1. *Mutatis mutandis* we can now rewrite the two paragraphs above in which I introduced the distinction between *observing* and *intervening*.

What is the change in expected utility of *observing* myself committing a single sinful action rather than refraining? Suppose that I observe myself committing such an action. Then I can infer that I am very likely not to be among God's chosen. Hence it is very likely that I am not destined for heaven and so my expected utility is (roughly) $\delta = 1/6$. Suppose that I observe myself refraining from this single sinful action. Then I can infer that I am very likely to be among God's chosen. Hence it is likely that I am destined for heaven and so my expected utility is (roughly) $(1 - \delta) = 5/6$. So observing myself committing a single sinful action rather than refraining entails a *drop* in expected utility of $(1 - \delta) - \delta = (5/6 - 1/6) = 2/3$.

What is the change in expected utility of *intervening* by committing a single sinful action rather than refraining? If I am not among God's chosen, then the expected utility of committing this single sinful action is 1/6 and of refraining is 0. If I am among God's chosen, then the expected utility of committing this single sinful action is 1 and of refraining is 5/6. So either way, intervening by committing the single sinful action entails a *rise* to expected utility of $\delta = 1/6$.

Hence the diagnostic utility of committing a single sinful action is negative but the outcome utility is positive. Prelec's two other cases can be dealt with in the same fashion.

Here is the smoking case: smoking a single cigarette is like the sprinkler being turned on; refraining from future smoking is like rain; being wilful is like wintertime in California. *Observing* myself smoking a single cigarette entails a drop in expected utility since I infer that it is very likely that I am not wilful and won't be able to refrain from smoking in the future. *Intervening* by smoking a single cigarette entails a rise in expected utility. The diagnostic utility of smoking a single cigarette is negative but the outcome utility is positive.

Here is the orphan scheme case: refraining from investing in an inefficient orphan scheme on the grounds that another investment has greater public utility is like the sprinkler being turned on; investing in caring schemes at large is like rain; being a caring society is like wintertime in California. *Observing* my society refrain from investing in the orphan scheme entails a drop in expected utility since I infer that it is very likely that we are not a caring society and that we won't invest in caring schemes at large. *Intervening* in my society by refraining from investing in the orphan scheme and investing in a scheme with greater public benefit entails a rise in expected utility. The diagnostic utility of refraining from investing in the orphan scheme is negative but the outcome utility is positive.

Prelec takes the agent's total utility to be her outcome utility complemented by her diagnostic utility. Then, following our calculation above, the total utility of turning the sprinkler on, committing the single sinful action ..., equals a δ-gain in outcome utility and a drop of $((1 - \delta) - \delta)$ in diagnostic utility: $\delta - ((1 - \delta) - \delta)$. And vice versa, the total utility of turning the sprinkler off, refraining from a single sinful action ..., equals a δ-drop in outcome utility and a gain of $((1 - \delta) - \delta)$ in diagnostic utility: $- \delta + ((1 - \delta) - \delta)$. This is somewhat different from Prelec's definition of total utility, but it is the closest that I can come to it.[1]

---

[1] Alternatively, one could calculate diagnostic utility as the change in expected utility from observing a third party leaving the sprinkler off rather than being

Interpretation

I take it that Prelec aims to construct a model of an agent who is partly guided by outcome utility and partly by diagnostic utility. Whether this agent is rational or not is a non-issue. This model has descriptive value – it captures the decisions of actual human agents facing problems that have this kind of structure. This is a valid pursuit. It is comparable say to the model in prospect theory showing that agents tend to make decisions by underweighting high probabilities and over-weighting low probabilities (Kahneman and Tversky, 1979). These are not rational choice explanations. We do not attempt to explain agency by showing that what the agent does is a rational action.

But one might ask another question that does belong to rational choice theory, namely are there any situations under which a rational agent would be advised to leave the sprinkler off, to refrain from committing the single sinful action, etc. In our simple model the answer is a resolute *no* – i.e. turning the sprinkler on, committing the single sinful action . . ., is the only *rational* option. The only thing that matters when deciding whether or not to turn the sprinkler on, to commit the single sinful action . . ., is that one raises one's outcome utility by $\delta = 1/6$ by doing so, no matter what season it is, no matter whether one is among God's chosen.[2]

But now, in real life, it may indeed be a good idea to refrain from turning the sprinkler on or to abstain from the single sinful action. So why is this? Well, in real life, the causal structure is often more complex and my singular agency does have causal consequences that go beyond immediate consequences.

In the smoking case, it is reasonable to assume that there is no fixed character. Today's character may be characterized by great resolve, but after smoking one cigarette, my character will lose its resolve. With less resolve comes a reduced chance that I will be able to continue

---

ignorant about whether she has turned the sprinkler on or left it off and representing this ignorance as equiprobability. Then the diagnostic utility of her leaving the sprinkler off raises my expected utility by $(1 - \delta) - (.5(1 - \delta) + .5\delta) = 5/6 - 1/2 = 1/3$. Again, this does not quite coincide with Prelec's definition.

[2] This is the advice of the causal decision theorist in the Newcomb problem in Nozick (1969). The Newcomb problem has the same structure. Substitute 'me having the character of a two-boxer' for 'summer', 'me taking two boxes' for 'the sprinkler being on' and 'the predictor putting money in the opaque box' for 'rain'. As a causal decision theorist, I take two-boxing to be the only rational solution.

abstaining from smoking. And this is why I should abstain from smoking a single cigarette.

In the Calvinist case, it is reasonable to assume that Calvinists tend to draw inferences from their singular actions about their chances of salvation and these inferences very much influence their peace of mind. A rational agent may need to work with such projected beliefs and if we include the agent's peace of mind in the description of the states of the world over which preferences are defined, then a rational agent may indeed need to abstain from the single sinful action.

But if we want to capture such features in our model of rational agency, then we need to construct a more complex causal network that includes downstream nodes from committing a single sinful action. For example, in our smoking case, this would be the future state of my character and its effect on long-term smoking. In our Calvinist case, it would be our future cognitive state and the resultant level of peace of mind.

The orphan scheme can be thought of in a similar vein. A rational society might want to invest in the inefficient orphan scheme. The reason for doing so is that turning one's back on such a scheme may make society redefine what kind of society it is. It may come to think of itself as a heartless society. And it will then lose its resolve to invest in caring schemes at large. Or its citizens may derive much benefit from the self-congratulatory state of mind that ensues from investing in highly visible caring schemes (even if they are inefficient). If we import this more complex causal structure into our cases, then it will become rational to invest in the otherwise inefficient orphan scheme.

References

Kahneman, D. and Tversky, A. (1979). Prospect Theory: An Analysis of Decision under Risk. *Econometrica* 47(2): 263–92.

Nozick, R. (1969). Newcomb's Problem and Two Principles of Choice. In N. Rescher (ed.), *Essays in Honor of Carl G. Hempel*. Dordrecht: Reidel, pp. 114–46.

Pearl, J. (2000). *Causality: Models, Reasoning and Inference*. Cambridge University Press.

Index